W9-AVS-694

Praise for
Power Up Your Profits

*If you are serious about making rain for your firm this is "must read"
material . . . very enjoyable, powerful and to the point. Definitely can help
any practitioner or consultant develop more business.*

—Allan Koltin, President
PDI, Chicago, Illinois

*Troy Waugh is a true professional. While working with Wolf & Company,
he consistently demonstrated depth of knowledge, understanding of
our problems, and most importantly, the ability to guide us in developing
practical solutions to marketing and selling obstacles.*

—Donald J. Figura, Managing Partner
Wolf & Company LLP

*This is an essential text for CPAs committed to growing their
practices. Regardless of your level of experience, it delivers practical,
down-to-earth advice.*

—Christian Frederiksen, CPA
Millwood, California

*The world of accounting is changing at record speed. With accountants
today selling everything from insurance to technology, we really have to be
ahead of the curve just to survive. With Troy Waugh's help, our practice
has grown by double digits the past seven years in a row. His experience
as a CPA and a marketer has really helped our firm adapt to this
dynamic environment. His book is a must for anyone in the industry.*

—Jimmy C. Averitt, Partner
BDO Seidman, LLP, Dallas, Texas

*Predictable results can only come from a marketing and sales
system and that is what Troy Waugh provides in* Power Up Your Profits.
*His proven system was designed for the professional services industry
and specifically accounting. I have witnessed sustained growth in firms
using his system. The book is a must read for partners and future partners.
It is a quick read with lasting results.*

—L. Gary Boomer, CPA, Chief Executive Officer
Boomer Consulting, Inc., Manhattan, Kansas

Troy Waugh is one of the leading marketing consultants to the CPA profession. In his new book, you can benefit from his accumulated wisdom in helping CPA practices grow, offer more value to their customers, and achieve a better quality of life. Since I believe we learn more from success than failure, I particularly liked the profiles of the most successful rainmakers in the profession. If you are interested in increasing your marketing potential, Troy's book is essential reading.

If you are like me, you appreciate a good read. Troy Waugh is one of the leading consultants to the CPA profession and his new book is an excellent source of marketing experience and wisdom. If you follow Troy's teachings, you will no doubt grow your practice, earn more, and enjoy a better quality of life.
—Ron Baker, CPA
Corte Madera, California,
Author of *The Professional's Guide to Value Pricing*

Waugh challenges accountants to become better communicators and thereby become more valuable to their clients. His book is a focused collection of practical, useful and profitable ideas.
—Gerald Marsden, Managing Partner
Eisner & Lubin, LLP, New York, New York

I cannot praise this book and Troy Waugh enough. This is a tremendous addition to the literature on selling. I can't wait to get this into the hands of professionals, including my clients.
—David Cottle, CPA
CMC

Troy Waugh is making us Certified PASSIONATE Accountants. He's innovative, logical, and inspirational. And, his simple, on-point advice is making us more money!
—Elizabeth B. Wiggins, CPA/ABV, Partner
BKD, LLP, Houston, Texas

Troy Waugh has the ability to offer very practical ideas which can be implemented fast and easily. Anyone involved in a professional service firm will find this book very rewarding.
—Werner E. Rotach, CEO
Horwath International

*In the complex world of the Profession Services firm,
the value of an ever-improving bottom line is constant. Troy Waugh's
knowledgeable insight of our industry provides an excellent
resource in helping attain bottom line results.*
—Jonathan L. Miller, Partner
Habif, Arogeti & Wynne, L.L.P., Atlanta, Georgia

*Troy Waugh is an excellent trainer for accountants in the development
of marketing and selling skills. His practical approach is easy to implement
in your practice. Utilizing Troy's techniques, our firm has developed
a marketing culture in our practice. We have identified marketing niches
and established committees to target these groups. Our partners are
not only bringing in new business but having fun doing it. Troy has proven
to us that even accountants can become highly successful sellers.*
—David M. Frazier, CPA, CBA
Yount, Hyde & Barbour, P.C., Winchester, Virginia

*This book should be required professional reading for any owner
or would-be owner who wishes to succeed in public practice today . . .
Troy Waugh has successfully demonstrated over and over again that
even the most reluctant CPA can be trained to acquire new business. . . .*
Power Up Your Profits *should be on everyone's desk for reference
and repeated reading.*
—Eugene M. Cohen
EM Cohen Associates

I just read Power Up Your Profits: 31 Days to Better Selling.
*I found it to be one of the most practical books on the subject
that I ever read. . . . Your ease of presentation and use of
real experiences by CPAs should make it mandatory reading by young,
and not-so-young, CPAs. . . . Great Job! Congratulations!*
—Frank P. Orlando, CPA Managing Partner
Parente, Randolph, Orlando, Carey & Associates

*I think your 31-chapter format is an effective way for your readers
to handle the reading and implement the learning. Of course, the real-life
stories from people we recognize prove the impact of the techniques.*
—Donald B. Scholl
B.D. Scholl, Inc.

A marketing book specific to the reader's industry, if done competently, is almost always more immediately useful than a generic marketing book. Power Up Your Profits is the authoritative guide to marketing for accounting firms — every page rings with the voice of experience and is packed with ideas that teach and motivate.

—Bob Bly

Power Up Your Profits

31 Days to Better Selling

Second Edition

Troy Waugh

WILEY

John Wiley & Sons, Inc.

This book is printed on acid-free paper.

Copyright © 2005 by John Wiley & Sons, Inc. All rights reserved.

Published by John Wiley & Sons, Inc., Hoboken, New Jersey
Published simultaneously in Canada

No part of this publication may be reproduced, stored in a retrieval system, or transmitted
in any form or by any means, electronic, mechanical, photocopying, recording, scanning,
or otherwise, except as permitted under Section 107 or 108 of the 1976 United States Copyright
Act, without either the prior written permission of the Publisher or authorization through
payment of the appropriate per-copy fee to the Copyright Clearance Center, Inc., 222 Rosewood
Drive, Danvers, MA 01923, 978-750-8400, fax 978-646-8600, or on the web at *www.copyright.com*.
Requests to the Publisher for permission should be addressed to the Permissions Department,
John Wiley & Sons, Inc., 111 River Street, Hoboken, NJ 07030, 201-748-6011, fax 201-748-6008.

Limit of Liability/Disclaimer of Warranty: While the publisher and author have used their
best efforts in preparing this book, they make no representations or warranties with respect
to the accuracy or completeness of the contents of this book and specifically disclaim any
implied warranties of merchantability or fitness for a particular purpose. No warranty may be
created or extended by sales representatives or written sales materials. The advice and strategies
contained herein may not be suitable for your situation. You should consult with a professional
where appropriate. Neither the publisher nor author shall be liable for any loss of profit or
any other commercial damages, including but not limited to special, incidental, consequential,
or other damages.

For general information on our other products and services, or technical support, please
contact our Customer Care Department within the United States at 800-762-2974, outside the
United States at 317-572-3993 or fax 317-572-4002.

Wiley also publishes its books in a variety of electronic formats. Some content that appears in
print may not be available in electronic books.

Library of Congress Cataloging-in-Publication Data

Waugh, Troy.
      Power up your profits : 31 days to better selling / Troy Waugh.— 2nd ed.
          p. cm.
      Includes bibliographical references and index.
          ISBN 0-471-65149-4 (cloth)
          1. Selling.   2. Marketing—Decision making.   3. Strategic planning.
      4. Customer relations—Management.   I. Title: Power up your profits: thirty-one
      days to better selling.   II. Title.
      HF5438.25.W2868   2004
      658.85—dc22

                                                                                2004011579

Printed in the United States of America

10 9 8 7 6 5 4 3 2 1

About the Author

Troy Waugh, CPA, MBA, CEO, The Rainmaker Academy, is a leading marketing and sales consultant to the accounting industry. Troy helps public accounting firms grow. He and his experienced team of consultants have helped firms add more than $500 million in new business through their consulting, training, and alliance services.

Troy's highly acclaimed book, *Power Up Your Profits*, has received praise throughout the world. His articles have been published in *Accounting Today*, *The Practical Accountant*, and numerous state society monthly newsletters. Troy has been publishing a "Marketing Moment with Troy Waugh" since 1992. He is one of the most sought-after speakers on sales and marketing professional services in the United States.

Troy is the founder of The Rainmaker Academy, the leading sales and marketing training course in the United States and western Europe. The Rainmaker Academy is a three-year intensive sales training program whose graduates have attracted over $300 million to their firms during the classes.

Troy received an MBA in marketing from the University of Southern California in 1973. He obtained a BS in accounting from the University of Tennessee in 1969. He became a Certified Public Accountant in 1970.

Troy joined the Nashville, Tennessee, office of Price Waterhouse (now PriceWaterhouseCoopers) in April 1969 and transferred to the Los Angeles office in April 1971. He served several of the largest clients of the firm and became an audit manager in 1974. During his years with PWC, Troy was active in the Los Angeles Junior Chamber of Commerce and many other activities.

In 1975 Troy became chairman and chief executive officer of Advantage Companies, Inc. During his eight years with Advantage, Troy guided a complete repositioning of the company's focus away from the budget motel business into magazine publishing. During this period, Troy negotiated over 40 acquisitions or divestitures of businesses.

In 1984 Troy became a vice president with Jacques Miller, Inc., a real estate investment firm. He was promoted to senior vice president and national sales manager during his years with Jacques Miller, Inc. Due to the tax reform act of 1986, Troy was instrumental in repositioning the company away from tax-advantaged real estate in 1987 into high-yielding healthcare real estate and again in 1989 into real estate management.

He is a member of the Advisory Board, a national consortium of leading consultants to the professions, the National Speakers Association, the American Institute of CPAs, and the Tennessee Society of CPAs.

Troy Waugh may be reached at:

The Rainmaker Academy
4731 Trousdale, Suite 12
Nashville, Tennessee 37221
615 373-9880
e-mail: troy@waughco.com

The Rainmaker Academy

Designed to put the up-and-coming future leaders of your CPA firm on the fast track to success, The Rainmaker Academy is a comprehensive three-year training program in leadership, client service, and practice development. Conducted at a level commensurate with an advanced degree program, The Rainmaker Academy develops graduates with the necessary skills to consistently attract and retain quality clients for your firm.

During their attendance in The Rainmaker Academy, our students have attracted over $300 million of newly generated revenue for their firms.

The Rainmaker Academy features:

- A curriculum specifically designed for accounting and consulting professionals
- Exposure to top Rainmakers from around the world
- One-on-one coaching between class sessions
- A requirement mandating that each student teach course materials, along with skills he or she has mastered, to other members of your firm
- A minimum of 48 hours CPE per year

To optimize interaction among participants and to ensure that each student receives maximum attention, classes are limited to 24 students.

Year 1

Most CPA firms already have tremendous opportunity within their existing client base and should be tapping into this lucrative source of additional revenue on an ongoing basis. Therefore, the objective of the first year of The Rainmaker Academy is to create "mistmakers," valuable professionals who understand the sales process and begin generating new revenue for their firms.

Year One focuses on developing cross-selling opportunities and building loyalty within existing client relationships.

Year 2

The second year of The Rainmaker Academy builds on the premise that an "interested introvert" can be a better salesperson than an "interesting extrovert." The introvert, however, must first develop effective selling skills.

Year 3

In today's business environment, a steady stream of highly qualified new clients is essential for any firm to remain competitive. Providing value, a crucial subject in this increasingly competitive market, is essential not only in attracting new clients but also in retaining existing ones. The third year of the Rainmaker Academy emphasizes major account development, proposal generation and related pricing issues.

Consulting from The Rainmaker Academy

The Rainmaker Academy is a sales and marketing consulting and training firm exclusively serving the accounting profession. On a selective basis, the associates of the firm provide strategic assessment, planning, and implementation of successful practice development programs for CPA firms. The Rainmaker Academy differentiates itself from its competitors by focusing on the successful implementation of that program within your firm.

Sales and Marketing Consulting Services

At The Rainmaker Academy, our consulting programs are designed to help you work smarter—not harder. Like the story of the goose that lays the golden eggs, it's important that our clients maintain a desirable balance between their personal and professional lives. While our consulting programs will certainly help increase the number of golden eggs in your basket, we'll also pay specific attention to your personal well-being in order to help maximize your performance.

Our consulting philosophy stresses the successful implementation of growth strategies to make your firm more profitable. We help clients attract better business, not just more business. We offer both broad and narrowly focused consulting programs including:

The Marketing Partner™ Relationship

The Permission Marketing Campaign

The Strategic Marketing Assessment

Strategic Marketing Planning and Implementation

Five-Star Client Service

Strategic Marketing Retreat Facilitation

Client Loyalty Surveys

Lost Client and Lost Proposal Analysis

Rainmaker consultants can also help your firm with industry niche and service-area development, competitor analysis, leadership succession, firm reorganizations, mergers and acquisitions, service-line expansions, keynote presentations, and the executive search process.

Customized for the specific needs of each client, The Rainmaker Consulting programs are designed to help your firm become a leader in the practice development and client relations arenas.

Contents

Preface

This book reveals principles, strategies, and techniques that can help you attract better clients to your firm. Better clients are necessary for an enjoyable life and a profitable business. If you want to enjoy your life more and become more profitable from your accounting practice, this book is for you.

You can master your life and your career when you learn to sell. Rather than be assigned work, you will be able to create exciting and interesting projects. Rather than be a victim of the leverage system, you can control the fulcrum. Maybe you have read general books for professionals on marketing, and you were disappointed. You probably noticed that most of the advice in the general books really didn't apply to you. This book is written for financial services professionals working in accounting firms.

The thought of being a salesperson does not usually conjure up positive thoughts. Recently I asked people in a seminar what came to mind when I said, "salesman." The responses were: aggressive, liar, pushy, flashy, and so on. That is not how you see yourself and that is not how selling is done in the accounting profession. You think of yourself as a skilled accountant or consultant— as well you should. Selling is a vital part of a thriving professional's daily life. Selling is performed to persuade prospects and clients to take advantage of the benefits of your world-class service.

This is a major difference between you and the typical salesperson. The salesperson's job is usually over when the contract is signed. You, however, must service what you sell. Selling is simply the first step in a long-term relationship between you and your clients. Selling accounting services is different from selling anything else. It is different from selling law services, brokerage services, or products of any kind. That's why this book is written specifically for CPAs.

Will you use everything in the book? Probably not. Many different styles can be successful. In preparation for the book, I have met with thousands of CPAs who have attended my training classes. Their input has been invaluable. I have personally interviewed a number of top business developers in firms all across the United States. You will see from their comments how differently people can approach the same obstacle.

My mission in life is to help transform the lives of accountants. This mission is embodied in the Mission, Values and Commitment of Waugh & Co., Inc., the company I founded in 1991:

Our Mission

The mission of Waugh & Co., Inc., is to transform the lives of accountants. We help our clients realize their lifestyle and profit potential through more effective communications.

Our Values

- To provide unsurpassed content excellence, marketing motivation and value.
- To promote a climate of trust, innovation, enthusiasm, teamwork, and open dialogue among our clients and associates.
- To conduct our business with the highest standards of integrity consistent with our Christian values.
- To seek to understand the critical needs of our clients and associates and to help create a sense of partnership among all.

Our Commitment

All of our work is fully guaranteed. If we fall short of your expectations in any way, please contact us immediately so we can work to assure your happiness. Or simply pay an amount you believe represents the value you received from us.

Our Difference

The basic differentiator in all we do is to help accountants change culture. Our Rainmaker Academy program extends over a three-year period because we have found it takes that long for a technical accountant to build the skills and discipline necessary to learn to sell. Our training programs are built with posttraining–day reinforcement (usually 12 weeks) so each program can be ingrained in the culture of the accounting firm. Our consulting extends over months and years as we help partners develop a winning strategy and then help them implement that strategy.

Many smart people urged me to write this book to appeal to all professionals so the commercial success would be broader. But that is not what I do. My mission is to help CPAs, not sell a lot of books. Likewise, many smart "politically correct" types have advised me to water down our statement of values. It is important that people who work with me know my values. When prospects know the "unwatered-down" version, they can make a more informed decision based on truth, rather than some meaningless mist.

This book is written to help you become a CPA who can sell, not a salesperson selling accounting services. Like our company's quarterly newsletter, "A Marketing Moment with Troy Waugh," the chapters are short and to-the-point. A CPA who can sell is a powerful person in today's business world. CPAs are the most trusted business advisors to owners and managers of businesses around the world. Combine the power of trust with the power of persuasion and you have a master.

The concepts in this book have been generated over a lifetime of experience and study. The concepts and techniques are taught in our many training courses and in the consulting we provide many CPA firm partners around the world.

In relationship selling, push selling is not as effective as pull selling. Push selling is the type of selling an untrained, interesting extrovert would deliver. Push selling consists of expounding, expanding, and encouraging. How many times have you bought from a fast-talking salesperson and regretted it within hours? Pull selling is the type that relies on pulling information from the buyer in order to understand the buyer's situation. Then, armed with good information, you tell your client how you can solve his need. Pull selling is much less threatening than push selling.

So there you have my fundamental vision of how an accountant can be an effective practice builder. This book is designed to help you, the practicing accountant, build your practice by building your client's business. Throughout the book, I will share with you specific examples of how you can expand your practice. Many of them will help you build your client base. But first you must obtain a client. So, really, this book is about the complete marketing process. Done well, a marketing program in your firm can create a tornado of profitable business for you.

Acknowledgments

My concept of the CPA began to form when I was very young. James Smith, CPA, was the most successful businessman in the small town where I grew up. He was very active in the community, and his ability to help people with their finances was legendary. He was well known for helping people save tax dollars (at a time when there were 90 percent marginal tax rates). He helped clients finance their businesses and then negotiated with their banks for rates and terms.

Smith helped establish the region's Industrial Development Board to increase the area's job base. Then he helped the companies that moved to the area to negotiate union contracts and tax abatement programs.

The first CPA I ever knew of made an impact on his client's businesses and on the little town of my youth. And although I never knew him personally, he created my image of a CPA. He set a large portion of the pattern for my business life. I wanted to become a CPA.

James Smith, CPA, was also a marketer, par excellence. Frequently he was quoted or featured in the local newspaper. I remember listening once as he was interviewed on the local radio station. Probably the thing that stands out most in my mind, though, was a large photo of Smith sitting on the back of his 1957 red T-bird convertible. What a car!

Once Smith came to visit my dad. After he left, my dad said, "That man is a great man, he really helps people."

William Waugh, my dad, set the other major part of my life's pattern. He was a grocery man and a great marketer. It was with him that I began my work life. He taught me that hard work and long hours were key ingredients in business success. My dad always worked six-day, 60-hour weeks. When I became an accountant, busy season never bothered me. I thought it was great to have a nine-month vacation of only 40 to 50 hour workweeks between tax seasons.

But my dad really worked at marketing. He taught me the best way to build a business is to focus on building customer loyalty. Rather than working in his office, he was walking the floor greeting customers most of the day. Yes, he had stock to arrange and order; reports and bank deposits to make; employees to hire, fire, and counsel; but much of his day was spent near the cash registers at the front of the store. He told me one day, "When a customer is paying their money is the most critical time for us in selling. If they feel good and appreciated at that point, they most likely will come back. If they will come back, we can turn a $20 sale into $1,000-a-year revenue."

It was with my dad that I was exposed to advertising. Every week he changed the store signs and the ads in the newspaper. Periodically he had advertising circulars printed. Then he would drive several of the store employees around town distributing the flyers directly to peoples' homes. He was also a networker. He was active in the local Civitan club (I still love those Claxton fruitcakes they sell) and in our church. People who met him in these circumstances grew to like him and often would then show up at the grocery.

When I joined PriceWaterhouseCoopers in 1969, the first partner for whom I worked had a blend of qualities that fit my vision. Tempered by an antimarketing environment, Fred G. Frick was deeply concerned with the success of his clients' businesses. While maintaining objectivity and independence, Frick viewed his clients from inside their business rather than from afar. He saw himself as part of his client's de facto management team.

More than a dozen of Fred's clients have since told me of his value to their organizations.

Fred Frick is not a natural-born marketer. He is, by nature, an introvert. Yet he was quite visible in the community, sought new business aggressively, and helped build his clients' businesses. He taught me the key to building an accounting practice was to build your client's business first, and then your practice will also grow. When you focus on your client's success, you cannot fail. I use his concept today in my marketing consulting work with accounting firms. It works.

Fred has a deep interest in business and in the elements that make them successful. He convinced me to join a smaller office of PW so I could learn more rapidly about businesses from the inside. Under his tutelage, I learned to ask the questions of the business owner that would get to the heart of the problem issues. Many times Fred could not solve the owner's problems just with an audit or tax return. But surfacing the issues often led to opportunities to help the client solve major business problems.

But most of all, Fred Frick taught me that an interested introvert can be a better marketer than an interesting extrovert can. He told me, "If you have good business sense and are truly interested in your client's business, the communication (marketing) permeates the relationship." An interested introvert asks questions and listens to the response. Most introverts are shy about overselling themselves; they abhor appearing pushy.

I owe a great debt to the late Ken Powers, who edited many early drafts of this book. Ken worked with me since 1977 and has been an inspiration to me. Ken counseled me, listened to me, and supported me throughout the many trials of life. He was a great editor and friend.

Dr. Rick Crandall challenged me to finish the book and edited the final versions and acted as my advisor on content. Without his expert advice and encouragement, the book would still be in draft format.

As a consultant, I have learned much from other consultants to the accounting industry: Jay Nisberg, Gary Shamis, Allan Koltin, Marc Rosenberg, Gene Cohen, Gary Boomer, Art Levy, Tim Beauchemin, and Ron Baker are the most prominent. But more important, I have learned from key clients of Waugh & Co.

Kevin Poppen, president of The Enterprise Network, an alliance of leading CPA firms, has made many special contributions and observations. I owe a special debt to several other colleagues, including Patrick Patterson, Guy Gage, Scott Bradbary, Charlie Flood and Graham Wilson, and Drew Crowder.

Better Selling Starts with You

1 A Nontraditional Attitude

The greatest discovery of my generation is that man can alter his life by altering his attitudes.

—William James

Much of the budget and effort for marketing and sales in accounting firms is wasted. Many accountants know something about marketing and sales because they went to business school. However, the standard consumer approaches they are taught in "B" School are not the most effective for professional service firms.

As a first overview of sales and marketing, let's look at the results of a general business survey of marketing spending as shown in Exhibit 1.1. This

Exhibit 1.1   Bar Chart

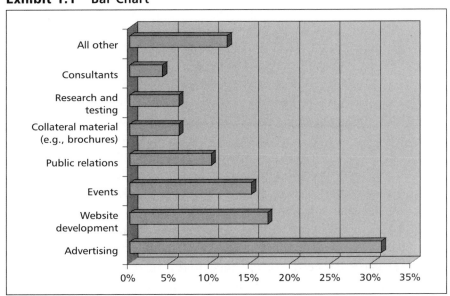

Source: Blackfriars Communications, 2004.

3

particular one is from 2004 by Blackfriars Communications. However, many other summaries would show a similar picture. In this survey, 100 senior executives reported how they budgeted their marketing dollars.

The only thing different in this marketing budget from one 20 years ago is the money spent on website development.

Eighty-two percent of those surveyed agreed or strongly agreed that marketing is important to their companies. Yet despite the fact that the companies surveyed averaged $280 million a year in revenues, only 37 percent had a VP of marketing or the equivalent. These companies are typical of an MBA approach to marketing: they spend millions a year on marketing, prefer costly approaches such as advertising, and don't supervise and track their marketing effectively. In addition, they separate sales from marketing so it does not appear in the survey.

As you'll see in this book, my approach is much more practical and effective than the general one for three reasons.

1. I consider marketing and sales together.
2. I focus your efforts and spending on personal sales where your biggest results are.
3. I emphasize marketing to your *existing* clients and contacts, not to strangers through mass media.

What Is Marketing?

One of the simplest ways to define marketing is as "anything you do to get or keep a client." That should include planning and research to decide what types of clients you want to offer what services. It can include advertising, publicity, networking, online referrals, and personal selling to get clients. And it should include, most of all, great customer service to keep your existing clients and develop new work with them, as well as get referrals from them.

A few years ago, I noticed a shift from accountants talking about marketing to their actually doing some activities. I formed The Rainmaker Academy and today, we employ a team of consultants who work with me to deliver marketing and sales consulting and training to accountants.

David Lill, author of *Selling, The Profession,* has captured the best definition of selling for me. David says, "Selling is the process of seeking out people who have a particular need, assisting them to recognize and define that need, demonstrating how one of our services fills that need, and persuading them to make a decision to use our solution."

Both marketing and sales involve communication. Marketing generally builds awareness of you and keeps in touch with people. Sales involves more personal contact where you sign up the clients.

A Marketing/Sales System

Even accounting firms with some talented rainmakers often don't handle their marketing and sales correctly. One of their weaknesses is the lack of a systematic approach. If you don't use your marketing dollars—and talent—within a consistent framework, you will not achieve optimum results.

The first step in a system is to realize that there are different audiences that you need to reach consistently. In general, to be successful, you need to handle three stages of marketing:

1. Finding prospects
2. Developing prospects into clients
3. Serving clients and developing new business and referrals from them

My use of these three stages here does not mean that all your marketing should focus on potential clients. Similar stages are useful for referral sources that are covered in other chapters.

Step 1, finding prospects, includes many of the marketing methods mentioned earlier that you're familiar with, such as advertising, publicity, and sales. However, the emphasis in this book is different from a typical MBA approach to marketing. In fact, just the use of the three steps shows a different approach. Most traditional marketing books focus on the first step, with some attention to the second. However, the third step is your most profitable approach to marketing. I often suggest that you devote up to 90 percent of your marketing budget to cultivating your existing clients. More on that later.

You can find prospects with many methods, from seminars, to referrals, to direct mail, to personal networking. Your job is to test a variety of methods and to systematize them. Different people in your firm will be better at different methods as well. And different people and methods will be more effective for different clients. To adapt a classic psychological formula for predicting behavior:

$$\text{Person} \times \text{Marketing Method} \times \text{Prospect} = \text{Results}$$

It's up to you to test marketing methods, find the ones you are comfortable with that work for your targeted prospects, and then set up a system to repeat your successes. For instance, if direct mail works, you will develop a schedule to mail regularly as well as test new mailing lists. If seminars work, you use them regularly.

The object of good sales and marketing is not to make you work more, but to make you work less. Each time you use the same method, it becomes easier and more automatic. That's what a system does for you.

Step 2, developing prospects, is where most marketing systems break down. It is also the most important area where permission marketing applies. It can take a long time to turn prospects into clients, and you need their permission to make this conversion go smoothly. This occurs for several reasons, not least of which is the fact that changing accountants can be difficult for clients. However, there is a more basic reason: Prospects must trust you enough to let you sell them. Yes, you need some trust even to be allowed to sell. The permission approach opens by helping prospects feel in control and rewards the first small trust step on their part.

Many prospects are wasted because firms don't have effective follow-up systems. The worst statistic in this area is that something like 75 percent of trade show leads are never followed up at all. I use this only as an example of lack of follow-up. Although local chamber trade shows can be effective, trade shows are not a major marketing method for most firms.

Let's take a more typical example. Say you meet a person at a business mixer. She seems interested in your services, she fits the profile you're looking for, and there is a level of comfort or rapport in your contact. You get her card and she takes yours. Now what?

If you're like most accountants, you stick the card in a drawer and hope she'll call you. After a few months, you've forgotten who she is, and eventually you throw out the card. If you're more effective at following up prospects, you call the person and try to set up a meeting. If she agrees, you try to sell her on your services at the meeting. If she isn't ready to act, you may or may not follow up again.

What you need is a *system* for following up prospects. Your system should gather information about prospects and their needs, help them become familiar with you, and give them reasons to want to hear from you. For example, a system might include a schedule of contacts like this: Initial contact, questions to determine the urgency of their needs, personal meeting to get acquainted, newsletters four times a year, and invitations to a yearly seminar.

An "A" prospect is one of your most highly sought-after prospects. "B"s are slightly less valuable. Some accounts use three grades, A through C, and others use up to six grades, A through F.

For A prospects, you might add occasional lunches, referrals *to* them, a meeting with another of their professional advisors, and going to one of their industry meetings.

Again, the specifics of your follow-up system will depend on your style, the methods you prefer, and what fits for the prospect. The point is that if you *have* a system, it is much easier to consistently follow up and build relationships and trust.

Step 3, serving clients and developing new business and referrals from them, is also covered in other chapters. When people are clients, you have permission to stay in touch with them. They don't want to be bothered by you, but they will want you to contact them whenever you have information of value to them—for instance, tax rule changes. By contacting clients with something of interest to them, when you're not trying to sell them more services, you come across as a trusted advisor with their best interests at heart. Different clients will prefer different levels of contact. We often forget to *ask* clients their preferences about contact from us. Some people would prefer a lot of contact; others, the minimum. It's up to you to find out what people want. Some will go for old-fashioned baseball tickets or the nice bottle at Christmas. Others will prefer business information or social contacts.

One certain statistic with which we contend is that the average sale is made after the sixth contact and the average salesperson quits after two contacts. That's a major problem for developing new clients when people don't hire you after a couple of contacts. But the problem is even worse for many professionals. For the biggest accounts, it is more likely to take a dozen contacts to make the sale. Clients don't make the decision to switch providers lightly. Unfortunately, many professionals quit before the first contact. They think to themselves, "I don't like selling, nothing is likely to happen from a few meetings, I have too much work to do—I'll just skip sales efforts for now!"

Although this book is full of proven information that can make you better at all aspects of selling and marketing, perhaps the most important thing it can do is give you the evidence to allow you to change your mind. To sell successfully, you must be willing to do it. Even more, you must find sales activities that you can be positive about doing. A positive sales attitude will help you succeed. Fortunately, you can practice your sales behaviors while your attitude is developing.

This book can guide you, but you must take responsibility for your own actions. Only by acting on what you know about sales can you make sales and develop your "sales attitude."

The Right Sales Attitude

The reason most accountants do not sell well is because they defeat themselves in their minds before they begin.

Several thousand CPAs have attended The Rainmaker Academy's sales training programs. It is rare to find a CPA attending one of our programs who has previous experience or education in sales.

Yet, everyone sells. The key to success in any business is the ability to persuade people to use you or your service.

Most CPAs did not study accounting or join an accounting firm to go into sales. Unfortunately, most high schools and colleges do not teach students that in today's world, everyone sells. You sell yourself to almost everyone with whom you communicate. You sell yourself to family members. Lawyers sell to judges. Students sell to professors. Workers sell to bosses.

Selling is far more than convincing someone of the merit of your ideas, company, plan, or whatever. It is how people experience you and your staff. Think about it this way: Anytime you interact with any business, the person with whom you come in contact is selling. Most of the time, the person with whom you interact is not the business owner, but an employee. How that employee treats you determines your desire to return to the business or to encourage others to trade there.

Terry Orr, a partner with BDO Seidman in Dallas, Texas, says, "I really view almost everything I do every day as selling. There are times when you are not in front of a client or a prospect, but I spend at least 50 percent of my time selling and marketing."

The salesman who thinks that his first duty is selling is absolutely wrong. Selling is only one of the two important things a salesman is supposed to do—and it is not the more important of the two. The salesman's first duty is to make friends for his house.

—Ellsworth M. Statler[1]

Why Sell?

The most important reason you should learn to sell is to be able to attract the kind of clients with whom you enjoy working. Selling is about getting more interesting and more profitable clients. It is not just about getting more revenue.

As long as you are unable or unwilling to sell, you'll have to accept whatever clients walk in your door, or your partners will assign you work. If you

PORTRAIT OF A SALES LEADER

DAVID MORGAN, comanaging partner of Lattimore, Black, Morgan & Cain, LLC (LBMC), never really thought he'd have to sell. Yet through an intense focus on personal selling, he and his partners have pushed LBMC into the top 100 accounting firms in America in less than 15 years. Morgan wanted to be a professional baseball player: "I couldn't run and I couldn't pitch, but I could knock the ball out of the park." Growing up, he developed a very competitive spirit through sports, a trait that he has brought to his public accounting career. "Jim Lattimore, Mike Cain, and I would play league softball, and we always played to win," said Morgan of his early days in public accounting.

Morgan is the comanaging partner, along with Michael Cain, of one of the fastest-growing firms in America. LBMC was founded in 1984 and is now ranked 54 in *Accounting Today's* Top 100 Accounting Firms in America "Morgan's leadership and competitive spirit has helped drive our firm to our position today," says Cain. Morgan went to Tennessee Technological University and joined KPMG. He had offers from all the big firms but chose the one that offered the most money. Being a very competitive person, Morgan saw the early money as a sign of winning.

Morgan learned early to network in the community and within his profession. He has served on many boards and committees, including the Private Companies Practice Section of the AICPA. He particularly wants to serve his profession and was the 2000–2001 president of the Tennessee Society of CPAs. Other competing CPAs will say of LBMC, "They own the Tennessee Society." Morgan says, "When our firm gets involved in something, I don't believe in dabbling in it. I want us to make a real contribution so we will work hard to be very active and participatory. We do the same thing in a variety of industry associations where we specialize."

After three years with KPMG, Morgan's entrepreneurial juices encouraged him to start his own practice with another friend. Then in 1984, Jim Lattimore, Charlie Black, David Morgan, and Michael Cain founded LBMC.

M. Lee Smith, a client of David Morgan, says, "He really focuses on working to solve my problems. David is intense around my issues and he really understands how my business operates. I can count on him to understand, creative, aggressive, and extremely helpful. He resells me every day."

enjoy the work you are assigned, no problem. However, much of the work that gets assigned is work that others do not want to do. The key to being able to work continuously with clients you enjoy, in areas you enjoy, is your selling skill.

In The Rainmaker Academy's consulting practice, we identify the type of projects that our CPA clients really enjoy doing. Then we help them find more of this type work.

Bob Gaida, a partner with BDO Seidman in Woodbridge, New Jersey, recognized this when he was recruiting. He said, "I have to recruit against the Big Five for the best people on campus. Telling them that our firm has white walls with beautiful pictures gets you nowhere. Many college students go through four years of indoctrination about the Big Five. It dawned on me that I had to come up with a clear benefit in students' eyes that would make them say yes to us. Otherwise, I would end up with the lesser staff. And that would translate in the clients' eyes to the students who were rejected by the finer firms. Those clients would have smaller margins, less profitability, and be more prone to get you sued. I had to sell to get the better students. The same is true with clients. If I want the better client, I must sell."

Harvey Mackay, author of *Swim with the Sharks without Getting Eaten Alive*,[2] describes the effects of downsizing during tough economic times. A bank officer had to dispose of one of three professionals. He terminated the most technically qualified professional and kept the two who had built personal networks. Mackay draws five conclusions:

1. Talent alone will not save you.
2. Training and education will not save you.
3. The government will not save you.
4. No matter how self-reliant, dedicated, loyal, competent, and well educated you are, you need more to save yourself.
5. You need a network.

> *High-performance net workers gain endorsements for reasons that go beyond the basic product or service. They do extraordinary things.*
>
> —Thomas J. Stanley, *Networking with the Affluent and Their Advisors*[3]

When Terry Orr wanted to ascend to partner, he was required for the first time to bring in $50,000 of new business. He had not attracted any new business in nine years. Orr says, "It shook me for about 24 hours. It was a real wake-up call. You have wake-up calls in your life, but despite all the things I had accomplished, all of a sudden my career was at stake. I had to take a different direction. I had to focus differently in order to move forward. And I realized that there were a lot of people who could read the textbooks and get the answers in public accounting. But being able to generate new business was a unique quality that would allow me to control the rest of my career. It was vitally important that I figure out how to do that."

Accounting Firms Have Responsibilities Too

Sadly, firms do not prepare young accountants for the realities of the business. Many accountants join firms that say that technical competence is all that matters. Later, when you have mastered the technical side of the business, you learn that selling is crucial to moving up. Accountants who are unprepared for this news often leave the profession. During 1999 the American Institute of CPAs sponsored a vision project. Two of the five core competencies dealt with selling:

1. *Communication and leadership skills.* Able to give and exchange information within meaningful context and with appropriate delivery and interpersonal skills. Able to influence, inspire, and motivate others to achieve results.

2. *Focus on the customer, client, and market.* Able to anticipate and meet the changing needs of clients, employees, customers, and markets better than competitors.

The 4 Cs and Ps of Marketing

The 4 Ps of marketing represent the seller's point of view. The 4 Cs reflect the customer's viewpoint.

1. **Customer value (versus Product):** Defining the characteristics of your product or service in terms of customers' needs.
2. **Cost to the customer (versus Price):** Determines customers' spending.
3. **Convenience (versus Place):** Looking at location from the customer's perspective.
4. **Communication (versus Promotion):** This includes advertising, personal selling, sales promotions, and other methods.

—Philip Kotler, *Kotler on Marketing*[4]

Your Unique Position

"Sometimes I feel defeated before I even begin the marketing process." I hear this statement often, in private, from accountants who are reluctant to step into the selling arena. Author Harry Beckwith points out that if you have not created a compelling distinction and benefits to people who use your service, your own people will not present a strong selling message.

Usually, when CPA firms have communicated to employees a compelling advantage the firm can offer clients, the environment for selling is well established. When employees feel passionately about a firm's partners and staff members, selling is easy.

I believe that anyone can conquer fear by doing the things he fears to do, provided he keeps doing them until he gets a record of successful experiences behind him.

—Eleanor Roosevelt

Call Reluctance

Accountants are not the only ones paralyzed psychologically and then unable to forge through the marketing process. The barriers to marketing or selling are real to all human beings. For over 20 years, I was responsible for a sales team. We had men and women who were highly trained in selling and marketing. And almost to a person, the key for each of them to dramatically increase their sales was to get over the hurdle of what we termed "call reluctance."

What is fear? The dictionary defines fear as a feeling of anxiety, misgiving, apprehension, phobia, dread, or horror caused by the nearness of evil or pain. Franklin Roosevelt said, "We have nothing to fear but fear itself." What he seemed to mean was that if America approached the world with timidity, that timidity itself would defeat us. In the rough-and-tumble game of football, many injuries are caused by tentative contact. Great running backs learn that the only way to deal with the obvious tackle by 1,200 pounds of defensive beef is to turn on the afterburners as if to knife right through the danger.

The fear of failure is a major stumbling block for us. Our profession is so insistent on perfection that the idea of failing at anything is so frightening that we will not even attempt a marketing activity. It is much more comfortable to prepare a tax return where there's little possibility of failing than to attempt a marketing activity that has a high probability of failure.

The fear of rejection is a deep-seated and debilitating feeling that is so unsettling that we find ourselves avoiding any situation in which we could possibly be rebuffed. This fear is so powerful that we even attach the fear of rejection to a situation where a prospect might turn our services down for very logical reasons.

The fear of success is the same fear that many politicians express when they take office for the first time: "Now that I've been elected, what do I do now?" We fear that if we succeed at marketing that we will add more hours, more drudgery, and more problems to our already crazy schedules.

Then, of course, we often lack the self-confidence necessary to step out and meet these fears head on. The lack of self-confidence can result from being unfamiliar with a particular activity. But even the top performers in any field deal with a lack of self-confidence. They speak of the jitters or butterflies before a game or a performance.

Another definition of fear requires us to analyze the letters F-E-A-R as False Evidence Appearing Real. A few years ago a man hijacked an airplane with a bar of soap. The evidence was false but, to the pilot, it appeared real.

Dealing with Fear

Reading this book will not banish your fears. You can learn only to deal with those psychological bugaboos, challenge them, and attack them head on to keep them from defeating you before you begin to sell.

Successful marketers are not fearless. My friend Ken Powers says, "Where there is no fear, there can be no courage." You can learn to channel your fears into emotions that help you succeed. The best antidote for fear is action. As the old adage goes, when you fall off a horse, the best thing to do is get right back on.

One of the first steps in dealing with any fear is to begin a pattern of positive self-talk. Give yourself a pep talk or a faith talk. Instead of defeatist ideas, give yourself success messages. Messages such as "I am an accountant and I am important. I know what I am talking about. I can help my clients. My associates are the best accounting firm team in town. My clients will be glad they retained my services."

Bill Jenkins, former CEO of Kennedy & Coe, LLC, of Goodland, Kansas, whom you'll meet in Day 7, worked hard to develop this self-confidence. He says, "As I approach a potential client situation, I give myself a little self-talk, I say 'I'm a stud, you're a stud and we can do big things together.'"

The second step is to stay away from the complaining negative people in your firm. When the people who sap your energy and get you down by complaining show up in your office, leave. When you are subjected to their complaints, say something like "What is good in your life?" or counter their complaint with a positive comment. Accountants as a group have a healthy skepticism. Some turn cynical or hypercritical. They tend to be critical of each other. Although some criticism is absolutely necessary, much of it is destructive in nature. Stay away from those people in your firm who are chronic complainers.

Handling Complainers

Dealing with negative co-workers can drain your energy. One strategy to turn them on a more positive track is to exaggerate what they say so that it sounds even worse. This will make them say that things aren't that bad and turns their thinking in a more constructive direction.

—*Executive Edge* newsletter

The third step in dealing with fear is to develop an action plan. When doing training for accounting firms, I separate people into breakout sessions to rehearse new concepts. It is only through concerted action that you will learn to channel your fears into constructive energy. Most accounting firms insulate their accountants from marketing responsibility until they have been around a few years. By this time their fears are built to an almost overpowering degree.

Other Benefits of Selling

Finally, let's discuss the rewards of learning to sell. Your income will soar. When you can sell, you will be able to create your own group of clients and staff members to handle those clients. Appropriately managed, your income will grow dramatically. One of my students made over $1 million in 1999, after only 12 years in the profession. She left one of the Big Five accounting firms in 1992 and began to sell her services. By 1999 her gross exceeded $2 million.

Selling skills are in great demand. If you become unhappy with your present employer, other firms will be standing in line to hire you if you can sell. Bob Gaida understood this when he worked with me to create a Sales College. He said, "I knew that we would be training people and the sales training would make them more attractive to other accounting firms. But the risks were greater in not training them and keeping them than training them and risking losing them. Most managing partners would rather not invest in training. We took the better business calculation."

Firms with CPAs who can sell will grow in good times and in bad times. In many of our classes at The Rainmaker Academy, our consultants ask CPAs,

"What happens in a business when revenues are flat or are declining?" The answers are:

- Money gets tight, so that raises and bonuses are lower.
- Owners start cutting corners to keep up their income.
- Training expenses are restricted.
- Computer upgrades are delayed or canceled.
- Client service suffers, because the owners try to serve more customers with fewer people.
- Advancement opportunities are reduced.
- The best people leave.
- The average people stay.
- The best clients leave.
- Hiring of new staff is reduced, so we have no one to whom we can delegate work.
- Because staff is restricted; we work on a lower level, in uninteresting areas.
- Personal growth is stymied.

Then we ask: "What happens in a business with double-digit growth?" The answers are:

- We have more opportunities to advance to manager and partner.
- We get better raises and bonuses.
- The partners invest in better computers and in better training.
- We are able to attract the best people.
- We have staff members to whom we can delegate work. The less experienced can find this work interesting, whereas we can assume new and more challenging and interesting projects.
- Clients hear about your success and are attracted to you.

Think about it: When you have the attitude "I will help sell our firm to clients and to prospects," you become a part of the solution for success, not a part of the problem.

Summary

Accountants have many reasons to be uncertain about selling. They usually have little preparation for it in their training or early work. Yet to grow as a professional, you must develop clients. Personal growth is challenging. There is no greater feeling than that of attracting a new client to your firm. Attracting a new client is strong testimony to your professional stature, your technical skills, your network, and everything you have worked to establish. Once you have attracted one client, you will enjoy the tremendous satisfaction and growth of learning selling skills. Sales guru Tom Hopkins says, "The better you are at sales, the more you benefit others—your clients, your family, and the nation's economy."

This book contains 31 sections, one for every day in the month. Read one daily. It will help you find new ways to promote your practice. Or, if you find yourself on the seventh day of a month in need of a sales boost, read the entry for Day 7.

2 Selling Is a Learned Skill

If you want to increase your success rate, increase your failure rate.

—Thomas Watson, Jr.[1]

Fear of failure, or the related fear of rejection, is probably the biggest obstacle that you have to overcome to learn better selling skills. To become good at a new skill, you have to fail. The more often you try, the more you'll fail and the faster you'll learn.

This concept is not unique to learning to sell accounting services. As we get older, many of us stay within our comfort zones. We don't want to learn something new that is difficult, whether it is surfing or snowboarding. Believe me, learning to sell your services is a lot easier than learning to surf, snowboard, water-ski, and so on. And you don't fall down as much! With your services you're selling something you know a lot about that can help others. If that's not true, you should get out of the business.

During the many years I have trained CPAs to sell, I have discovered that the most successful rainmakers have certain characteristics. Most of these characteristics are the result of learning and environment, not genetics. Tom Hopkins, the noted motivational speaker, once told me, "An interested introvert can be a better marketer than an interesting extrovert." This is indeed true in the accounting industry. I have found that most accountants can be solid rainmakers—if they are willing to study, practice, and focus on improving their selling performance.

Jeff Everly, a partner with Yount, Hyde & Barbour in Winchester, Virginia who is profiled in Day 4, says, "I think anybody can learn to play golf. If you practice hard, you can play a good game of golf, but not everybody is going to be able to go on the PGA Tour. By the same token, I think anybody can learn to sell. You just have to make up your mind to do it, work really hard, and have some fun."

Deborah Bailey Browne, a graduate of The Rainmaker Academy from Newburgh, New York, who is profiled in Day 19, says, "I think that everyone can learn to become a Rainmaker and to use their assets, their strengths and weaknesses in different ways. I do feel that certain people are better rainmakers. For example, I have a friend who is an artist. He tells me that I need to be a painter to relax. I can't draw. He said 'No, everyone can learn to draw.' So I said, hum, maybe one day I will take some classes. I don't think I could ever paint or draw as well as someone who is naturally gifted. However, I could to learn draw enough to do some things. So I think I'm using the analogy with the rainmaking and I think that you've got to still do some rainmaking. I think you can learn to sell. Perhaps your strength is more technical. If you are also rainmaking, coupled with the technical skills—that's a huge positive."

PORTRAIT OF A SALES LEADER

BILL FINGLAND is managing partner of Baird, Kurtz & Dobson, in Springfield, Missouri. Growing up in a small town in Missouri, Fingland wanted to be a lawyer. His love of debate, speech, and theater classes steered him toward a career in communications, and he thought the law might be a good fit for him. Working in his father's business, Fingland Glass Company, he developed a strong work ethic. Bill says, "My dad worked long hours and my mom was a nurse. Working with my dad in the glass company helped me to develop an interest in business. Maybe because the office was air-conditioned and the warehouse was not, I gravitated toward the office during my younger years."

Fingland's cousin wanted to be a lawyer but, in college, he changed to accounting. This influenced Fingland to study accounting at the University of Missouri, where he received his BS and MA degrees. However, he was still very interested in speech, debate, and theater. Fingland says this training was very instrumental in him being comfortable making presentations today before boards, committees, and other groups. "Every successful CPA must be able to communicate," Fingland says.

Fingland joined Baird, Kurtz & Dobson's (BKD) Springfield, Missouri office directly out of college. At the time, BKD's revenue was less than $30 million. The firm now reaps nearly $120 million in annual billings. Said Bill of his early years at BKD, "I worked in the Springfield office under three people who had a major influence on me: Dave Henderson,

Like and Trust

Businesspeople do business with people they like and trust. They don't do business with someone they don't like, no matter how great that CPA might be. If you are unwilling to meet personally with prospects, "like" doesn't have a chance to develop. Spending time with prospects, so they come to like and trust you, is crucial to building a strong sales machine.

Often, I have the opportunity to follow up on a winning or losing proposal in a competitive situation. In over 70 percent of the winning proposals we have analyzed, there is a strong correlation between the length of the personal relationship between a key decision influencer and the winner. The decision influencers report things such as: "We had known Anne for a number of years and just felt comfortable hiring her firm." Or "I worked with Brad during the United Way campaign and found him to be a class person." Or

Dick Donaldson, and Jim Glauser. Each of them taught me a different aspect of marketing and selling."

In the mid-1980s, Fingland moved to the firm's Tulsa office to develop a healthcare practice.

The office had a tiny amount of healthcare work when he arrived, but a few years later had gross billings of nearly $5 million. Fingland became the firm's director of the healthcare practice in 1994 and managing partner in 1997.

Fingland is a strong believer in training his firm's employees to be strong communicators. "You can be the best damn CPA in the world, and if you don't tell somebody about it, you'll starve to death," he says. In 1999 his firm initiated the BKD Sales Academy for managers and young partners. Selling is as vital in public accounting as it is in any other business, according to Fingland.

During his years of developing the Tulsa practice, Fingland learned to pilot an airplane. "I wanted to be very efficient with my time, and the plane could get me several hundred miles very quickly," he says. Whenever he flew to a client's business or hospital several hundred miles away, Fingland would make stops along the way to visit with clients and prospects. He'd call ahead and suggest a meeting with the prospect, saying, "I'm flying just over you to visit a client and I'd like to stop in for a short visit to catch up with you. Would you pick me up at the airport?" "Not only was this a little different to many people, it helped me to cover a lot of Oklahoma territory very efficiently," Fingland says.

"Our chairman knew your partner, John, from a former business relationship." Although in most cases a deep friendship does not exist, the buyers almost always genuinely like and trust the winner more than they do the loser.

 There's a world of choice out there. People are looking for products they can trust, not just ones that meet their needs.

—Lou Pritchett[2]

12 Steps for Recovery

We teach a 12-step selling process for accountants that we call our 12 steps for recovering accountants. Developing "like and trust" actually is step 5, after qualifying (step 4) and before discovering needs and wants (step 6). Often accountants begin the discovery phase of the work before gaining the trust of the prospect. When this happens, the prospect may be evasive about real needs. After all, company owners may not want internal financial problems spread about. And until someone likes and trusts you, it is unlikely that you will gain access to his or her real needs.

Bob Gaida, whom you will meet in Day 15, says, "One of the most important aspects of early selling is: If I could only do one thing for this person, what would be the one that wins his heart." Winning the heart early in the sale is what power sellers believe and practice.

During our proposal follow-up, we have discovered that gaining access to a key piece of information is critical to winning proposals. In many cases, the losers never gained access to this critical information. You obtain critical information on which you build a winning proposal through an effective like-and-trust phase of selling or during an effective investigation phase (discussed in Days 23 and 24). Getting a prospect to state a need, in the form of a desire or want, will enable you to respond with a strong benefit statement.

Accountants who are effective at steps 4 and 5—developing like and gaining trust, and discovering needs and wants—rarely prepare written proposals. Many buyers in these situations form such a strong bond with the seller that the competitors are ruled out early in the process.

Mike Kruse, of Kruse and Associates, says, "When I go on a sales call, my first thought is to make a friend for life, even if the prospect does not work out now. In some cases, I am laying the groundwork for a future business relationship. I know if people trust me, they will share, sometimes secret, key information, with me." Kruse founded his firm in 1993; now it has grown to nearly 100 employees. Kruse partners sell all of the time, but most of the proposals are done on a laptop computer. A partner enters data and then prints a summary of recommendations for the prospect. In seven years of phenomenal growth, partners in Kruse's firm have done fewer than five formal written proposals.

12 Steps to Selling Success for the Recovering Accountant

1. Prospecting for leads
2. Gaining access to prospects
3. Qualifying prospects
4. Identifying decision influencers
5. Developing "like and trust"
6. Discovering problems and needs
7. Creating wants
8. Handling objections
9. Demonstrating capabilities
10. Creating value perceptions
11. Persuading decision influencers
12. Closing the sale

Accept Responsibility for Results

Too many people use a variation of the old line, "The dog ate my homework." Today it is in vogue to blame your parents, or your grandparents, or your partners, or your competitors, or the client's personnel for your own failures. But the best rainmakers don't blame something or somebody; they take full responsibility for results they achieve.

If you don't succeed at winning a new account, you must program your mind to not blame. Instead, learn from the situation and work harder next time. Bob Gaida says, "Leadership and sales have a high correlation. Leaders take responsibility for success. You've got to be in it to win it. You must try. It doesn't matter that you fail, just get up and go and you will have your fair share of success. Good leaders and sellers say, 'Okay, now I understand that I have to get up and bat in order to hit a home run, but my challenge is how many times can I hit a home run those times I get up to bat. I'd like to have a good batting average.' But people who can't sell will say, 'The reason I won't even get up to bat is because everybody knows I can't hit a home run.'"

Process beats substance. . . . The rhythm of the unfolding relationship, the way you are handled (informed, misinformed, belatedly informed, not informed) explains more about how you react to a product or service than the so-called result itself.

—Tom Peters[3]

Failure Is Necessary

Programming your mind for selling success requires that you handle the fear of failure. Fear of failure paralyzes many great people. The key to overcoming your fear of failure is to redefine what constitutes failure. If you allow the depression that comes when a prospect says no to your proposal to defeat you from making more proposals, then it is the fear that holds you back. With any selling effort, there are going to be a number of proposals that you will not win. Learn from them, and then move on. Don't let fear stop you from making another sales call.

If you view each sale as a life-and-death situation, then be prepared for a life of depression. In the business of selling, there are going to be more defeats than victories. So we must broaden the definition of success by tracking your proposal success rate over multiple selling situations or each year's proposals. Then calculate your percentage of success. Now you can focus on your overall record.

Bob Fifer, in his book *Double Your Profits,*[4] says: "The ability to see successes and failures in groupings is a valuable game to play." You learn to see the bigger picture and to balance the failures against the successes. Doing so will cause you to worry less about rejections. The result will be bigger successes as well as fewer failures because your confidence will become a self-fulfilling prophecy.

Be realistic. Would you rather have 100 percent success on 1 proposal or 30 percent success on 10? A major league team will not hire the ballplayer who can bat once a year and hit one home run even though his average is perfect. If you are going to play in the major leagues, make a resolution to double your failure rate. By doing so, I promise that you will more than double your successes.

Selling is a numbers game. The only way to be successful is first to insure that you are engaged in a sufficient amount of activity to have a success rate. As Bob Gaida says, "You lose 100 percent of the proposals you don't make."

Selectively target your marketing efforts. The most successful marketing has a high failure rate. Even the best direct mail campaigns obtain only a

3 percent response rate. If you focus on the 97 percent failure rate, you'll never launch the campaign, but if you focus on what you can do with a 1 to 3 percent response rate, you begin to see the possibilities.

Progress Requires Action

To be successful in selling, you must take responsibility for your actions and be willing to fail. For accounting firms to succeed in training their staffs to sell, there must be a climate that encourages action. If accountants are as critical of your lack of success each time you attempt a marketing initiative as you are of your accounting work, most of you will not even try. We must encourage everyone in the firm to try marketing by encouraging people to fail more often.

For many of us, a better understanding of the marketing process will enable us to better deal with the fears that hold us back. When you feel the need to come back from a chamber of commerce business mixer with a new client in tow, the pressure is too great. Yet if you talk with several people at the mixer and increase their awareness and familiarity of you and your firm, count this as a success.

You will be rewarded for your successes in marketing. When you achieve a small percentage success rate, often the clients you obtain bring in big-time fees. You will not be rewarded by the percentage of successes, but by the number of successes.

Above-Average Willpower and Ambition

Any person who has the willpower to pass the CPA exam has an enormous amount of ambition. Self-discipline is a key for top sellers to succeed. No matter how tempted they were to give up, they persisted toward their goals.

Recently I met with a successful music producer. He told me that for every top-selling music star, there were hundreds of people with more talent than the star who made millions. Fascinated, I asked if there was anything that set the stars apart from the talented but average musicians. His answer was startlingly simple. He said, "The superstars have remarkable self-confidence." Many of the "stars" believed in themselves so strongly, or had someone else believe in them so strongly, that they were able to persist, even when the odds were against them.

Every year I meet talented CPAs who manage practices far below their maximum potential. Why? In my view, it's not because of lack of opportunity or of talent. Instead, it's because these CPAs do not believe in themselves.

Lack of self-esteem will hinder the most talented CPAs from reaching their goals. An accounting firm full of people with low self-esteem can't be highly successful in marketing.

Be Intensely Goal Oriented

Goals crystallize and energize your selling. We ask students in The Rainmaker Academy to write 21 reasons they want to succeed in selling. With each personal marketing plan, we ask people to write specific goals. We do this because I have found that goal setting is crucial for people to be top sellers.

Goals help us overcome and work through some of the energy-sappers of successful selling: lack of time and the fear of success.

We All Have Time

Once at a presentation, I heard Zig Ziglar[5] say, "Son, if you are going to have to eat a frog, you don't want to have to stare at the sucker too long." In other words, he was saying, do the most difficult things first in your day.

Time constraints seem to be a huge barrier for lack of selling by accountants. Time is an accountant's most precious commodity. And although a continuous supply of time is available, it cannot be stored for future use. You cannot manage time. You can manage your activities and yourself, but time is and will be the same forever. Many accountants, however, feel trapped and manipulated by the demands others make on their time. When you have clearly established goals for your selling, you will tend to place a priority on achievement of the goals and not allow time to slip away.

Many successful sellers focus on the activities that demand no extra time. The way in which you communicate with your employees and clients can be positive marketing encounters. When you communicate management recommendations, internal control weaknesses, or adjustments, do you consider the selling impact they have?

 Any fact facing us is not as important as our attitude toward it, for that determines our success or failure.

—Dr. Norman Vincent Peale

Fear of Success

The fear of success is really the fear of failing in the future. What we really fear is obtaining a new client and not being able to provide great service. Of course, some accountants believe they are not worthy enough to build a great practice. They suffer from the guilt of past deeds. So their continuing procrastination, which results in continuing failure, is atonement.

To deal successfully with the fear of success, you must plan to bring in new clients. To do this, you must leave holes in your schedule so that you are able to accept attractive work. If you fill the factory with junk work, you will not have the ability to add attractive work.

Many accountants are worriers. They ask, "If I bring a new client into the firm, will I be able to provide better service than the client has received in the past? Will I be able to meet the client's needs? Do I really have the time, or will this new client overwork me?" A more positive way to look at the fear of success is to see it as an opportunity for growth.

Fear of success can be understood and managed as positively as other psychological fears are managed. A thorough and objective analysis will assure that you, your partners, and your staff have the technical abilities to meet the client's needs, or will indicate where additional expertise is needed. Then you can make appropriate adjustments, if any are needed. Managing the fear of success is a road to improving the capabilities of you and your firm, preparing you to capitalize on any opportunity of interest.

Just because your prospect is currently being served by a first-class local or national firm does not mean the prospect is getting first-class service. Recognize this fact. Furthermore, if you focus on selling services that your firm is providing to other clients in an excellent manner, contact the prospect and stress how valuable those services could be to the prospect. Last, match the prospect with the appropriate person in your firm.

Make one of your personal goals to eliminate 50 to 100 hours of junk work every year. Then focus your marketing effort to bring in the kind of work you clearly love. Your clients will steer you in the right direction, you will be more attractive to new clients, and your enthusiasm will excite you so much that you will not fail.

Every year, you will grow to enjoy your work more and more as you act on overcoming your fears. I have trained thousands of people over the years to improve their selling abilities. Many of them held a false idea that they could not succeed, but when they began to step out and try, their success in marketing excited them.

Ability to Approach Strangers

Every seller has some level of call reluctance. But the best rainmakers train themselves to overcome their butterflies and get out of their offices and meet people. Harvey Mackay, author of *Dig Your Well Before You're Thirsty,* says,

"If I had to name the single characteristic shared by all of the truly successful people I've met over a lifetime, I'd say it is the ability to create and nurture
a network of contacts."

Your greatest asset in successful marketing is a strong belief in yourself and
the great service that you are providing your clients. Armed with strong confidence in yourself and a determination to meet people, you will be able to
attract the type of clients you want.

*Character consists of what you do on the third and fourth tries
after you've failed.*

—James Michener

When CPA Terry Orr's managing partner told him that to make partner
he would need to bring in $50,000 of new client business, he went into action.
"My first attempts were simply going around to people that I knew, friends
and people I'd worked with, saying, 'I need help, can you help me?' The response was overwhelming. Everyone wanted to help, and then I would explain
what the situation was: 'I've got to generate new business.' So I started going
out to my contacts who were clients and asking, 'Do you know of someone?
I've given you great service. I need your help.' And they started making referrals. I went to bankers and attorneys and people who I didn't know. The grat-
ifying thing was I never had one person say, 'No, I won't help you.' Every single
one said, 'Of course I'll help you.' They started sending me referrals and, all
of a sudden, this thing started to flow and my eyes were finally opened to
the fact that this was not something that was that difficult. It was as easy as
sitting down with someone and asking for their help on a personal basis: 'I
need help, can you help me?'"

Fear of Failure

Let's talk about channeling the fear of failure into energy that will drive you
to succeed. Discomfort or mild anxiety has some positive aspects. When we
are mildly anxious, we work at peak performance levels and actually accomplish more than when we are comfortable. So if you are uncomfortable meeting strangers, push yourself into these mildly uncomfortable situations. Start
by associating with your client's executives who are outside the accounting
department. Get to know the sales force, the manufacturing team, the design
group, and any of the other people who work with your client.

Once you learn to put yourself into mildly uncomfortable situations, teach your staff to do the same. As you become conditioned to the discomfort, you will be able to increase your marketing prowess dramatically. Trying to force people straight into situations where high anxiety sets in will create avoidance behavior, the source of procrastination and disorganization.

Bill Jenkins, former CEO of Kennedy & Coe, says, "Not everybody is going to be the same. Not everybody is going to be as creative as others. Some are going to do better, but I think all of them have a significant potential for selling. But if it is left just to them—if they don't see somebody else do it, if there is not somebody else in the room encouraging it, if they are not having their hand held—they may have difficulty.

"The only way a CPA learns to sell is to take her selling. He or she has got to be with people who know what they are doing, see other people do it . . . then they follow your lead . . . they try it themselves. When they do try, they have some luck; when they do, you celebrate it and give them encouragement, and they try it again and they get better at it.

"You have to be careful with young accountants. A young person goes out there and finally sells something, but he typically underprices the work by at least half. But he's made a sale and is pretty fired up about it. He can't continue to go on underpricing jobs, so you've got to talk to him. But you've got to be careful about reprimanding him for underpricing it. Otherwise, he won't sell again because he's experienced negative consequences for selling."

Fear of Rejection

All sellers must cope with the fear of rejection that comes before the contact and feelings of rejection after the contact has occurred. The fear of personal rejection prevents many accountants from making a marketing contact. Most marketers can separate themselves from the product to overcome fear of rejection. Because our services are our products, however, we are the product, and detachment is harder for us.

Research has shown that moving a prospect from contact to contract will take about nine actual positive marketing interactions with your firm. These contacts might include dozens of ads or mailings because the reality is that your prospects miss many of your attempted interactions.

The first technique to deal successfully with the fear of rejection is: Don't go for the kill on the first call. Set the objective for the first interaction at a very low level—maybe just creating awareness. Then if you can build each successive call into a sales strategy, the overwhelming fear of rejection won't stop you.

Most people give up just when they're about to achieve success. They quit on the one-yard line. They give up at the last minute of the game, one foot from a winning touchdown.

—H. Ross Perot

The second technique in dealing with fear of rejection is planning your response to rejection. Your contact may have a rational reason for not doing business with you right now. She may be having a bad day and her lackluster response is not your fault. A steady, consistent approach will win out. The average sale in American commerce is made on the fifth sales call, but the

Of Self-Esteem, Self-Respect, and Pride

The most important single quality of success and happiness is a positive mental attitude, a general feeling of optimism about yourself and your future.

There are four universal principles, or laws, that determine your levels of self-esteem, self-respect, and personal pride.

1. **Law of Belief.** Your beliefs become your realities. Biggest single challenge? Self-limiting beliefs.

2. **Law of Expectations.** Whatever you expect, with confidence, becomes your own "self-fulfilling prophecy."

3. **Law of Attraction.** You are a "living magnet." You attract into your life people and circumstances in harmony with your dominant thoughts.

4. **Law of Correspondence.** Your outer world is a mirror of your inner world.

There are three key ideas that explain your levels of self-esteem, self-respect, and personal pride:

1. All causation is mental.

2. You become what you think about most of the time.

3. If you change your thinking, you change your life.

—Brian Tracy

average marketer makes only two or three calls. My experience shows that for accountants, it takes more than five contacts to achieve a sale.

The feeling of rejection you have when someone does not respond positively to you can be depressing. However, if you expect that over 90 percent of your marketing activity will not close the sale at that moment, the feeling will not overwhelm you. As accountants, we are trained to avoid making mistakes. We avoid low-payoff activity. We must make the mental shift to seeing marketing as a numbers game.

Teach yourself that marketing that is not successful today will be successful tomorrow. The activity of teaching yourself will help you build the potential client relationship or will prepare you to market better. Engage in positive self-talk and separate your ego from the sale.

Last, maintain a healthy balance of positive client interaction with new prospect activity. The client relationships will enable you to be confident with prospects. The fear of rejection is a very powerful psychological force that affects persons in every walk of life. It often prevents accountants from initiating any marketing activity whatsoever. Many accountants experience this fear before meeting with a prospect, imagining that the prospect will not be interested. Success at marketing requires, first, recognition that the fear of rejection exists, followed by action to deal with it and overcome it.

The best way to overcome the fear of rejection is to adopt a positive attitude and actively market your services with the belief that some prospects will indeed want to engage you.

Remember that all fear is conquered through experience. If you have a positive frame of mind when you encounter prospects, you will experience an increasing level of acceptance. The fear of rejection will steadily diminish as your experience and expectation of acceptance increase.

High Level of Empathy

Until you are able to put yourself in your clients' shoes, understand their needs and concerns, and then respond appropriately, you will only be a minor league rainmaker. Mark Kaland, partner at Clifton Gunderson in Milwaukee, Wisconsin, says, "I am still uncomfortable with the side of selling that seems pushy. I prefer to listen to my client's needs and then match these needs to a Clifton Gunderson solution. Just looking out for the client's best interests always results in increased business for us. That is the type of selling I like."

Sometimes we get so involved in the technical side of public accounting that we overlook the human side. Michael LeBoeuf, in his powerhouse book *How to Win Customers and Keep Them for Life,*[6] says that clients only buy two things from us: solutions to their problems and good feelings.

Most CPAs are great at solving problems; after all, that is what education and training have prepared us to do. We are extremely valuable to our clients because of this ability. However, when it comes to providing good feelings, we often fail to recognize the tremendous profit potential.

Clients will pay premium fees, will pay on time, and won't complain as much about our bills when we provide them with good feelings. Tax season is a good time to plan to improve your dedication to giving your clients good feelings.

Summary

Selling is a skill, and, like any other skill, improvement comes with focus and practice. Just as you wouldn't expect to get better at golf without practice, you can't expect your selling skills to improve without practice. Failure in the selling situation is not failure if you learn from it. Even a no can begin to develop the relationship. In fact, someone who has turned you down is more likely to hire you later over someone they meet for the first time because you are both familiar and persistent.

Developing a solid bond of liking and trust is a key factor in getting commitment from clients. It is one of 12 steps in the selling process.

3 Start a Consistent Marketing Program

Things come to those who wait, but only those things left by those who hustle.

—Abraham Lincoln

If you could add a dozen clients a year who were similar to your very best clients, would you be happier and have a more profitable business? Of course you would! It is likely that you have 100 hours of billable client work that you could delegate to someone else in your firm. If you invested these 100 hours in marketing and sales activities, you could create new work that would equal 100 hours, or more, times your billing rate. If you're not doing this, you are losing megabucks because of your lack of sales activity.

Attracting desirable clients is one of the key benefits of marketing and sales. If you simply wait for the business to walk in, you will get clients no one else has targeted. The best way to add the "good" clients to your firm is for you and your staff to always be prospecting for qualified leads. Aggressive lead generation or prospecting is usually the difference between an average firm and a super one.

Jim Belew, former managing partner of Belew Averitt, LLP, in Dallas, says, "We were coasting along in the late '80s and early '90s letting other professionals take away business from us. The accounting culture was really anti-marketing, the state board of accountancy did not allow selling, and we weren't very good at it. But we woke up one day and realized that we had to take steps to start an aggressive marketing program."

Check out the profit levels under the two scenarios shown in the table on the next page. Consider the relative impact of "Doing the Billable Work Myself" versus "Delegating the Billable Work and Selling 100 hours of New Work."

Here is the comparison between the two scenarios:

Doing the Billable Work Myself	Delegating the Billable Work and Selling 100 Hours of New Work	
$20,000 (100 hours × $200 rate)	$15,000 (100 hours × $150 rate, delegated)	
	5,000 (Mark-up)	
	−5,000 (Cost of staff doing work)	
	$20,000 (100 hours × $200 rate— new work brought in)	
$20,000 Net one-year profit	$35,000 Net one-year profit	
$140,000 Net seven-year profit	$245,000 Net seven-year profit	

Calculate what the compound effect would be if you invested 100 hours per year, every year, in selling new accounts. Your profit would amount to over $800,000 more during the period than if you did the work yourself. Then calculate the effect if you invested 200, 300, or more hours. You will clearly see why the firms that invest in marketing and sales are the most profitable year after year.

Five Key Elements of Accounting Sales

The best strategy in accounting sales is composed of five elements:

1 Generate a steady stream of leads into your firm.

2 Network deep into your prospects' organizations and enlist champions.

3 Satisfy clients' wants and desires as well as their needs.

4 Consistently train your entire staff to market and sell.

5 Always give a little "something extra" when working with clients, prospects, and referral sources.

Satisfied customers are an organization's most successful salespeople, because they do not stand to benefit financially from recommending the organization to others.

—Eberhard E. Scheuing, *Creating Customers for Life*

Generate a Steady Stream of Leads into Your Firm

If you are generating enough leads so that you screen out over 50 percent as being nonqualified, your lead generation machine is working well. If you accept anything that comes your way, the quantity of your leads is not adequate. Robert Bly, author of *Marketing Your Services,* says, "Many established service providers spend 10 to 25 percent of their time in self-promotion. Beginners must devote even more effort to establishing a reputation, getting clients, and making a name in the local community." We discuss lead generation in depth in the Days 6 and 7, so I will make only two points here.

1. Sales leader Terry Orr says, "There is a part of marketing that is just gathering the business cards and making the calls. Contacting and staying in touch with people you've met is an essential part of selling."

2. The absolute best source of quality prospects is through your referral network.

PORTRAIT OF A SALES LEADER

JIM BELEW's early training meeting the public and providing excellent customer service had a profound effect on his future success. Belew said, "I worked in a service station when service really meant something." He had a unique experience in the service station. One of the owners was a fastidious mechanic. His tools were all in order. His shop was spotless, and he went home each evening without a drop of oil or grease on him. This owner taught Belew the value of quality. He said, "People sought out this guy because he was so careful and clean. That was a big difference for mechanics. He exuded quality and I wanted to be like that."

The other owner, who ran the business side of the station, also intrigued him. Belew says, "The other owner supervised the other attendants and me and taught us how to greet our customers, how to do something a little extra for them. I worked for him for a number of years, and he started showing me more about how he ordered products, how he paid employees, how he scheduled, and other aspects of running the business."

After majoring in accounting at Oklahoma State, Belew joined Arthur Young in Dallas at a time when selling was not allowed in the accounting profession. He learned from the partners for whom he worked that

(continues)

the key to selling was paying great attention to your clients and achieving the clients' goals. He related this to the experience he'd learned as a youngster working in the service station.

Jim Belew and Jimmy Averitt were friends at Arthur Young. They opened their offices in 1976 with no clients and have grown to become the second largest local firm in Dallas. "Jimmy and I have been very fortunate to have attracted some of the brightest partners to our team," says Belew. He has often had a need to fill but waits until the highest-quality person came along. "If you compromise your quality standards, you compromise your business. The day you compromise your standards is the day you start going out of business. We want to build our business on solid ground with the best people," says Belew of his team of successful partners.

"I have never met a man with such an intense desire to help his clients and partners succeed," says Brenda Sellers, a former partner in Belew Averitt. This intense focus to help others succeed is the key to Jim Belew's firm's dramatic growth to a leading status in the Dallas market.

Belew established a firm-wide marketing plan in 1993. Each partner championed a focused area of development. He says, "During the first year we barely attained our planned results, but in the second year we reached our annual goals in five months. Since then we have learned to be much more predictable in our marketing goals." Belew Averitt grew from $2 million in net revenue in 1992 to over $11 million in 2000. Then, in 2000, Belew Averitt merged with BDO thereby expanding BDO's presence in the Dallas and Texas markets. BDO-Dallas is now one of the fastest-growing offices In the firm. Belew says, "Much of our growth came as a result of establishing a plan, then executing the plan daily."

Although clients remain the single best source of referrals, attorneys are a close second. We surveyed 274 accounting firms and found that client referrals accounted for 48 percent of referral business and attorneys account for 22 percent (almost twice as many as banker referrals). A growing number of referrals are also coming from other CPAs. And even though there hasn't been a study to determine the total impact, alliances and networks of accounting firms are growing to foster such referral work. The BDO Seidman Alliance and the McGladrey Network are two examples of associations of CPA firms established to stimulate the referral of clients to other firms.

In some very successful firms, attorneys account for as much referral business as do clients. Greg Anton, a partner at Anton, Collins & Mitchell in Denver, Colorado, says, "Many people in the profession would say your largest development opportunities are within your existing client base. I would say that this has not been the case with me. Most of my referred leads come from attorneys, bankers, and investment bankers."

Network Deep into Your Prospects' Organizations and Enlist Champions

The greater the number of decision makers, the longer the selling cycle. When deliberations to engage you take place in your absence, the marketing process becomes more complex. These factors make it critical that you have good contacts throughout a prospective client's organization.

Having to deal with multiple decisions makers is a barrier to selling public accounting services. Corporations and other organizations seldom have a single decision maker; more often, several persons are involved. Each of those decision makers may have a different view of the economy, a different view of the business, a different set of values, a different set of contacts and personal relationships, and a different set of goals.

Generally, the higher the price of the product, the longer the sales cycle.

—Tony Alessandra et al., *Non-Manipulative Selling*[1]

Harvey Mackay, author of *Swim with the Sharks,*[2] says, "Recently I've gotten better results by not even trying to talk directly with Mr./Ms. Head Honcho." In the modern business world, decisions are often made at lower levels in an organization. Obtaining a small assignment and proving your worth may enable you to move up in the organization later.

Dealing with multiple decision makers extends the selling cycle—and a long selling cycle is in itself a real barrier to selling success. The best clients don't change accountants that often. You have to plan a multiyear sales campaign for many prospects.

A third barrier to selling public accounting services is that much of the prospect's decision-making process occurs in your absence. You are not there to influence the decision. You prepare a written proposal, present it, and leave. Then the decision makers discuss their alternatives. You must learn to influence the engagement process even when you are not there. You must find ways to make your firm stand out so that the prospect will remember you.

Not-Yet Prospects

Most companies spend about 90% of their marketing budget on producing sale leads—but only 10% to follow up on them. Other studies show that about 26% of inquirers say they will buy within six months, 56% say they will buy eventually, and 18% have no plans to purchase, according to Wilson & Associates.

Over the long term, the group that plans to buy later produces four times more buyers than the 26% who say they'll buy soon. If people say they plan to buy later, keep in touch and use the extra time to build the relationship.

—*Executive Edge* newsletter

Depending on the prospect's urgency to hire, I use a different selling strategy for different stages. Many of my target prospects will not seem to be in a hurry to change accounting firms. I may not want to rush things either. In the early stages, I want to enlist a person in the organization who is receptive to me. The receptive person will give me information that will enable me to identify power influencers and discover problems and needs. He or she will introduce me around and may become my champion. If I begin to interact with the CEO too early in the process, my access time and in-depth conversation may be limited.

If the organization is nearing a change of service providers, a more intense sales effort is required. When a more rapid and intense sales effort is required, you may not have the time to develop the personal relationships you'd like.

Satisfy Clients' Wants and Desires as Well as Their Needs

Clients *need* financial statements. They *want* to make better decisions. Clients *need* to file a tax return. They *want* the convenience of having someone else prepare it. Clients *need* strategic planning. They *want* to take advantage of opportunities and avoid catastrophes.

Accountants who deal only in the *needs* of clients will earn a modest living. CPAs who satisfy the *wants* will be paid handsomely for their labors.

David Morgan says, "I try to learn something the prospect really wants. While I may not be able to get it for him, I can send him an article about it. That lets him know that I want him to have it too. Basically I am a shy person. Throw me into a room of people who I don't know and I am very uncomfortable. But I say to myself, 'I am here to find a want or need that I can help with.' And that motivates me to network."

Through the years, I have interviewed hundreds of clients of accounting firms. When I ask clients what they want, their number-one answer is: "I want my CPA to understand my business beyond the financial and tax reporting requirements." It makes sense, doesn't it? One of the fundamental needs of human beings is to be understood.

Sell Benefits, Not Features

CPAs spend many hours reading, training, and working on unique client matters. In many cases, CPAs understand a great deal about the client's business. But the client isn't aware of it. Strong CPAs must make clients aware of their understanding of the business.

Your services include features such as tax work and consulting. It should be obvious that clients don't care about your features; they care about how those features benefit them. Although you've probably heard that you should focus on client benefits in your selling, it's a point that's easy to forget. You show your understanding of your client's business by talking about the benefits that they want to achieve. These may be as general as "protection" from the IRS to as specific as helping them determine the true profitability of different product lines.

You also show your understanding and interest when you attend an industry meeting in your client's area, read a relevant trade journal, or take a training course relating to her business. Good selling is communicating your understanding to the client in subtle ways, such as chatting about the seminar you attended or the article you're reading.

The number-two answer we get when we ask clients what they want is "a more aggressive CPA." Clients define "aggressive" as being a proactive service provider and an advocate. One client of a CPA firm said to me, "Phil Scissors earned 10 years of his fees last year when he handled the IRS representation for me. I don't want to deal with those people and divert my attention from my business. He kept them out of my business and off my back." Some clients will actually get a bit angry when they learn their CPA could have performed a service, or knew of some technique, and didn't tell them.

Focus on what clients really want. Terry Orr of Belew Averitt says, "When I focus on wants, I receive a much higher price for audit or tax work. It's usually been the result of sitting down and understanding where the company is going. We understand they need an audit, but before we start the process of giving a bid we want to spend some time talking to them about where the company is today—what their objectives are for the company over the next three years and five years. We're not just coming in to do an audit. We are there to help accomplish the company's vision."

> *When you create an alliance with the vision, values, and core competencies of your customers, their business becomes your business. Their dreams become your dreams. Their goals become your opportunities. By understanding who they are and where they are going, you can say, "This is how I can help you get there."*
>
> —Barbara Geraghty, *Visionary Selling*[3]

Tony Zecca, of J. H. Cohn, tells the following story.

I was asked to go on a marketing call to a company called in the hardware business. I was referred in by one of the local banks to the company that was a distributor of hardware. They were having some difficult times. I walk into this building and it's like stepping back in time. The building is just a huge room and all these old gray-looking metal desks and all these people sitting there with piles and piles of paper all over the place. So I am escorted into the conference room. I'm sitting in this huge room and there's dust all over the place, cigarette butts lying on the floor, and I'm saying to myself "What the hell, what am I doing here? Who's going to sell to this guy, do we want to sell anything to him?" But this guy walks into the room and he's about 75 years old. He had a dirty old vest on and I thought he was the janitor. Turns out he was the president of the company.

So he sits down and, you know, one of the other lessons I've learned early on that I try to teach my people now is that you never know, when you're in a selling situation conditioned to listening a lot, you just never know where the connection is going to be, but unless you connect to the person you're selling to you're not selling them anything. So, we just started talking and we spent about two hours talking about everything in the world other than the business. And we just went on and on and on, and I noticed out of the corner of my eye that in the corner of the room there was a big pillow, one of those pillows that dogs lay on.

And after about two-and-a-half hours. this golden retriever comes walking into the room. I love dogs, and he comes over to me and sits down next to me. I pet him on his head and I reach down to say hello to him and he gives me a lick, and the guy says to me, "Well, if you're good enough for the dog, you're good enough for me."

He hired us and it had to be about a million dollars in fees that we collected over about four years. And I was up against all the big [firms], whatever they were at that point, big sticks, big cheese, I don't know what they were. But that was a true story. So I use that story a lot when I give seminars on marketing. Every once in a while, I use that story just to illustrate that you never really know where that connection is going to come from. And you know, I think it's a great story. He ended up being a wonderful client of mine, and I worked with him for about four years.

Consistently Train Your Entire Staff to Market and Sell

Marketing and selling are skills you can learn. The way to become a good marketer is the same way one would become a good golfer. Lessons from a pro are helpful. You can pick up a few tips by watching golf on TV. But the most productive way to improve your game is through practice, practice, and more practice. So it is with marketing. The only way to become a great marketer is through practice.

Many accountants have a comfort zone with marketing techniques. Good marketing training will allow them to expand their comfort zones in a safe environment. Good training allows each accountant to be challenged to try new techniques and provides positive feedback and support, not criticism.

"We talk about wanting your comfort zone plus 10 percent, when it comes to marketing," says Bill Fingland, CEO of BKD. "At BKD, we understand that everyone is different, but selling is a crucial part of your success in today's business world."

Greg Anton says, "Sales training over an extended period of time has been the most beneficial thing I have done to help me become a consistent business developer. I believe it strengthens all CPAs in their marketing efforts. But it cannot be a one-shot effort. That's a waste."

All marketing training programs should have a follow-up program that includes objectives and measurements of progress. Everyone gravitates toward new techniques. But as in learning golf, accountants should emphasize the basics: in this case, planning, prospecting, qualifying, relating, interviewing, handling objections, trial closing, and closing.

Accountants respond well to marketing training when:

- They receive it in manageable amounts.
- The training is participatory.
- They can visualize a model.
- They receive favorable results.
- They anticipate follow-up supervision to measure results.

The follow-up supervision is often labeled coaching. Many partners believe in miracles. They believe that staff members, most of whom have received little training in personal marketing during their careers, will miraculously begin bringing in new business the day they are made partners. Guess again.

If you really want to create a culture in which selling is "just part of the job," you must foster that culture from day 1. And the best way to do that is to give your staff on-the-job training.

Eight Tips to Help You Be a Better Marketing and Sales Coach

1. Ask staff members to report marketing activities to you on a weekly basis.
2. Take each staff member on a "live" sales call at least once each month.
3. Coach when business is great—and when it's not so great.
4. Always give your staff member some responsibility during each marketing call.
5. Perform a "postmortem" on each call (preferably while you are driving back to the office), and find something positive and something negative to say; ask the staff member to analyze your combined performance first, and then contribute your own insights.
6. Teach your staff members to think marketing all the time.
7. Keep coaching people as they move into management positions— the stakes will be even higher for them then.
8. Ask your staff members to give you feedback on your selling methods—teach them how to coach in the process.

Start with in-house training sessions that look and feel like coaching. That means one-on-one meetings with your staff, in which you discover which skill areas need some work and you create vehicles for the staff member to hone his or her skills.

Jim Belew believes in the power of training and coaching. He says, "I think practically every CPA can learn some degree of ability to sell. Some will be better than others and some sell differently. I think some CPAs are so brave that they don't mind knocking on doors and making cold calls. I think other CPAs are so cautious that they don't think they are selling but yet they do such a superb job of client service that their clients keep coming back to them more and more. Clients refer work to them. I think many times those CPAs don't realize that they are really selling. I think educating a CPA on the realities of selling is crucial. Too many of us have the picture that I've got to go knock on doors and make cold calls. That is really not what selling is—not in public accounting anyway."

Suppose you discover that several staff members need to improve their telephone skills. Get a small group of people around a phone, and then ask each person to call several prospects and try to schedule an appointment. When the call is over, evaluate what went right and not so right with the call. Staff members may be a bit intimidated, but their telephone skills will improve— and so will their confidence.

Your next step is to let your staff practice their personal marketing skills in a real, but nonthreatening, environment. The best way to do this is to ask staff members to help you present the firm's capabilities to existing clients.

Then move out into the streets: Take your staff members with you on your business development calls—and not just with referral sources, but with prospective clients as well. Then let them work their way up to playing more important roles in the sales calls.

And don't be afraid to "fail" in front of your staff. They will learn as much from your unsuccessful marketing appointments as they will from your successful ones.

 All purchase decisions, all repurchase decisions, hinge, ultimately, on conversations and relationships. . . . All dealings are personal dealings in the end.

—Tom Peters[4]

Always Give a Little "Something Extra" When Working with Clients, Prospects, and Referral Sources

If you mail tax returns, consider a personal delivery service. By all means call each client two days after the return is mailed to verify its receipt and review the key tax issues. Point out all the ways that you saved your clients tax dollars.

If you install computer software, provide an inexpensive additional piece of software after the sale at no charge. If you provide audits or reviews, find ways to give each person with whom you deal good feelings about you. Give them ideas to save personal tax dollars, provide them with free forms, take an advertising specialty item to them, or provide cookies or other goodies the last day on the job.

The Louisiana concept of lagniappe, giving a little something extra, will improve your clients' perceptions of your value. Harry Beckwith, author of *Selling the Invisible,* suggests, "Say p.m., deliver a.m. The first time you have something to deliver for a client, try this: Say you'll have it to him at 1 P.M. Then deliver it by 11 A.M."

Be safe, not sorry, by providing the good feelings that keep your clients coming back. In most instances giving good feelings only takes a minute. Realizing that clients can get their problems solved by competitors will encourage us to reach beyond quality work and provide our clients with quality service.

Bill Fingland says, "We see selling as a three-legged stool. First, you must give great service so your client will come back. Second, you must look for opportunities with your existing client. Third, you have got to go out and attract brand new clients to the firm."

Summary

Spending all of your time doing billable work keeps you on a treadmill—active, but going nowhere. Budget time for selling to new clients and delegate more of your billable work to others. Set up a marketing program that creates a regular flow of new prospects. Network widely in clients' and prospects' organizations. Look for wants *and* needs to satisfy. Keep your focus on the benefits the clients want to achieve, not on your services. Plan to give little extras on every job. And, most important, expect everyone to sell, and set up a training program to support them.

Mind Share = Market Share

You need a share of the mind before you can earn a share of the market.

—Jay Conrad Levinson[1]

Let's face it; a large percentage of the population doesn't know what an accountant does. Ask any high school student what a lawyer or doctor does, and you'll be more likely to receive an accurate response than when you ask the same teenager about a CPA. In 1991 the Gallup organization surveyed high school and college students for the American Institute of Certified Public Accountants (AICPA) and found that 37 percent of the students could not provide any explanation of what an accountant does. CPAs were ranked sixth out of six professions based on the students' opinions.

Lawyers and doctors are regular role models in television and other media. Accountants are relegated to arcane and maladroit parts. Even the largest accounting firms in the world have ceased using the designation CPA in its advertising during the past few years.

The mind of the average citizen is not conditioned to receive advertising about accountants. The human brain can absorb only a few of the thousands of marketing messages thrown at it every day. Psychologists tell us that a major cause of stress in today's society is the inability of the human brain to manage all the information that's thrust at it.

And yet, capturing a portion of the prospect's or client's mind share is what selling is all about. Lou Mills, whom you'll meet in Day 9, says, "Marketing is creating a public image in the mind of the prospect—making sure that when people decide they need to look for new consultants or CPAs, that our name is at the top of the list." Robert Bunting, chairman of Moss Adams, reinforced his partner by saying, "From a strategic standpoint, we decided that it wasn't enough just to be in a niche. Rather, you should be the dominant player."

When you are the dominant player in a niche, prospects will think of you. This is the essence of capturing mind share.

> *Positioning is not what you do to a product. Positioning is what you do to the mind of a prospect.*
>   —Al Ries and Jack Trout, *Positioning: The Battle for Your Mind*[2]

Advertising researchers have a term for media overload: They call it "noise." They estimate that from 3,000 to 6,000 marketing messages a day are available to the average person. Advertisers like Coca-Cola, Nike, General Motors, and McDonald's are flooding the print, postal, and electronic media. McDonald's reportedly spent over $200 million in the United States in the first year to launch a new hamburger. How can you compete with McDonald's for space in the mind of your prospects? How can you get through the noise and get anyone to notice you in this overcommunicated society?

Some advertisers paid $2 million for a 30-second spot on the Super Bowl broadcast in 2004. Many of them were dot-com companies advertising nationally for the first time. Were they effective? Can you name one of them? (The day after the Super Bowl, many viewers couldn't recall what company sponsored an ad they liked.) Al Ries and Jack Trout, in their book *The 22 Immutable Laws of Marketing,* say, "More money is wasted in marketing than in any other human activity (outside of government activities, of course!)."

Researchers have further discovered that for any of the new information to be retained and used, the mind must associate it with another piece of information already there. Couple this fact with the limits on our brain's capacity to absorb information and you can further understand how difficult it is for a general marketing message to penetrate the fog.

Actually, we use only a very small part of our brain's capacity. The brain's power is thought to be limitless, and so are the wonders we could accomplish if we could fully harness that power. But most people don't want to harness their brains to understand accounting.

"Only by studying how perceptions are formed in the mind and focusing your marketing programs on those perceptions can you overcome your basically incorrect marketing instincts," say Ries and Trout. In Rick Crandall's book, *Marketing Your Services for People Who HATE to Sell,* Rick Crandall reviews a set of famous letters in marketing: AIDA. They stand for:

Attention

Interest

Desire

Action

Crandall explains that before a prospect takes any physical action, three steps (AID) must take place in the prospect's mind.

In Day 16, I talk about the AIDA process using the following steps:

- Awareness
- Familiarity
- Differentiation
- Positive perceptions
- Development of needs
- Sale

You must win the battle of the mind before you can win the client. Sometimes you can do this in one call. For example, the national firms have developed some "black box" tax products designed for specific types of companies or individuals. If you have a product that will save a business owner a million dollars, you can move through the mind-development steps rather quickly. However, more often than not, multiple interactions are necessary to build a long-term relationship with a company for core services. Rarely do you have a product or service that will bowl your prospect over.

How many times have you heard "I'm happy with my present CPA"? The reason you hear this so much is that the current accountant has a solid share of the client's mind—so solid, in fact, that the client is regularly acting on the mind share. In order for you to get the prospect to act, his or her mind must go through the steps of attention, interest, and desire. Author Harry Beckwith says, "People choose what seems most familiar."

Most marketing experts agree that repetition is the key to developing awareness. Direct mail marketers, for example, can receive a higher response rate from subsequent mailings than from first mailings. In my years of experience, I have found that the right repetition will open the mind of the prospect so you can have a chance at action being taken.

Lou Mills says, "Creating a public image is very important. When I meet someone who has heard of my firm [Moss Adams], that person is much more open and receptive to me." Deborah Bailey Browne, CPA of Newburgh, New York, says, "You're selling whether you like it or not, but I think that in public accounting it boils down to personal and institutional relationships. I think that's very important. It's not just the firm name or the price; it's relationships."

Don't Compete Where You Can't Win

Last year I performed a marketing audit for an accounting firm in a large metropolitan market. The firm's $11 million in annual revenue had stagnated over the last three years, and yet the metro area in which it was located was expanding at nearly 14 percent per year. Total revenue for accounting firms in the market exceeded $1 billion.

Why was this firm not growing in an expanding market? Was it because it was not marketing? No. This firm was spending nearly 4 percent of its annual revenue on marketing—which is above average—trying to attract new business. Over the previous three years, in an attempt to stimulate sales, the owners had increased their marketing commitment. Many of the firm's owners and senior managers were active in the community. The firm employed a full-time marketing coordinator. And yet nothing much was happening.

Normally, an accounting firm making this size of commitment would be growing faster than the market. The reason for the no-growth results was in the manner in which the firm and its owners were investing their time and money. They were trying to compete with McDonald's for the mind of

PORTRAIT OF A SALES LEADER

JEFF EVERLY, a partner in the Winchester, Virginia, accounting firm of Yount, Hyde & Barbour, says: "I work in the banking niche of our firm. We are active members of three statewide banking organizations. When anyone in a bank thinks about accounting, tax, auditing, internal auditing, or profit improvement, we want him or her to think of us first."

I first learned of Jeff Everly when I was working for another client that I will call Smith CPAs. Smith CPAs had lost in the proposal process against a small firm in northern Virginia by the name of Yount, Hyde & Barbour. Smith asked me to assist them with a lost proposal review, a service that I frequently perform for clients. During the lost proposal review, I spoke with the CEO and the CFO, both of whom related this story to me. "We initially thought Smith would be the winning firm for several reasons, but we asked our present Big Six firm and a small firm to propose. David Frazier and Jeff Everly made a terrific presentation on behalf of Yount, Hyde & Barbour. We felt they'd really understood us and could help with many issues in our bank. Smith made a good presentation as well. But Frazier and Everly did something else. At the end the general public. In order to spend eighty cents per consumer (the amount McDonald's spent just on its Archburger rollout in 2000), its ad budget alone would have been $1.6 million—totally out of the question for an $11 million firm.

These well-intentioned owners were grasping for business by spending heavily on general market advertising and networking. A large portion of their advertising had been placed in newspapers and magazines. Partners were active in chambers of commerce and civic clubs. The firm was a huge supporter of general business fairs and high school yearbooks, and it advertised heavily with large display ads in 10 yellow pages.

When all its marketing is directed at the general marketplace, no accounting firm can spend enough in a huge market to make an impact. There is just too much competition for the attention of the average person.

A Winning Plan to Capture the Minds of Your Prospects

How then can you design a marketing program to condition your prospects' minds so they will take action?

of their presentation, they shook hands with most of the audit committee members and with us. In a gentle way, they said, 'We really want your business.' At the conclusion of the audit committee meeting, the vote was three votes for Smith and three for Yount.

"About 4 P.M. that afternoon, Everly called the CFO and asked, 'After all your interviews, did you develop any other issues that we failed to address?' The CFO said, 'Yes, there were two key issues to which I'd like you to respond.' Everly sent a fax later that afternoon and followed up with a phone call the next morning. The CFO told me, 'We circulated the fax to our audit committee and told them about the phone call. They were so impressed that when we met the next week, the vote came down to six for Yount and zero for Smith. We didn't hear from your team. We really decided you were not interested in our business.'"

Everly joined Yount, Hyde & Barbour in Virginia, in 1980, and was promoted to partner in 1993. Today he leads the practice development efforts for this five-office, 14-partner firm. Everly is a strong rainmaker in his firm. He said, "The days are gone when people can become partners in accounting firms without the skill to sell."

Kruse & Associates did not employ a marketing person until it recently merged with Crowe Chizek. The firm did no general interest advertising, and yet it has grown an amazing 30-plus percent a year for the last four years.

To get started, it is important to select a qualified group of suspects (people you suspect may be prospects) and begin communicating with them. You could plan a series of personal calls. Or you could advertise in the publications they read. You could write them. You could send them gifts. There are myriad ways you can communicate with prospects. I generally prefer to use a combination of methods.

In order to penetrate the fog of your prospects' minds, your marketing (including advertising) should have four attributes.

1. All of your marketing should work together.
2. Marketing should be repetitive.

Keeping in Your Prospects' Minds

Bob Gaida uses the technique of sending articles of interest to prospects. He says, "Any time I am reading the paper or a magazine, I try to keep clients and prospects in mind. While reading, I think 'Who will find this article interesting?' But the power that I add is a pen. Not a ballpoint pen, not a typed letter, but my fountain pen. I find that fountain pens are powerful, because people can tell when real ink was used, therefore, that you really wrote it. I want them to know that I am reading about their interests."

Gaida continues: "Voice mail is a powerful tool. You're at home watching the 11 o'clock news, but before going to bed you call that prospect's voice mail and say, 'I've been on the run today and I could not get you. But I did have some ideas about some of the challenges you're facing—very shortly I'd like to talk to you about this.' What's the first thing your prospect hears in the morning? 'You have a voice mail; it is November 20, 11:30 P.M.' Pretty powerful. Your prospect is probably thinking, 'Boy, this guy is psychotic—he's working so late. But I don't really care if he's psychotic. . . . I want that kind of delivery. This guy is a winner.'"

Gaida says, "Gifts are also nice little things if they make sense, and are tasteful and appropriate."

3. You must be different.

4. Keep it simple.

All of Your Marketing Should Work Together

Advertising and public relations should support networking. Networking should support selling. And selling should support your repeat client base. When your marketing efforts work together, you will compound the potential effect of each separate effort.

Marketing Should Be Repetitive

Researchers have discovered that repetition is the only way to penetrate the mind. Remember when you were in school and the teacher had you memorize the times tables to twelve. To memorize something, you repeated the problem over and over. Now you have nine times nine embedded in your mind. This is why Bud Light, Coca-Cola, and Toyota run multiple ads on the same television program.

Now, quickly! What is 14 times 14? Perhaps once you worked out the answer to 14 times 14, but the answer is slow in coming because you haven't repeated it enough for it to lodge in your brain. Never, never run an ad or a marketing program only one time. It's like whispering to the captain of an airplane when you're sitting in row 25 next to the engine and he is in the cockpit with the door closed.

You Must Be Different

When your prospects think there is no difference among accountants, they select based on the lowest price.

 Anybody who is any good is different from anybody else.

—Felix Frankfurter, U.S. Supreme Court Justice

Keep It Simple

When you only have a few seconds to penetrate someone's mind, you must boil your message down to its simplest form. Politicians call these sound bites. The politician who masters the simple sound bites can move an enormous electorate.

Bill Fingland, CEO of BKD, says, "I try to keep my contacts small, focused, and simple. Whenever your contacts are personalized, they have a higher priority than brochures. Everyone is trying to find the magic bullet to attract new business today: advertisements, brochures, the Internet. I think in our business, it is our people who make the difference."

Your Permission Marketing Program

At The Rainmaker Academy, we have developed a 12-step selling plan for those suspects you do not personally know. You would not use this plan for suspects or prospects you know or can meet through a referral. How many steps you use will vary depending on your strengths, but in all cases they include multiple contacts by mail followed by telephone contacts and personal visits. The mailings are specifically designed for the target market and may include brochures, newsletters, or product sheets of potential interest to the audience. The telephone call is only to arrange a meeting. And the first meeting is designed only to meet and fully qualify the prospect.

The personal meetings should become progressively more in depth. They generally are designed to build "like and trust" with prospects before diagnosing needs and wants. Typically, we attempt to have prospects actually come to the CPA's office. If a prospect comes to your office, it is a strong sign of interest. During the meetings we arrange a "Business Review" or "Operational Review" or a "Business Physical." These reviews enable us to determine the needs and wants of the prospect's decision makers.

Last, we make two proposals: one in draft format and one in final format. These proposals do not have to be in writing. If they are not in writing, the final proposal is made with an engagement letter.

By using this permission selling plan, we have obtained 5 to 15 percent of the suspect list as new clients within a two-year period. This is more than double the results of a simple mail-and-wait campaign.

Variations on this program are many. PDI of Chicago, Newkirk in New York state, and Mostad & Christensen in Washington state have developed a variety of mail marketing tools. These tools help CPAs penetrate targeted account lists. Although these customized programs work rather well, we have found that adding telephone and personal visits accelerates the results.

Summary

You can't throw money at general advertising and expect good results. You need to do more focused marketing that gets people's attention because it applies to them. Then you need to repeat that focused marketing to achieve top-of-mind awareness among prospects and clients.

5 Selling Takes Time

Generally, the higher the price . . . the longer the sales cycle.
— Tony Alessandra et al., *Non-Manipulative Selling*[1]

One of the things that can be discouraging about selling efforts is the extended time it can take to sign up a new client. Many companies are very slow to change accountants. According to some estimates, companies change only as little as every 12 years. This is just one of the reasons why selling accounting services can take a long time. Although some people will sign up with you quickly, some of your best prospects will take years to develop.

Naturally, when you first target prospects, you don't know what their situation is and how long their decision process will take. If they come to you as the result of a referral, often they are ready to hire you immediately. These are your easiest prospects to convert to clients. People who come to you after having met you or heard you speak are also very likely to hire you. When prospects come to you from other sources, such as advertising or publicity, they are often considering several firms.

Even though people who come to you are the easiest sales prospects, they are not always the ones you want. That is, those who come to you may not be of a size, industry, or profitability to make the ideal clients. There are also some clients who "shop" accountants regularly. Often they are impossible to please or are using you to put pricing pressure on their existing accountant.

To build the kind of practice *you* want, you need to select your own clients. You can educate some referral sources to bring you these clients, but the largest pool will come from your efforts to appear in front of and then select the types of clients you want. You will have to start "cold" with some of these prospects. This is where the long sales cycle often comes into play.

The simple answer to this "problem" of long selling cycles is that you must have a system in place to keep in touch with desirable prospects who are

51

worth waiting for. The extended selling cycle can work to your advantage. Many of your competitors will drop away over time. The firm that has your prospects as clients now will tend to take them for granted. You'll have time to educate yourself about prospects and their industries. And, best of all, you'll have time to build a relationship and establish a bond of trust with the prospect.

Why Prospects Don't Buy Quickly

You face four major challenges when selling services to today's busy executives:

1. *You have many competitors.* Until people really know the benefits you provide that others don't, it is very hard for you to stand out from the crowd.

2. *Your prospects usually see changing accountants as another job on top of their regular jobs.* They are hesitant to invest their mental energy and due diligence in hiring you if they can "get by" with what they have. In fact, often they will settle for a status quo that they know is inferior just to avoid making a change.

3. *They can't be sure what they're getting.* Any difference in your services compared to their current provider is unproven and intangible. Prospects have to be very motivated to make a change, either by dissatisfaction or by the promise of a very clear gain.

PORTRAIT OF A SALES LEADER

TERRY ORR, an amazing practice developer for Belew Averitt, LLP in Dallas, Texas, tells it like this: "I think the important thing is to develop pipelines of new business. We market and sell inside a pipeline with other CPAs, lawyers, investment bankers and venture capitalists." Terry's story is an interesting one. He never expected to be a rainmaker. He'd been in the accounting industry nine years and had never attracted a single client. Within a few months of his managing partner telling him that to become a principal (basically a nonequity partner), he'd need to create $50,000 of new business, he attracted the business and became a principal in Laventhol & Horwath, Las Vegas. Orr, now a senior partner in the Dallas firm of Belew Averitt, LLP, is one of the leading sellers in the accounting industry.

Orr is like most practicing CPAs in most accounting firms around the world. He is bright, well mannered, service oriented, unassuming,

4. *Making a change is painful, even with all the help you can offer.*
   Your best prospects have many other priorities that are more urgent
   than changing accountants. Your toughest competition is not from
   other accounting firms, it is from the many other tasks and decisions
   your prospects have to deal with. Often getting them to put you on
   their agenda is your biggest challenge.

What If All Prospects Were Ready Today?

Many accountants wish that every prospect they came in contact with was
ready to buy immediately. Believe it or not, there would be several drawbacks
to this situation (unless the prospects come from strong referral sources).
Let's look at the traditional side first. If prospects were ready to buy immediately, why would they choose you? Without the foundation of a solid relationship, how could you differentiate yourself from other accountants? When
prospects don't know you, they are price buyers who treat your services as
commodities. That's not where you want to be.

Now, let's look at it from the other side. How would *you* know if you wanted
to work with them? If prospects came to you ready to buy, you wouldn't
have the time to get to know each other. By taking time to research their situation and meet the key personalities, you have a better chance to see if they
are the right type of client for you. Many clients who look good on the surface
are hard to work with, never satisfied, and don't pay their bills. *Part of good*

introverted, principled, loyal, and very motivated. Accounting is one
of the few professions where a self-motivated person with modest
resources can achieve great success. Orr's family was close knit and of
modest means. Orr said of his childhood, "I was very shy." If you met
him today, you would not be bowled over by the power of his presence. Yet with his unassuming smile and easygoing manner, you would
be drawn to him as you would to a good friend.

After high school, Orr went on a church mission in a foreign country where he "had the opportunity to meet a wide breadth of cultures
and people." While still a very shy person, Orr developed an interest in
people.

What has helped Terry Orr become a leading business builder in the
accounting industry? Orr says, "I think it's simply a strong desire to succeed. I think there is a basic desire to want to accomplish goals. If you
have that desire then you can succeed."

marketing is screening prospects by your criteria. By taking some time, you can sift out the best prospects to develop your practice the way you really want it.

Having a variety of prospects in your sales pipeline gives you a variety of contacts and allows you to set your own pace. And as you gain in experience, you'll find it easier both to keep your pipeline full and to judge the readiness of prospects.

How to Handle a Long Sales Cycle

You need a system when dealing with a sales cycle that could take an unknown length of time. Different prospects will be at different stages in their buying cycles. It's up to you to create a communication program that is easy to run, keeps in touch with prospects, and builds your credibility and the prospects' trust in you.

Prospects will be more open to hiring you at specific points in their situations. For instance, when there is a change in executives, often there is a change in accountants. The situation is similar when a company plans to go public, when a sale is contemplated, when companies are being acquired, and so on. It's up to you to keep your name in front of your prospects regularly and to be aware of upcoming changes that might benefit you.

Your system for contacting prospects over a potentially long sales cycle will include getting permission up front to keep in touch and a series of communications that fit your style. We often start with a series of mailings and then seek a series of meetings that can lead to a proposal. (See Day 8 on permission marketing.) A newsletter or e-zine is ideal for regular contact. Perhaps you can invite people to in-house seminars. You may issue occasional advisories about changes in the tax laws; you may invite prospects to lunch regularly. You may attend groups they belong to. You may write articles in their trade magazines. And you may make regular visits to key prospects. These are only a sampling of the methods you can use to keep in touch with prospects, learn about their situations, and build their trust in you.

Identifying Your Best Prospects

Your overall marketing program may have many components. In fact, each professional in your firm (and support staff as well) may be responsible for specific methods of contact. Each person probably will use a variety of methods, but it may be easier to think of each accountant specializing in an approach. One person may speak a lot, another write, another cultivate new business from existing clients, another have an industry focus, another edit the newsletter, another go to networking events, and so forth.

Prospects may "hold up their hands" to identify themselves to you when you meet them, or they may respond to an outreach effort. But you also should develop a target list of prospects that you'd like to have. For all your prospects, you should put together a database of prospects and document what you know about them. Supplement this list with information from their websites and questions asked of your regular contacts.

Develop a system to prioritize prospects as to their value. Use simple and inexpensive contact methods with B prospects, such as newsletters and holiday greetings. Save your more expensive personal selling methods for A prospects. And use still other approaches for prospects whom you have reason to believe are close to hiring a firm.

It's tempting to focus on the last group of prospects who come to you and say they're ready to hire a new accountant. However, often these "short-cycle" sales are not your best prospects, and you end up with a ragged assortment of small clients and industries that you don't know much about.

Although it is common to bemoan long sales cycles, often they can be a good sign. Because the A target clients you really want will seldom come to you, your long sales cycle marketing often is your most valuable tool in the long run. This is when you are going after the big clients who can really build your practice.

Your first job with prospects who don't know you is to introduce yourself and your firm. You can do that with a series of mailings, with a phone call, or by seeking them out at an industry meeting. If the prospects are very important and you build a file on them, you will find other ways to meet them, such as serving on a committee for their favorite charity.

Once prospects are aware of you, it's up to you to build the relationship over time. Normally you do this by demonstrating your value to them even though they're not clients. Your newsletter, seminars, advisories, and informal advice can serve you well here. For example, many accountants and financial planners serving the individual market offer retirement or financial planning seminars. One recently overbooked three dinner seminars at a local restaurant and had to offer a fourth session in their offices.

Their Buying Cycle versus Your Selling Cycle

When you meet a new prospect, it's worthwhile letting them know you'd like to do business with them. If they are interested at that point, you're in a short selling cycle. For the many more who aren't open to a proposal at the beginning, that's when your long sales cycle starts.

Although I've talked mainly from your perspective about the sales cycle, it is crucial to note that prospects' *buying* cycles are more important than your selling system. You need to ask them about their situation. For instance, few larger companies will decide to change accountants within a tax year. You need to find out how they evaluate firms. Who makes the decision to evaluate new firms? You need to find out if there are small projects that aren't handled by their main accounting firm. The more you know about their situation and how they buy, the better you can adapt your sales approach. When you try to sell at the wrong time in a buying cycle, not only are you not successful, you annoy people and can come across as pushy and unprofessional.

Many people make this distinction between marketing and sales: Marketing communicates, keeps in touch, and creates leads. Sales closes leads. Using this distinction, most of what you do during a long sales cycle is marketing— you're not trying to sell yet.

Effective marketing can help overcome your most important challenge with people who don't know you—becoming a familiar and trusted source. Research has shown that familiarity leads to acceptance, which is the first step on the way to liking and trust.

When you are known and accepted, prospects will consider you when their buying cycle is at the purchase point. Although sometimes you may be able to encourage them to consider you sooner than they normally would, don't push. Be content to become trusted over time and positioned to move when they are ready for you.

Be sure to have an overall system and a coordinated approach. In many firms, each partner runs his or her practice like a separate business. Once a prospect is in your database, make sure that all marketing and sales efforts are coordinated and make sense. It is counterproductive and unprofessional looking if a prospect who has received information from the firm or one partner for a year or two is suddenly "sold at" when another partner meets the prospect at a conference for the first time.

Getting on Their Priority Lists

Often the main reason prospects don't consider your services is because they have many other priorities. Changing accountants doesn't make their top 10. And unfortunately, as they handle their current priorities, others will develop that are more demanding than your case for change. This can mean that you never move up the priority list.

Fortunately, as prospects become more familiar with you, the risk of a change goes down. When they are comfortable with you, the effort involved in making a decision in your favor can become minor.

Another way to move yourself up the priority list is to help prospects with their current priorities. Of course, this means you have to be in close enough touch to know their priorities. You might help them thorough informal advice. You can help them with quality referrals to sources who can support their priorities. Or a referral to a profitable client for them may buy time—and interest—to consider you.

You also can use the long sales cycle to educate yourself about their business and industry. If you're suddenly writing articles in their trade magazines or speaking at their industry events, your status for consideration will rise.

Traditional sales training tells you to keep selling, even when prospects tell you they are not ready to buy. You are much better off believing them and having a plan to move forward in a nonpushy way. When you aren't trying to sell the prospect, you are a better listener and more likely to become a source of advice.

Sometimes you can expand your services to deal with prospects' other priorities. Accounting firms that help clients install new computers are an example. Once you have established a working relationship with a prospect, you'll move up the readiness continuum regarding their accounting services more quickly.

Build the Relationship Broadly

You have many possible contact points within an organization. While you are keeping in touch with your prime contact during a long sales cycle, you also should be building other contacts. Take the secretary of the person you're cultivating as a simple example. Often this person can be enlisted as a source of friendly information. When you don't act like the typical salesperson who tries to avoid or manipulate gatekeepers, you have a chance to gain useful information. Secretaries and administrative assistants can tell you about other people in the prospect company who may be influential. If you're going to stay in touch for a year or more, take advantage of the time to cultivate several people at the prospect's firm. Sending your newsletter or information about your services to an expanded group of people can pay off.

Summary

With a few exceptions, it is natural for the best prospects to take a longer timeframe to sell. They want to get to know you on their schedule, and you should want the same thing. You can use the time in a long sales cycle to your advantage to educate yourself on prospects and their situation, to build in-depth contacts, and to assess their needs. Instead of expecting a "one-call close," know that it can take 5 to 12 years for the average company to change accountants. Focus on long-term relationships and build trust and like. When you show that you don't expect a quick sale, prospects will take you more seriously as a professional.

Target Better Clients

6 Leads, Leads, Leads

Here's a pointer culled from the careers of men who have attained notable success: Don't sit in your office during the hours prospects can be seen. Do your office work before or after the hours during which possible customers can be reached.

—B.C. Forbes

You need three major marketing systems in operation to make your marketing superior: (1) a system to generate leads, (2) a system to stay in contact with good prospects, and (3) a system to build strong relationships with clients. The second and third areas are more important than the first, but without the first stage, you can't do the rest. The problem I find in most low-growth CPA firms is a shortage of leads. Lead generation is difficult and confusing. Many partners would prefer to spend time working on uninteresting and poor-paying clients than venture into the cold waters of lead generation.

Willie Sutton had the right idea. Asked why he robbed banks, the infamous bandit replied, "Because that's where the money is." Willie had prospecting down cold. To mine for clients, you have to be where prospects are plentiful. Prospecting for leads isn't quite as easy as finding money in a bank. But Sutton's wry logic still applies. Here, I want to discuss ways to generate a high volume of leads (or prospects).

Change Is the Only Constant

With the rapid pace of change in today's business world, businesses are being sold, companies are going out of business, and some of your clients are downsizing. Others may outgrow your service's capability or will be attracted to another service provider. Some clients you will "outplace." (I hate the words "fire a client.") Couple your need to grow (even modestly) with the natural attrition, and you'll find you need to grow 10 to 15 percent just to net 5 percent growth. If your target growth rate is 20 percent, add 5 to 10 percentage points to the target to obtain the growth you desire.

What is the probability that someone you meet today perceives she has a need for your services? When I ask this question during training classes, the answer usually is "less than 5 percent." If you agree with this percentage, then you agree that you must have 20 prospects in the pipeline for every client you expect to create.

Finding Prospects

Confucius said, "Dig the well before you thirst." Harvey Mackay adopted this theme in his book on networking, *Dig Your Well Before You're Thirsty.* Often the need for lead generation does not seem urgent. The task seems

---

PORTRAIT OF A SALES LEADER

MIKE KRUSE is partner in charge of the Nashville office of Crowe Chizek, LLP. Growing up on a farm in western Kansas, Mike Kruse learned the value of hard work. During his early college years, he took an introductory accounting course and enjoyed its structure. Working his way through college, he learned to be very efficient with his time. Kruse said, "To work an eight-hour shift, go to school, and complete my homework every day built an internal tempo in me. Working my way through Kansas State University taught me how to make every minute count for something."

Kruse joined Touche Ross & Company in Kansas City after his graduation from Kansas State University. I first met Kruse when he moved to Nashville in 1979. At the time, I was CEO of a small publicly held publishing company, and Kruse was managing partner of Touche Ross's local office. Prior to Kruse's arrival, Touche Ross was a respected but sleepy office. It had about 20 to 25 people and was the smallest of the Big Eight national accounting firms. Within five years, the Nashville Touche Ross office became one of the largest.

Today, Deloitte & Touche, Nashville, has revenues of nearly $50 million and is the largest accounting office in the state. The current Deloitte & Touche managing partner, Bill Hawkins, says of Mike Kruse, "Mike really was the catalyst that jump-started the growth of our office back in the early eighties. His unrelenting focus on sales and marketing helped every partner recognize that we needed to build a new dimension to our technical capabilities. Mike attracted millions of dollars of new work for us."

difficult, of low payoff, or even demeaning. In this chapter, I want to convince you to develop a lead-generation system that is effective, efficient, and professional.

Generally speaking, there exists a five-level hierarchy of leads:

1. Qualified referred prospects
2. Referred prospects
3. Warm prospects
4. Cold prospects
5. Suspects

In all cases, you want to be in a position where your prospect may ask you to help. If you have to beg for the business, your position may not be as

Kruse's partner Larry Morton says, "Mike is one of those guys who means what he says. Clients trust him and his partners trust him. He builds trust quickly with prospects because he does what he says and he does it on budget and on time. He is a man of his word. I think that is the single biggest reason Mike is successful." John Colwell, also a partner, says, "Mike's goal is to help people run their businesses better and to make friends for life. Whenever we start out on a call to a prospect, Mike will say, 'Let's go make a friend for life.' He means that too. Whether the person becomes a client or not, Mike builds trust and friendships wherever he goes."

Kruse, along with partners Larry Morton, Marc McKerley, John Colwell, and Larry Williams, started Kruse & Associates in 1993. The partners had worked together in another firm for a few tumultuous years. Kruse & Associates completed its first fiscal year with $1.8 million in revenue; by 2000 its annual revenue was over $10 million, the firm merged with Crowe Chizek in 2003.

Kruse says, "We wanted to be the best we could be for businesses in the construction industry. We believed that our experience, contacts, and love for the construction business would enable us to build a significant firm. So we have focused most of our attention on construction and related businesses." Although the firm has branched out into a variety of other business types in recent years, the partners believe that their intense focus in one industry is a major reason they have enjoyed a strong growth rate.

strong. When prospects ask for your help, you can be sure that you have the proper amount of mind share, which was discussed in Day 4. Bob Gaida, a partner with BDO Seidman, says, "If I have taken the time to understand their needs and wants and have given them true benefit statements, I've created a high desire. I will sometimes wait for the prospect to say 'Can you help me with this?' Then I know that our minds are together and the client will be willing to pay a fair price."

Jeff Everly, a partner with Yount, Hyde, and Barbour, says, "Sometimes it will take four or five years to really develop a cold lead into a warm one. The prospect has to go through a comfort process before you can get to first base. It has taken over six years just to be able to call up a prospect and get an appointment sometimes. But we nurture those leads in many ways to warm them up."

How to Generate Leads?

Compare your sales activity to the performance of a funnel. New prospects (suspects) enter the sales cycle at the top of the funnel. Over time, these suspects turn into qualified prospects, then into interested-qualified prospects, and then into clients. At times, the process is quite short, but other times, several years are required.

There are many ways to find suspects. Here are some ways to attract suspects to fill up the funnel (others, such as online marketing, are covered in later chapters).

- Advertising
- Public relations
- Cold calling
- Direct mail
- Telemarketing
- Referrals
- General networking
- Industry networking
- Trade shows
- Seminars and speeches
- Tip clubs

Advertising

I rarely hear of an accounting firm getting a new client from advertising. The leads you receive from advertising and publicity generally will be cold and unqualified. However, I do know that when you meet a person who has seen or heard your ad, that person is more receptive to you. Meeting a receptive person is an important aid in capturing mind share of potential clients.

Advertising is salesmanship . . . the only purpose of advertising is to make sales.

—Claude C. Hopkins[1]

Most marketing and sales experts in the accounting industry warn against investing heavily in advertising. Yet some of the Big Five firms are spending over $100 million a year on advertising. Magazine, newspaper, airport terminal billboard, television, and radio ads from the big firms are everywhere. Marketing author Rick Crandall says that advertising is the least effective of various marketing methods for professional services. The real answer lies in the total size of your marketing budget. Our Rainmaker consultants generally recommend that clients spend 10 percent or less of total marketing costs on advertising. For a total marketing budget of $300,000 or less, 10 percent is like whispering in the wind in the world of advertising.

To invest appropriately in advertising, accountants must use as many creative, low-cost, and targeted approaches as possible. Jim Belew has used a testimonial advertising campaign for a number of years in the Dallas business newspapers. He says, "The testimonial campaign is almost as strong as obtaining a referred lead in the market place. Prospects recognize our clients, then when we meet, receptivity is high from the beginning."

Print advertising in magazine and newspapers is good because it is relatively low cost and can be used in reprints for years to come. Reprints can be used in brochures, direct mail letters, and proposals. Trade magazines are particularly good for accounting firms focusing on an industry. However, general print advertising in newspapers can have a short life. Seth Godin, author of *Permission Marketing,* describes the downside of most "interruption marketing" today—it gets missed or it creates a negative message. Several large accounting firms have learned the hard way that expensive ad campaigns can be a deep money hole, with little payoff.

Accountants are readers and are cost conscious. Print advertising comfortably fits these two traits. But most Americans receive their information electronically, if you include broadcast. It is important to tiptoe into the electronic advertising world. *Newsletter on Hold* is an audio newsletter that people hear when you place them on hold on your telephone; using it is a great way to dip your toe into electronic advertising. An interactive Web page, National Public Radio sponsorships, or selected business talk radio or cable television ads can be reasonably priced. However, don't buy these venues just because they may be inexpensive. Buy them only if you can reach your target audience through them.

Public Relations

Public relations (PR), like advertising, appears in various print and electronic media. Unlike advertising, consumers perceive PR as less intrusive—and you don't have to pay for the space or time. Generally, studies of PR effectiveness show that PR is more believable than advertising. But good PR is much harder to obtain. With advertising, you select your media, pay your money, and you're in. With PR, you may try a number of times to attract attention and not receive a mention.

Public relations is anything you do in the marketplace to get attention that does not appear to be advertising. Stories about people in your firm, promotions, and specialized services training or offerings are all potential PR activities. Some of the best PR opportunities come from articles you write about interesting business topics.

Create Your Own Directory of Experts

Provide media with a "sourcebook" of experts from your organization. This sourcebook should include not only listings of your staff's technical expertise, but also human interest items, such as unusual hobbies or sports. For each individual, list contact information and a brief summary of qualifications.

There are many ways to obtain good PR. Any time you have a speech or seminar, make certain to let the business reporters in your community know about the event. Even in the largest markets, a handful of people controls the business press. Whether these people attend or not, send each one a copy of your presentation. Make certain that all the business reporters receive any newsletters and general client communications you send out. When reporters get to know you, they're much more likely to write about you. If you produce a client newsletter, reproduce one article a month for distribution to the business press. Hire one of the freelance business writers in your community to help you write your firm's newsletter.

Cold Calling

In his book *Guerrilla Marketing Attack,* Jay Conrad Levinson describes the difficulty with cold calling. He claims that moving a person from apathy to the point of being ready to do business with you takes 27 attempts at a marketing interaction. Levinson says that it takes 9 marketing interactions to move a prospect from unaware to ready to buy. He says that most people miss 2 out of 3 marketing attempts; so to insure you get the 9, you must plan for 27. In other words, to get 9 good interactions, you must be willing to allow 18 attempts to fail. All cold calling starts with call number 1 out of 27. Any intelligent partner understands the significant investment necessary to move from call number 1 to call number 27. Most sane CPAs conclude that it is much easier to dust off the desk, clean out the files, or call for a tee time than be subjected to 26 potential rejections.

And yet, remember when you founded your firm? You called on whoever would talk with you. Jim Belew says, "When Jimmy Averitt and I founded our firm, we made contacts with everyone we knew and many people we didn't know, asking for business." Mike Kruse said, "Five of us started together in 1993, we fanned out to the construction companies and people we could think of. We had to get business to put food on the table." Bob Gaida said, "When I opened the New Jersey office for BDO, the firm blessed me with about $400,000 in business, and I appreciated that. But that wouldn't support the office. So I developed a target list of prospects based upon some thorough prequalification factors that I established. I began to call on the owners of these businesses."

If I were a salesman, I would double my possible calls, for some of the best business comes through an unexpected source. Where well-laid plans have failed, persistent plugging has won.

—F.D. Van Amburgh

If you do a good job of target selling, there will be some businesses on which you will have to make cold calls. The key for success is to make as many of the contacts as efficiently as possible. Rather than making all the calls in person, use other marketing tools. Plan to use the phone on 4 to 8 of the 27 contacts. Use letters, newsletters, and clipped articles for 8 to 12 of the contacts. Advertising your prospects may read also counts as an interaction. A strong testimonial letter or a phone call from one of your satisfied clients to your prospect could be worth up to 10 contacts with just one interaction. Today a number of firms successfully employ a telemarketing salesperson. In some cases, the telemarketer makes personal visits to qualify and probe the needs of prospects.

To be efficient, you must have a series of marketing tools and you must use them appropriately. This is where firms like PDI in Chicago, Newkirk in

New York, and Mostad & Christensen in Seattle come in handy. These firms will provide you with marketing materials on a consistent basis so you have something to mail.

Cold-Calling Strategies

When you make cold calls, it makes sense to have a reason to call. Here are a few:

Reconnaissance

- You appeared on a special list and I wanted to meet you.
- I am doing a research project for the _____.
- I'd like a brochure or annual report from your company.

Introduction

- We have mutual friends in high places.
- We have mutual friends in low places.
- I was just prospecting.
- You oughta be in pictures. (Ernst & Young uses this concept quite well with its Entrepreneur of the Year awards.)

Presentation

- Try our business review or our tax review—you'll like it.
- We have a staff person available to help straighten out your books and records for a week. We'll lend him to you.
- I am writing a newspaper column and would like to interview you.

Direct Mail

For many CPAs, some form of direct mail advertising makes a great deal of sense. In Days 18 to 20, I thoroughly discuss the use of letters, newsletters, and other forms of direct mail. Generally, we recommend that each partner in an accounting firm mail to about 500 persons quarterly. Of this 500, about one-third each should be clients, referral sources, and prospects.

Telemarketing

Telemarketing has gotten a terrible name in recent years because of the harassing phone calls we all receive during the dinner hour. But let's face it, the telephone is a very powerful sales aid, particularly for business-to-business selling. Done well, telemarketing can be a powerful tool to help you develop leads galore. (Incidentally, the federal "Do Not Call" registry only applies to residential calls, not business-to-business calling.)

Most CPA firms are not set up to be executive telemarketing firms. So it makes sense to send one of your staff members to a telemarketing school like the one put on by New Clients, Inc., in New Jersey or to hire an executive telemarketing agency. Many of the national accounting firms, including PricewaterhouseCoopers and Ernst & Young, have internal telemarketing departments.

Five Key Rules for a Successful Telemarketing Campaign

Once you have a good script that highlights your benefits, consider these five rules:

1 The telemarketer's voice must be near–radio announcer quality.

2 The telemarketer must understand your business, your personnel, and your services.

3 Prospects should not be able to hear any background noise.

4 Mature-sounding voices get better responses than youthful ones.

5 Slower speech patterns work better than rapid ones.

Referrals

The Day 9 chapter is devoted to building referrals. Qualified referred leads are the strongest category of prospects you can develop, which is why I have devoted an entire chapter to the subject.

General Networking

General networking is best performed with strong centers of influence—people who know many prospects for you. Harvey Mackay has built an industry and a science around networking. Mackay describes the concept of "six degrees of separation" (originally developed by psychologist Stanley Milgram), which refers to the fact that there's a chain of no more than six people that links every person on this planet to every other person. Rarely will you ever need to use all six links. In most cases, you can get to a prospect in your community with just one or two contacts.

Cultivating as few as four solid centers of influence can supply you with plenty of prospects. In The Rainmaker Academy we generally advise people to develop seven "aces"—centers of influence or referral sources with whom they develop a deep relationship.

Civic clubs, country clubs, charities, boards, college associations, and many other organizations provide significant opportunities for general networking. General networking is essential for people starting out to build a network of business contacts. Once a CPA has a solid set of seven aces, it's generally more profitable to spend more time nurturing the aces than finding new people.

> *You can close more business deals in two months by becoming interested in other people than you can in two years trying to get people interested in you.*
>
> —Dale Carnegie[2]

Once your network is established, you may want to move on to higher forms of prospecting, such as industry networking.

The chapters for Days 10 and 11 are devoted to building and managing a strong network.

Industry Networking

For the experienced networker, involvement in an industry group is a way to multiply successes. Being known as an industry expert within a group is a way to attract prospects who may be similar to your most profitable clients. Industry groups help you stay on top of business trends, governmental intrusions, tax events, technology developments, and many other aspects of running a specific business.

In general, every partner in an accounting firm should be involved in some type of industry or trade organization. Lou Mills says, "The targeted leads we are tracking are primarily industry focused. Once we became more industry focused, our leads became stronger and we became better known."

Trade Shows

When you're seeking a lot of good prospects, it makes sense to exhibit at an industry trade show. Planning and implementing a trade show effort can be expensive and time consuming. Here are a few pointers to help you make your trade show a winner.

Focus on the Result.   You want to end up with new clients as a result of your trade show activity, right? Remember, the trade show encounter is only the first step in about 9 marketing interactions that you should plan with new prospects before they will buy from you. As mentioned earlier, since your prospects probably will miss 2 out of 3 attempts, in order to get 9, you really should plan for about 27. When you understand this critical point, you will feel better about the immediate results of your trade show if you return home with an ample supply of leads.

Coming away with good leads often requires you to evaluate the trade show's potential for generating leads. Ask the show promoter for a list of last year's exhibitors and call two or three of them to find out the rest of the story.

Rarely will your attendance at the show result in immediate business. According to Kathryn Clark, writing in *Personal Selling Power* magazine, "Two-thirds of all sales from trade shows aren't achieved until 11 to 24 months after a show." So, set a realistic expectation for lead generation. If you accomplish your target number, count the show a success.

Predetermine and Qualify Your Leads.   Before you attend the show, decide what type of leads you will seek. Then set your show's marketing strategy to focus on these leads. For example, when you attend a trade show for your primary industry niche, the attendees at the show may be your predetermined targets. At a general business exhibit, the exhibitors themselves may be your targets.

Convey Your Message

Make sure your sign says exactly what benefits you offer to attendees. People only take one second to see what your booth has to offer. Put borders around your signs—borders help the reader concentrate on the information on the sign.

—*Executive Edge* newsletter

Every time you meet people at the trade show, attempt to qualify them as potential prospects for your firm. Ask planned questions that will enable you to follow up appropriately after the show. Find out whom prospects are using now for their accounting work.

Ask prospects pertinent questions about the relationship: Has your accountant helped you be more profitable? Has your accountant helped you deal with new technology? Has your accountant helped you streamline your operations?

Ask the people you are qualifying about other decision makers: Is there an audit committee? Is there a bank or bonding requirement for work? Is the decision entirely up to the person with whom you are talking? According to Simmons Market Research Bureau, more than 70 percent of trade show attendees can significantly influence a decision to purchase.

If you know for whom you're looking and know when you've found them, your follow-up after the show will be more successful. Proceeding through a successful qualification will be a memorable event for your prospect and can be another step on the road to earning the prospect's business.

Trade Shows = Good Prospects

Did you know that:

- *91 percent of decision-making attendees consider trade shows as an extremely useful source of purchasing information.*
- *90 percent of attendees have not been seen by your sales force within the last year.*
- *90 percent plan on making a purchase within the next 12 months.*
- *80 percent of attendees are decision makers or influencers.*
- *30 percent have a definite interest in your product or service.*
- *It costs 33 percent less to generate a lead at a trade show.*
- *It costs 62 percent less to close a lead generated from a show than one originated in the field.*

—Center for Exhibit Industry Research

Follow-up Is Critical.   Allocate a portion of your time and dollar budget to the follow-up after the trade show. Unless you also set aside this time and money for the follow-up, you shouldn't waste your money to attend the show. Sometimes the proportion is 50–50. Some experts recommend a one-third, one-third, one-third budget: one-third before the show (mailing to registered attendees to attract them to your booth), one-third at the show, and one-third for follow-up. Set and plan all of your follow-up activities before the show occurs. Without such planning, the likelihood of your timely and effective follow-up is low.

If you plan your follow-up activities ahead of time, you can fax qualified leads to your office each day so that the appropriate follow-up letters and materials are sent. Nothing is more impressive to prospects than to return to their offices and immediately receive your materials.

Incidentally, keep the letter and the materials short. Remember, prospects are retuning with a pile of show materials to go through and are likely to be facing an overflowing in box. A big package of "stuff" will not get read and may not even get opened. Within 10 days of sending your letter, phone your prospects to make sure that they received the information. Then ask for an appointment to visit the prospects in their offices.

In their offices, you will have the best opportunity to further qualify your prospects and to begin to learn about their problems. Problems are "seeds of a need," the small indications that you may be able to help. If you do not find any problems, any attempts to proceed to proposal will be ill timed.

According to the Trade Show Bureau, 80 percent of exhibitors never follow up. If you do not follow up, you are wasting time and money going to the show.

Seminars and Speeches

Brian Tracy says that when people read something you have written, they perceive that you have about 4 times the amount of knowledge as displayed in the article. When you give a speech, the factor is 10 times. I am not sure of the scientific accuracy of this statement, but I do believe in its general intent. In the Day 19 chapter, I cover many of the things you will need to know to become well known as a capable speaker.

Tip Clubs

Formal tip clubs have become popular in recent years. Some organizations start locally, but there are also organizations that sponsor the formation of the tip clubs. Tip clubs generally meet weekly for the purpose of exchanging leads. Typically tip clubs are restricted to one representative of each business per group (e.g., one CPA, one banker, one contractor, one real estate agent, etc.). To belong to the group, you must agree to contribute leads. A tip club with 10 to 20 other "bird dogs" working for you can be a powerful source of new business. Most tip clubs are run like franchises, but some CPAs have started their own.

Summary

Leads are necessary to feed your marketing system. There are so many ways to generate leads that every accountant can find methods that are comfortable (or, at least, not too uncomfortable). If you allot time for planning lead-generation activities, doing the activities yourself, and following up, you will produce solid leads and new clients.

7 Focus on "10s"

Affluent consumers use different criteria than the nonaffluent in selecting services. They place more emphasis on knowledgeable, experienced people who can offer a variety of services. And they value personalized relationships.

—Journal of Services Marketing

This chapter is devoted to selling to high-quality clients and prospects—"10s." Whether you are beginning a new practice or revving up a mature one, the principles in this chapter will be very profitable for you.

Periodically, good businesspeople analyze their client bases and prospects and make certain they are focused on high-quality clients. When you focus your sales and marketing activities on a high-quality market, your payoff (in terms of high-quality new clients) will be maximized. You also will find that clients of lesser quality will be attracted to you at higher prices.

David Morgan says, "We want closely held businesses that are very successful, that would refer us to additional clients, and that are 'off–calendar-year' companies. We have to be careful with our staff members to not be too rigorous. We have a strong marketing culture throughout our firm, and when a young person attracts a 1040 client, we welcome that client into our firm. We want the young person to develop selling skills. If we did not allow them to bring in clients that are of lesser quality, many of them wouldn't have a chance."

In 1989 the Kanthal Corporation of Sweden discovered a vital statistic about its business: It found that 5 percent of its clients generated 150 percent of its profits. This concept is referred to as the 5–150 rule.

The 5–150 rule does not necessarily mean that the largest 5 percent (in terms of their operations) are included in this rule, just the most profitable. The rule applies to many accounting firms.

If your firm has some very large clients, you probably are devoting special attention to them. How you manage these key clients and how you sell

PORTRAIT OF A SALES LEADER

BILL JENKINS, former managing partner of Kennedy & Coe in Goodland, Kansas, says, "Generally the best businesspeople in many of our 22 markets are doing some business with us. We are the dominant accounting firm in most markets because we are not for everyone."

Working in his father's service stations, Bill Jenkins learned that "a man who loves his work is never lonely." His father's entrepreneurial spirit was a major influence on Jenkins. His dad suggested that he study accounting when he went to Kansas State University. Jenkins said, "The more I studied accounting, the harder time I had seeing myself doing a lot of the detail work. I was not real accurate and so I had a more difficult time than most."

He considered teaching and spent a year after obtaining his accounting degree in the teaching program at Kansas State. "I really enjoyed teaching. It was a way to help other people develop themselves and I learned that you could have a much more meaningful conversation with a person who is educated." This experience may have had a profound effect on Jenkins's marketing approach during his accounting career. Through Jenkins's leadership, Kennedy & Coe has developed a series of educational programs that members of the firm, plus a few invited speakers, give to their clients each year.

The most successful program, The Lions Den, is a program for family business owners. Each year the firm hosts about 400 clients and prospects in this three-day program designed to help business owners and their families cope with the complexities of owning, leading, managing, and passing on a successful family business. The firm runs about 25 other programs during the year at various places around its 22-office system in Kansas, Nebraska, Oklahoma, and Colorado.

After obtaining his MBA at the University of Colorado, Jenkins worked for Arthur Young & Company for over four years before joining a small firm in Nebraska. Unhappy with the differences in the two firms, Bill sought improvement by moving to his present firm. He was fortunate to start work in the Goodland, Kansas, office under a future managing partner of the firm. Bob Wilbur was a strong tax accountant and was very involved in the Goodland community. "Bob trained me well to take over as manager in charge of the Goodland office when he became managing partner of the firm in 1977," says Jenkins of his tutelage under Wilbur.

(continues)

PORTRAIT OF A SALES LEADER *(Continued)*

Jenkins learned to enjoy bringing in new clients. He gained some recognition within the firm as a business developer. That recognition earned him a reputation, and people started to ask him how he did it. That reputation caused Bill to want to do more. During his 23 years with Kennedy & Coe, he has helped open nearly a dozen small offices and trained a number of the firm's current owners to be rainmakers. Jenkins says, "You learn to sell by selling. I think every CPA can learn to sell and I think everyone should sell to some degree. You either have to attract new clients or convince your existing clients to buy more services. Selling is crucial in today's CPA firm."

to others who are similar is one of the most crucial marketing decisions you can make.

Although the first cut in separating clients is based on revenue, evaluate these two clients:

	Client A	Client B
Annual fees for the CPA firm	$50,000	$50,000
Gross fees at standard	$40,000	$60,000
Year end	April 30	December 31
Distance from CPA office	10 miles	300 miles
Profitability of client	High	Marginal
Growth rate of client	15%+	± 2%

Anyone can clearly see the profitability difference in these two clients. There are many other factors to consider besides just the financial side. Some clients are difficult and demanding. Clients located far from you can be a problem—what toll will travel take on your staff? It's hard to measure these things, but they do have a meaningful impact.

Bob Gaida says it this way: "While it's nice to have a big funnel and just put stuff in, if you put all garbage in, you'll get nothing coming out but garbage. You have to prequalify. Who am I going to be with? What is their sphere of influence? Can they lead me to clients? Are they a potential client? There are two fundamental items I look for: Does the client have the ability to pay a premium fee and do they have a thirst for knowledge?"

What Kanthal Corp. learned is a valuable lesson for all CPA firms: A small minority of clients was masking the heavy losses from other customers.

I learned from the Kanthal lesson and have applied their study to our CPA firm clients. Generally, we classify clients as A though F or 10 through 1. A clients compare to 10s, B clients = 9s, C clients = 7–8s, D clients = 5–6s, E clients = 4, and all the rest are Fs.

Generally, I find that 5 percent of an accounting firm's clients make up 50 percent of the gross revenue. (Obviously, this is not profitability, but it is a place to start.) After separating out these A clients, we generally find that the next 15 percent of clients account for about 30 percent of the total revenue. These are B clients. By totaling the amount of revenue for the A and B clients, we can see the Pareto rule—the 80–20 rule—come into play. Separating clients in this manner allows us to begin to define a good target market. C clients will account for another 5 percent or so of your revenue.

To obtain the most bang for your buck in marketing, you need to focus your firm's marketing budget. A $3 million firm with $90,000 to $150,000 to spend on marketing will obtain its best return when the budget is focused on a segment of its total market. Some professionals call this segmentation process "niching." I find that CPA firms obtain the best results from their marketing investment when they invest those dollars in marketing to A, B, and C clients and to prospects who would be A clients for the firms.

Rating Your Prospects with the MADDEN Test

In Day 7, we are going to help you evaluate your best clients and segment them into finite categories. But first let's think about what makes a good client. Years ago Dr. David Lill, author, speaker, and professor of marketing, invented the MADDEN test for a good prospect. Both David and I are fans of John Madden, former pro football coach and current sports announcer, and this analogy has stayed with me.

A good prospect under the MADDEN test has:

Money
Accessibility
Desire
Decision-Influencing Power
Eligibility
Need

Money

Be alert to various factors that will answer these questions:

▪ Will this prospect have the ability and willingness to pay premium or full fees?

- Who have their previous accountants been?
- Who are their other advisors?
- What do their facilities look like?
- On what scale are their products and services?

Accessibility
For you to sell your services, you must be able to talk to the company. You must have contacts who can refer you to the firm, industry contacts, or other access.

Desire
Next, ask yourself: Does the prospect have the desire, or interest, to work with me or our firm? If the client has the money and you can access the decision influencers, but they do not desire to work with you—guess what? They won't.

Decision-Influencing Power
The next qualifier relates to the decision influencers. Not only must you have access, you must be able to sell to people who can decide to hire you. In other words, if you are selling organs, don't waste your time talking to the monkey! You must have access to decision makers and influencers. Untrained CPAs waste an enormous amount of time talking to low-level employees who are not decision influencers. Generally, if you cannot access the key decision influencers, your message will not get through. Also, if key decision influencers will not talk with you, most times they are not serious about changing accountants.

Eligibility
Is the prospect eligible to do business with you? This question relates to risk, industry, expertise, enjoyment, and many other factors you may set for eligibility. David Morgan says, "If we come into contact with a municipality, we will stop right there. We do not do government agencies. They are not eligible to work with us."

Need
Does the prospect have a need for the services you provide? Do not reserve this question for last. Often it will be the second or third qualifier.

Analyzing Your Clients
When selling to 10s, it is important to follow a manageable eight-step pattern:

1. Set revenue objectives.
2. Identify target prospects and clients.

3. Determine which marketing tools will reach your prospects best.

4. Create an integrated marketing strategy.

5. Set specific objectives, activities, dates to complete, person responsible, and budgets for both time and money.

6. Use your personal contacts.

7. Market deep in the client's organization.

8. Measure your results.

Let's assume that you or your firm has a solid client list. Without a great deal of analysis, select five of your "best" clients. You decide what "best" means to you: large size, enjoyment, low risk, and so forth. List those five clients in the first column of the chart shown in Exhibit 7.1.

Exhibit 7.1   Your Five Best Clients

Name	Retention probability + (0 to 4)	Expansion possibility + (−1 to 3)	Desirability rating (−1 to 3)	= Total score
1.				
2.				
3.				
4.				
5.				

Once you have listed your five best clients, dig a little deeper by analyzing them. One good method is to use retention, expansion, and desirability as measurement tools. Use the following retention, fee-expansion, and desirability keys to rate the five clients on these three issues.

Retention Key

4 = Client has given me a referral in last two years.

3 = Client has expressed high satisfaction with my work.

2 = I think client is happy.

1 = There has been a service, fee, or accounting problem.

0 = Client is very unhappy.

Fee Expansion Key

3 = Premium fee realization and fees growing over 15% annually.

2 = Fee growth over 5% annually, full realization.

1 = Fees flat, ±5%, 90%+ realization.

0 = Less than 90% realization.

−1 = Intense fee pressure.

Desirability Key

3 = Low risk, on retainer, great people who seek our advice.

2 = Moderate risk, pay within 30 days, normal people who take our advice.

1 = Average risk, pay within 60 days, people who use us most of the time.

0 = High risk, or slow pay, or difficult people.

−1 = High risk, and slow pay, and difficult people.

Now, add the scores together for each of the three measurement tools for each client. You now have a ranking of clients. A perfect score is 10.

Another method you can use to qualify your clients as 10s would be to define what each numerical rating means to your practice. The following chart (see Exhibit 7.2) lists the elements and qualities that would constitute various levels of qualification for the fictional ABC Accounting Firm. Look at the example and make your own judgments for your practice.

Once you have evaluated the types of clients you want or would be willing to accept, the next step is to begin to identify prospects who are very similar. List the best 10 of these prospects in the next chart (see Exhibit 7.3). Then, using the visibility and CPA strength keys that follow, rate each prospect on their visibility and how strong their current CPA is.

Visibility Key

5 = Would hire me tomorrow. I am in second place with no competition.

4 = I could propose but there may be competition.

3 = Prospect knows us fairly well.

2 = Prospect is aware of us and has been qualified.

1 = I have had no interaction and do not know suspect.

CPA Strength Key

5 = I know, and prospect knows, that current CPA is not adequate.

4 = I know of some potential weakness in the relationship.

3 = I do not know of any problems, but I am going to keep searching.

2 = I think the relationship is strong.

1 = Prospect has told me that he loves the current CPA and do not want to have a second.

Exhibit 7.2   Client Rating

Client Rating	ABC Accounting Firm	Your Accounting Firm
10	Interesting industry matches our core skill set Interesting company to which we can contribute Innovative leaders and managers Will use at least four services of our firm Will pay premium rate Highly profitable business Low risk Non-calendar-year end Owners and managers have a good reputation Will generate quality referrals Seeks and values our advice and counsel Total fees in excess of $75,000	
9	Interesting industry matches our core skill set Interesting company to which we can contribute Innovative leaders and managers Will pay premium rate Will use at least three services from our firm Owners and managers have a good reputation Will generate quality referrals Seeks and values our advice and counsel Total fees in excess of $75,000	
8	Interesting industry matches our core skill set Interesting company to which we can contribute Will pay full rate Profitable business Will use at least three services from our firm Owners and managers have a good reputation Will generate referrals Seeks and values our advice and counsel Total fees in excess of $50,000	
7	Interesting industry Interesting company to which we can contribute Will pay full rate Profitable business Will use two services to begin Owners and managers have a good reputation Seeks and values our advice and counsel Total fees in excess of $50,000	

(continues)

Exhibit 7.2   Client Rating *(Continued)*

Client Rating	ABC Accounting Firm	Your Accounting Firm
6	Interesting industry Interesting company to which we can contribute Will pay full rate Profitable business Will use two services to begin Owners and managers have a good reputation Seeks and values our advice and counsel Total fees in excess of $20,000	
5	Interesting company to which we can contribute Will pay full rate Profitable business Will use one service to begin Owners and managers have a good reputation Seeks and values our advice and counsel Total fees in excess of $10,000	
4	Company to which we can contribute Will pay rates with 10% discount to start Profitable business Will use one or more services to begin Owners and managers have a good reputation Seeks and values our advice and counsel Total fees in excess of $5,000	
3	Will pay rates with more than 10% discount Will use one or more services to begin Owners and managers have a good reputation Seeks and values our advice and counsel Total fees in excess of $1,000	
2	Wants a discount larger than 20%	
1		

Exhibit 7.3   Prospects Similar to Your Clients in Your Markets

Name	Current	Relative Strength	Visibility of Current CPA
1.			
2.			
3.			
4.			
5.			
6.			
7.			
8.			
9.			
10.			

Starting Out

What if you are just beginning your practice or are beginning to build a new niche within your firm? Where do you start?

First you must evaluate your skill set and your interests. What value can you contribute to prospective clients? Some very successful practitioners begin with highly selective client criteria. Others set their initial criteria lower until they capture a share of the market, then begin to upgrade. If you select the second method, you must follow through on your upgrading plan.

Summary

However well developed your practice is, deciding on the kinds of clients with whom you want to work is crucial. As the Cheshire Cat told Alice in *Alice's Adventures in Wonderland,* "If you don't know where you're going, any path will take you there." Your best clients will be far more profitable for you than your worst clients. Defining and working to develop your perfect 10s will help you grow a successful practice for the long term.

8 Marketing with Permission

I can get more cooperation with a kind word and a gun than I can with only a kind word.

—Al Capone

One of the main reasons that accountants and other professionals sometimes don't like to sell is because they worry about being pushy. That is, they don't want to impose on others or be pushy about selling their services. That's where one of the newer concepts in marketing comes in. *Permission marketing* was developed by author Seth Godin for online marketing in a book of the same name. However, the permission concept applies to most of marketing, online or offline.

In brief, in permission marketing, you ask permission to stay in touch with prospects and clients. Prospects opt in to receive information from you. In Godin's model, you offer people rewards for receiving messages from you, such as money, free reports, or products.

Standing Out in a Crowded Marketplace

Every decision maker is subjected to thousands of advertising messages every day. Out of the thousands of messages, a few bits of information may be retained. But they are hard to distinguish amid the clutter of impersonal messages that swamp us.

As an accountant, you are not just affected by marketing and sales attempts of other accountants, consultants, tax lawyers, and other competitors. You are competing for the *attention* of your prospects and clients. "In Dallas–Fort Worth, there are thousands of practicing accountants competing for every client I have," says Terry Orr. "Permission marketing enables me to get heard through the noise of the marketplace."

And you're not competing just with thousands of commercial messages every day. You are also competing for people's attention with their boss, spouse, kids, hobbies, and need for sleep. It's a busy world for most people, and their needs for your services are not always high on their lists of priorities.

The better your marketing and sales are, the easier you make it for people to cut through the clutter and distractions in their lives to hire you. They'd like to make a quick, painless decision that improves their situation at no risk to themselves. That's why referrals from people they respect are so effective — they reduce risk and time to decision. Your goal with your other marketing and sales efforts is to help people make the same easy decision. Selling your services is so much easier with permission than without it.

Interruption Marketing

Even if you haven't been aware of Godin's work, you've been applying the concept of permission marketing. And it's when you don't apply it that you can feel pushy. When you try to cultivate people as possible clients, they have to *allow* you to do so. You have to *interest them* in talking with you. You need to enlist their cooperation. The sales methods that are preferable for you are generally less pushy and more inviting for prospects.

Godin refers to traditional marketing and sales efforts as "interruption marketing." Television, radio, and Internet commercials interrupt the program you're enjoying (or the search you're doing). The dinnertime telemarketing call is the classic image of pushy sales. Accountants don't interrupt people as dramatically as this. However, it's worthwhile to rank your marketing techniques on a scale of "interruptability." For instance, sending an unsolicited mailing for your services is more interruptive than offering an invitation to a free seminar on tax issues. When people attend your seminar, they know you will make a sales pitch of some sort, but they are accepting that because of the value of the seminar. (And you can surprise them by keeping your pitch very low key—say, just mentioning that you'd be happy to meet with them individually at no charge to apply the seminar principles to their own situation).

Godin makes the distinction between traditional marketing and permission marketing clear when he says: "Interruption marketers spend all their time interrupting strangers, in an almost pitiful attempt to bolster popularity and capture attention. Permission marketers spend as little time and money talking to strangers as they can. Instead they move as quickly as they can to turn strangers into prospects who choose to 'opt in' to a series of communications." Joe James and David Coker of Coker James in Atlanta, Georgia, have used a permission marketing campaign to aggressively grow their practice for over three years. "We waited for the clients to show up on our door step, we got active in trade groups and we initiated many things. When we began to use the consistent, low-key approach of seeking permission to sell, our results started to soar," said James.

Godin tends to pay people fairly explicitly for receiving marketing/sales messages. Pay can include entry into a drawing, coupons, points toward purchases, cash, and so on. Although your offers are likely to be more subtle, you do need to make it worth people's while to take your calls. Normally, you would "pay" people in some sort of "information currency" about accounting—for instance, a company newsletter or e-zine is very useful for keeping in touch with people. You are giving them useful information and they are reminded of you regularly.

Permission marketing has several good things going for it. It is *anticipated*—people expect to hear from you. It is *personal*—your messages are customized for each individual's situation. It is *relevant*—your communication includes useful information for the prospect. Exhibit 8.1 shows how this contrasts with typical marketing efforts.

Exhibit 8.1   Permission Marketing versus Typical Marketing Efforts

	Interruption	Permission
Anticipated	No	Yes
Personal	Seldom	Yes
Relevant	Sometimes	Yes

Permission Develops Prospects

To put permission marketing in a fuller perspective, let's review a few basics about the overall process of marketing and selling. Doing so will show you how useful the permission concept is.

As we discussed in Day 6, to be successful, you need to handle three stages of marketing:

1. Find prospects.
2. Develop prospects into clients.
3. Serve clients and develop new business and referrals from them.

Step 1, finding prospects, is covered in other chapters.

Step 2, developing prospects, is the most important area in which permission marketing applies. It can take a long time to turn prospects into clients, and you need their permission to make this conversion go smoothly.

This occurs for several reasons, not least of which is that changing account-ants can be difficult for people. However, there is a more basic reason as well: Prospects must trust you enough to let you sell them. Yes, people must have some trust in you even before they allow you to sell. The permission approach opens by helping prospects feel in control and rewards the first small trust step on their part.

Step 3 is also covered in other chapters. Generally when people are clients, you have permission to stay in touch with them.

Developing Prospects into Clients

It is in step 2 that the permission marketing concept is most important and valuable. To carry out step 2, you need to *enlist prospects' cooperation* at some level. You need to obtain their permission to "court" them. It is possible for you to keep in touch with prospects without their real consent. You can seek them out at industry meetings. You can call them on the phone. You can mail them newsletters. But without their cooperation, your efforts may be counterproductive.

Online marketing is the perfect arena to see why enlisting prospects' permission to stay in touch is important. In the online arena, there are laws against contacting people without permission (such mail is known as spam). And it is easier for people to ignore your unwanted contacts. It is in this con-text that Godin developed the concept of permission marketing. You need to gain prospects' permission to send them e-mails. When people "opt in" to your online newsletter (ezine) or other messages from you, you are legal and prospects should pay more attention to your messages.

Godin lays out four tests of permission marketing:

Four Tests of Permission Marketing

1. Each of your marketing efforts should invite prospects or customers to "raise their hands" about their interests. You learn something about them each time they respond.

2. You keep a permission database. You can track each communication with prospects and customers and what they gave permission for.

3. When people give you permission to communicate with them, you have to have something to say.

4. How will you teach people about your services and particularly about how they are unique?

Once people become clients, you need to work to deepen the communication with these people—again with their permission.

All these permission criteria are applicable to offline marketing efforts as well. They amount to obtaining permission to build a relationship and then having the system in place to follow through with the job.

One-to-One Marketing

Notice that permission marketing has nothing to do with your technical competence in delivering accounting or consulting services. Although some of your communications with clients may be about accounting issues, the permission approach focuses on prospects' granting you permission to communicate with them. This is more about interpersonal relationships than about accounting issues.

The use of a permission approach to build relationships with prospects and clients fits well into what Don Peppers and Martha Rogers of the Peppers and Rogers Consulting Group have called 1–1 marketing. They recommend thinking of each client as unique. Ideally, your marketing would use a different message for each prospect and client based on their unique situation, personality, and so on. Ideally, each client or prospect is a target of one. Although this amount of personalization may seem hard to accomplish, the process emphasizes the specific and interpersonal nature of selling accounting services.

Peppers and Rogers take the 1–1 concept much further. Your goal is *not* to develop a sales message that is tailored perfectly to the client. That is part of the fuller 1–1 process. Your goal is to customize your services for each client. If your services are too generic, clients will buy you as a commodity and be highly price sensitive. That's not what you want.

I know from my years of work that clients take a firm's generic accounting abilities for granted. One of the main things they want is for their accountant to understand their businesses and proactively help them achieve their specific goals. For you to do this, you need to do research on their industries and issues. But you also need to become educated in the specific issues that each business faces.

By 1–1 marketing, Peppers and Rogers mean that the clients invest in *educating you* about their businesses. When they've done this, you are no longer a commodity. Put another way, when you have been educated about the specifics of their situation and needs, your knowledge becomes a unique selling proposition for you. No other accountant can equal your fit for the client. And the client won't want to spend the time training other accountants about their businesses, so your competition will have a very hard time breaking into your accounts.

Another important concept from 1–1 marketing is the idea of "share of client" versus share of market. When you know your clients really well, you can add new services the clients want. You don't need to sell them because you are helping them obtain what they want. Your goal is not to increase your share of market by adding new clients; your goal is to increase your share of each client's business.

Sample Permission Program

At The Rainmaker Academy, I have operated a dozen permission marketing campaigns for our clients. In our permission marketing programs, our team lays out 12 steps that finally result in a sale. Although you may not be able to carry out all the contacts in every case, you can complete the process with interested and qualified clients. Contacts 1 to 4 are letters, starting with an introduction and ending with a gift. You determine the number of letters to send out based on the number of meetings you can handle. About 10 percent of these prospects should "take a meeting" with you.

The Rainmaker version of permission marketing is very intense but very productive. In our version of permission marketing, we are very careful about obtaining and cleansing the databases. They use only experienced business telemarketers to set appointments, and they focus on insuring the accounting firm clients actually close business from the relationships developed.

Contact 5 is a phone call designed to obtain a lunch appointment with prospects. Contact 6 is the lunch, where you qualify them as a prospect and try to get them to visit your office for Contact 7. If you are able to move ahead, Contact 8 is a visit to their office, where you gather information to make a solid proposal. This information gathering includes a needs assessment. Contact 9 is a meeting with decision influencers. Contact 10 identifies outside influencers such as bankers, attorneys, and board members. Contact 11 is to present a draft of your proposal, and Contact 12 is to present a formal proposal.

You'll notice that there is a fair amount of research between the prospect showing interest and you actually making a proposal. Many firms simply put together a stock proposal when the prospect is open to it. Many of these proposals fail because no one has learned the real needs of the prospect, no one has presented a solution to those needs, or no one has asked key influencers for help.

Advancing the Relationship

The general permission marketing concept can be extended to the entire relationship spectrum. At the beginning of a business relationship, you want to enlist potential prospects' permission to become prospects. They are aware of your interest in doing business with them, and they agree to let you stay in touch. If you offer value and match your skills to their needs, eventually they hire you for some task.

There are many models of the stages of relationships with clients. I use the hierarchy of:

Suspects

Prospects

Clients

Former Clients

The key point to remember is that, unlike many sales and marketing efforts, in permission marketing the first business meeting is not the *end* of your marketing efforts. Rather it is the *beginning* of the most important stage. The loyalty you create now drives profits and referrals as you deliver great service and expand the relationship. At first this means taking on additional tasks. But as discussed, later it means adapting your services to clients' needs or developing new services. As you achieve the status of most trusted business advisor, you may even coordinate the services of others to provide needs that you don't do yourself.

At each stage of the developing relationship, you are earning permission to move to the next stage. You are building trust. Done well, you will have an unassailable competitive position. And you'll have clients who value you.

Building Trust

Developing the loyal client base you need for your best possible client relationship relies on building trust. Of course, the best way to build trust is to put the clients' interests first in a very visible way. Interestingly enough, when you put clients first, they reward you with more business. So, paradoxically, when you let clients know they are uppermost in your actions, you benefit yourself the most!

Building trust of this sort takes time for two reasons. First, it takes time for you to demonstrate your commitment to clients' interests. Second, time itself works on your side. A good deal of research has demonstrated that the more familiar we are with people, the more we like them. This is even truer in uncertain situations. And what could be more uncertain than tax and financial issues!

By consistently staying in touch with clients (and prospects), you have both a chance to give them rewards and a chance to let them get to like you. When you are in touch only when you are billing them, you do not build the trust you need. You need to be in touch more consistently. A newsletter or ezine can do this, but you also need some personal contacts.

It's easy to think of your marketing program in impersonal terms: You contact a large number of people, and some respond. Techniques like advertising and direct mail reinforce this thinking. I think it's more useful to think of your marketing efforts as personal. It's your job to find a few individuals you want to work with and cultivate them. Even more important, from *their* point of view your marketing is very personal. It's about trusting you and how you treat them.

Permission marketing and 1–1 marketing emphasize that what the Godfather said is still true: "All business is personal." It's up to you to build those relationships that will allow you to build a great business. Once you have permission to engage people, you're on your way, one person at a time. Terry Orr says, "If I try to slam a close on a prospect during our first meeting, he or she will usually clam up. I will never have a chance to develop trust because I did not allow time for the relationship to develop."

Getting Started

The biggest problems in implementing permission marketing are the same problems of doing effective marketing in general. You need a system. As an individual you can have bursts of sales and marketing activity—you can send mailings, take ads, give speeches, and so on. But your best marketing will be regular and systematic. Once you make a contact, you should have a system to follow up. You should have a number of ways to keep in contact planned.

Adding the permission concept to your marketing system reminds you to involve prospects or clients at each stage. Make sure they are interested in hearing from you, and create clear value for them in each contact. Build the relationships and trust one person at a time for success.

Summary

Although the concept of permission marketing was developed for the Internet, it has been around forever. It has been applied by people who take a personal approach to marketing and sales. And as Seth Godin notes, the concept is as old as the concept of dating, where you need permission to pursue your love interest!

To apply permission marketing, you explicitly reward people for receiving communications from you. Doing this reminds you that no one wants to receive a sales pitch. What people want is information that can help them from people who care about them. In addition, you must advance your knowledge of their situation so that you can deliver increasingly relevant information to build a 1–1 relationship. When you've achieved this, clients will not want to invest in training your competitors and you will have a solid client base.

9 Referrals Are Nuclear Power

Referrals are the most reliable, most rewarding, least expensive way of rounding up business.
—Ivan R. Misner and Robert Davis, *Business by Referral*[1]

Referrals are your most powerful and least expensive source of new business. That point is so important that I'm going to rephrase it. Referrals are your best source of new business and your least expensive source!

A qualified, referred lead can be better business than a client expansion or cross-sell of services in two ways. First, you are likely to obtain a larger client if your source is strong and you have educated him or her well as to the type of companies you want as clients.

Second, a new client expands your client base, making you less vulnerable to client attrition and giving you a new center of influence.

Why are referrals such a powerful source of new business? If you ask any top rainmaker this question, her answer would be something like this:

"When I receive a referred lead, the prospect is presold. Somehow the credibility of the referrer rubs off on me. If I have communicated well with my source, the prospect is ready to buy. All it takes is making sure my referral source knows what types of clients I work with. Nine times out of ten, when a prospect calls as a result of a referral, I have no competition. I am usually the only person the prospect is talking to. I am in a more powerful position with the prospect in many ways. I can say no to the prospect and send him to an appropriate CPA either outside or inside my own firm. Or if the prospect is someone I'd love to work with, I can say yes. In most cases, fees are not an issue. The prospect needs and wants something done, so I am usually able to collect full fees. We do not spend time preparing a written proposal. And, of course, the best part is, of the clients I choose to work with, I have a very high closing ratio."

Why referrals are your least expensive source of new business is fairly obvious—other people are doing the selling for you. This make the whole sales process a lot easier on you. You don't have to sell your services directly, you just have to develop people who want to sell for you! This concept also relates to why referrals are so powerful. The other people who refer you are perceived as relatively objective. Their opinion is more credible and trusted than yours is. They can say you're the best accountant in town and be believed. You can't. They don't feel ego-involved when they're selling you; it's easier on them.

Why don't you receive more first-rate referrals from clients and others? There could be one or more reasons:

- The person isn't motivated to promote you.
- They may not think you want new clients.
- They may not think about you.
- They may not be happy with your work.
- They may not know about all of your services.

PORTRAIT OF A SALES LEADER

LOU MILLS has been one of the most prolific business builders at Moss Adams for years because of his strong referral network. Lou is now retired.

Lou's father was concerned about raising his sons in the tough streets of a Chicago neighborhood, so he sent them to Washington state to live with relatives and attend school. Lou Mills says, "I really enjoyed the Pacific coast. But I took a job with Arthur Andersen in Chicago right out of school. About five years later, a horrible snow hit Chicago and I called a headhunter in Seattle. He got me on at Ernst & Whinney, and I was happy to be back in Washington."

Mills was one of the top rainmakers in his firm. "Some years you seem to get on a roll. Our firm is very niche-focused, and I really enjoy working with manufacturers. I have found that it's fun to see how things are put together and how the financial side of the business relates to the manufacturing process," said Mills. During his 15 years with Moss Adams, Mills has helped the firm grow from about $6 million in Seattle to over $22 million. The firm is dominant in the northwestern part of the country.

"My first sale was when I was a tax supervisor. The sale was to a well-known company that was using a national firm for their accounting and tax work," says Mills. This first sale created an excitement in Mills

Most of these reasons boil down to the potential referrer's perceptions about you and your relationship with him or her. Given the high value of referrals, it will pay you to think about different types of referral sources and how you can build the relationships that will motivate people to want to refer you.

Four Ways to Get Referral Sources to Send Business Your Way

If you are not getting your fair share of referred leads, here are four great ways to stimulate your referral sources to send you business:

1. Ask for a referral.
2. Build relationships with other service providers.
3. Enhance the revenue of your referrers.
4. Stay in touch with your referrer.

to develop his rainmaking skills. Today he serves as the leader of the Moss Adams firm-wide manufacturing and distribution services group.

Mills says, "The system I was using was developing relationships with the commercial bankers in the Seattle area. I would open relationships with banks, then I'd go out with the banker and I'd say, 'I'd like to develop a relationship with you and have a really nice chat.' But basically I'd say, 'The reason why I'm here is to generate some leads. I'd like to help you too. Anytime there is an opportunity, I'd like to go your way and have you work on it and that way it can be a mutual relationship.' Some banks would be okay, but primarily I focused on younger bankers who were aggressive and had the same desire I had. So when there was an opportunity that came up, they would tell me about it.

"Then we would host some get-togethers. We would have our networking meetings, informal meetings, and then what I would do is just kind of tag on to one or two people and figure out what their interests were.

"The meeting would generally be off-site. We try to do something that is fun. I remember one time we went with a bunch of lawyers to a Mariners game and we had a box. Sometimes that works. The key is that, after the event, you need to make sure you follow up and continue at least a monthly meeting process via lunch or breakfast with those referral sources. If you don't commit to regular contact after the event, you've lost your investment."

Ask for a Referral

Many CPAs tell me they don't want to offend their good clients by hitting on them for new work. The truth is, these CPAs are really too timid to ask for the referral. Actually, everybody enjoys the feeling of doing something for someone they like. So don't deprive your good clients of this pleasure.

Some of your clients may think you don't have room for another client. Let them know your doors are open for business by asking for a referral.

Many bankers and attorneys feel that CPAs, as a group, are timid and afraid of asking for business. Bankers and attorneys are usually more aggressive. When you are meeting with another professional, you must strengthen your personal style—be bold—so that you relate to the professional on his or her level.

Six Direct Ways You Can Ask for a Referral

Ask a client:

- *Bill, you have been a client of mine for over six years and you know that I work strictly by referrals. I would be honored if you would do me a favor and give some of your business acquaintances one of my brochures. Here are the kinds of clients we want to serve.*

- *Jean, thank you for your flattering comments about my work. Who do you know who might need their tax situation reviewed next year as I have done for you?*

- *Sara, I am going to send you an extra tax organizer this year. Would you take a moment and pass this extra organizer along to your next-door neighbor or one of your family members? We are growing our practice this year and I would really appreciate your help.*

- *Jere, you have been a great friend. We are expanding our business this year, and I need your help. Who do you know who could benefit from the same type of assistance I have provided you?*

Showing your clients your list of targeted prospects is a good way to ask for referrals. Here are some examples:

- *Tom, we are expanding our business in the coming year and we have identified some companies that we would like to add as clients. [Show the list to the prospect.] Do you know anyone at these businesses? If so, tell me about them.*

- *Leslie, will you introduce me to Bill Jones at Acme Construction?*

Bob Gaida, a partner at BDO Seidman who you'll meet in Day 15, describes the routine he has perfected over the years to get referrals: "If a client had not referred me in a while, I would start my conversation with 'You must not love me.' And they would say, 'Why?' And I would say, 'Well, you're not happy, it must be my fault, I'm sure.' And they would say, 'What are you talking about?' And I would say, 'If I was really doing a good job, you would refer me to a good client just like you. And you haven't, so I'm not doing a really good job.' Of course, then they would want to refer."

Terry Orr says, "It was as easy as sitting down with someone and asking for help on a personal basis: 'I need help, can you help me?'" Terry Orr's strategy is simple and to the point, and it works.

Build Relationships with Other Service Providers

Get to know all of the other professional service providers your best clients use. This is one of the quickest-producing and most profitable market-ing activities in which you can engage. Find a way to meet and work with each of the lawyers, bankers, bonding agents, insurance brokers, and other service providers your best clients have hired. These professionals are natu-rally open to you. You need no excuse to meet with them on behalf of your clients.

Easy Cross-Referring

Do as one professional does and arrange for other service providers to put a P.S. at the end of letters they send to prospects who are appropriate for you. The P.S. simply says:

If you need the services of an excellent accountant who specializes in _____, I'd like to recommend my friend _____. She has room for a few new clients and has given my clients first choice to fill those spots. If you would like to speak with her, call her at _____.

—Rick Crandall, *1001 Ways to Market Your Services: Even If You Hate to Sell*[2]

These professionals have a natural inclination to help their clients' busi-nesses—and that means meeting with you to generate new ideas for the benefit of your mutual client. During brainstorming sessions, business rela-tionships get built that lead to referrals for you.

Most referrals come from people who are impressed with your work and who trust you to handle their friends well. After you have thoroughly networked with these referral sources, you can begin to network with nonrelated sources of referrals.

Enhance the Revenue of Your Referrers

When you get to know your clients' other service providers well, you can find ways to enhance their revenue. Send them a referral, include them as a team member on decisions affecting your mutual client, or ask them to help you (e.g., prepare your will).

When you enhance their revenue, you create a due bill of which you will be the beneficiary. There are many ways to enhance the revenue of your referral source. Here are a few:

- **Do business with clients and encourage your staff members to patronize clients.** When you or your staff members trade with clients, make sure the client knows you were there. Encourage your staff and employees to trade with clients by placing coupons, business cards, and ads from clients in your break room or in employees' paycheck envelopes.

- **Encourage clients to trade with clients.** Introduce at least two buyers per year to your best clients and referrers. As part of your marketing plan each year, identify two prospective customers for each of your best clients. Introduce the two businesspeople to each other.

- **Refer potential clients to your best referral sources.** Most people think of this step. In some cases, you can refer potential clients to more than one lawyer or banker. But don't play this game with your best referral sources: Treat them the way you want to be treated. "Tee it up" for them alone. Communicate the referral yourself with a phone call or a note.

Stay in Touch with Your Referrer

Asking for a referral is difficult for many CPAs. Opportunities to enhance referrers' revenue may be limited. But anyone can stay in touch.

I've conducted many interviews with attorneys who give referrals to accountants. These attorneys tell me they send most referrals to the accountant they think of first. That means the person who stays in touch regularly through a newsletter program, a letter campaign, a seminar, personal visits, and phone calls—for any business reason—is going to capture a portion of the referral source's mind. When you capture a share of their minds, you will get a share of their referrals.

If you want an attorney or banker to become a powerful referral source for your firm, he or she must get to know you well. To begin a development program, you might want to arrange get-to-know-you luncheons or breakfasts with an attorney or a banker on a regular basis.

Jim Belew describes the referral receptions his firm has hosted for five years. "We host at least one reception a month for our key referral sources. Our staff members are invited, and the ones who are serious about their careers attend. We stage the reception so that during the tour of our offices, we tell the group something about our firm. Then during the cocktail hour, we have something serious to talk about. It has really helped our partners and staff members get to know attorneys and bankers in Dallas."

A Program to Cultivate Attorney Referrals

Here is a strategy for setting up a serious referral program. I'm focusing on attorneys because we find they are the best source of referrals for many CPAs.

Prepare for a Meeting

A good attorney never goes into court unprepared, and you shouldn't wing your first meeting either. Do your homework—use the Martindale Hubbell Law Directory to get an up-to-date bio on the lawyer. Review your client files: Do you already have common relationships? Once you have this basic information, you can plan what you will say, ask, and do during your first meeting.

What are you going to accomplish at this meeting? Count the first meeting a success if you are able to make the attorney aware of your capabilities. Also, you should learn as much as possible about the attorney and the extent to which he or she refers clients to CPAs.

Rate Referral Potential

The next step depends on whether you've classified the attorney as a C, B, or A prospect.

A C attorney is one who says he or she rarely refers clients to CPAs, or one who has a well-established relationship with another CPA firm. At least initially, about half of the attorneys you meet will be Cs. Count these as successful calls anyway, because now you know where not to spend further marketing capital. Just calendar C lawyers for a call-back one year from now and put them in your keep-in-touch program (e.g., send quarterly newsletters).

A B attorney is one who might be able to make from one to five referrals to CPAs with your expertise each year. This attorney may have a relationship with another firm, but you sense potential. Initially, as many as 40 percent of the lawyers you meet will be Bs. These attorneys are ideal candidates for receiving your firm's client or specialty law firm newsletter and for invitations to seminars you sponsored. Then contact these attorneys twice a year, just to stay in touch. If your talks prove fruitful, schedule another face-to-face meeting.

An A attorney (we call them aces) either needs accounting services for his or her own practice or has the opportunity to refer clients to a CPA more than five times a year. Of course, you probably won't meet too many of these—probably 10 percent or fewer of all the contacts you make will begin as A contacts. But, for these few, you will want to undertake the highest level of follow-up.

You can invite an A prospect to your office right away. To convince the attorney that he or she will also benefit from such a meeting, you might say: "Our associates are always looking for excellent attorneys to whom we can send our clients. Could you come by for an informal meeting?"

Build the Relationship

What are the objectives of this second meeting?

- To communicate how your firm is different—and better—than your competitors
- Perhaps to ask for a referral

If, during this meeting, you discover that the attorney you thought was an A is really a B, you might say something like this. "We share many clients with attorneys just like you, and we hear they like our service. If you have an opportunity to refer one of your clients, I assure you they will receive the best personal service I can provide." After saying this, wait for a response. Many times an attorney will say something like this: "We send our clients to Chasem and Crook." Respond by saying "I'm glad you respect them so much. I hope one day to earn your trust, and I'm willing to wait for you to be comfortable with me."

If the attorney remains an A prospect, you can afford to be a bit more subtle and take the long-range approach. Take the time to get to know the attorney's practice better, make sure he or she meets all of your associates, and establish mutual trust and rapport.

When the meeting is over, there are three possible next steps:

1. Invite your new attorney friend to meet with a client who may be a good match for him or her.
2. Offer to host a "mixer" for all of the attorney's associates.

3. Invite the attorney to an upcoming special event, such as a play, concert, or sports event.

At this juncture, it is vital that you move to enhance the relationship. Do not let the relationship drop now.

From the Horse's Mouth: What Attorneys Say They Want from CPAs

I recently worked with a panel of attorneys to help CPAs stimulate referrals. Here's what they said:

- *Take charge.* Attorneys respect CPAs who help them anticipate the future and prevent problems. CPAs who are overly cautious will not earn an attorney's respect.
- *Produce results.* Vague statements about quality don't impress attorneys. Give them clear examples of ways you can make a difference.
- *Shoot straight.* Get to the bottom line, and never sugarcoat the bad news. Tell attorneys what is wrong, so it can get fixed.
- *Understand the attorneys' needs.* Talk to attorneys about how to improve their own profits and how to satisfy their goals.
- *Share your professional expertise.* Teach attorneys how to use your services to their benefit. Allan Koltin, CEO of PDI Global, has developed deep experience in helping accountants consult with and develop referrals from attorneys. His firm publishes several newsletter programs accountants can purchase to send to lawyers.

Once you have established this kind of relationship with an attorney, you shouldn't have to come right out and ask for referrals. They should begin to flow. Remember, there are three attorneys for every CPA in America, and most CPAs are not courting any attorneys. Your chances for success are excellent.

Use Attorney Panels to Get Staff Involved

If you've been looking for ways to encourage staff members to ask for referrals, they might appreciate a few pointers from the very attorneys they are to approach.

When you've established a solid relationship with an attorney or a law firm in your town, you might want to ask them to serve on a panel discussion attended by your staff. Invite the attorneys to tell your staff members how they should go about asking for referrals. Encourage the attorneys to provide stories and examples of people who have successfully tapped into their referral network.

Your 12 Aces

"Twelve aces" is the systematic approach I recommend to obtain a steady stream of referrals. If every partner and manager in your firm focuses on deepening relationships with 12 referral partners, you will unlock the doors to steady business.

Each of your aces can generate millions of dollars in business for you over your business career. Just think: If you can get one of your aces to refer one client to you with $15,000 in recurring fees, over a 10-year life span this client will generate $150,000 of fees. If one referral partner can lead you to just one new client like this per year, over a 10-year span, this one ace will bring you $1.5 million in potential business. What is that worth to you?

Now work those numbers out with 12 aces.

Your 12 aces program begins by building on what you have. If you have no relationships, establish one referral relationship this year. You may have to sort through 5 or 10 prospects to find your ace, but if you focus, you will succeed.

After you have one ace, focus on adding two more until you have three. Each succeeding two will be easier and faster to obtain as you learn what to look for and how to create the deep trust you need for this program.

The 12 aces program will provide many benefits to you. It will:

- Eliminate the need for expensive advertising
- Build long-term solid relationships with other professionals
- Decrease the pressures of bringing in new business

There are many ways of initiating and staying in contact with referral sources. The key to success is to use a variety of methods. The most successful referral developers focus their attention on a few sources (your 12 aces). Lee Iaccoca said that he turned Chrysler around with 12 good managers. You can build a large firm with 12 aces (referral sources) working for you.

Keep in Touch with Your Aces

Your aces will be the most helpful in building your business over the long term. Here are a few ways to stay in touch:

Mail.   Send your aces a personal note at least four times a year.

- Newsletters, personalized with sticky notes
- Articles of specific interest
- Idea letters, referral letters, and thank-you notes

Meetings.   Meet with your aces at least four times a year.

- Personal, one-on-one meetings for lunch, breakfast, or coffee
- Meetings to introduce your partner or a prospective customer
- Seminars in your office or theirs
- Receptions, dinners, and cocktail parties
- Client business reviews, focus groups, advisory boards

E-mail.   Add your aces to your ezine list. Forward items of interest and send quick notes or thoughts.

Telephone.   Speak on the phone with your aces as often as possible.

Staying in Touch with Specific Types of Referral Sources

You can use letters, phone calls, e-mails, breakfast, lunch, dinner, and coffee for all categories of referral sources. Use these suggestions to stay in touch with specific groups.

Clients

- Client seminars and reverse seminars
- Client business reviews
- Focus groups and client surveys
- Advisory boards

Attorneys

- Attorney newsletters
- Continuing legal education (Cle) courses
- Mutual client meetings
- Office receptions

Bankers

- Banker newsletters
- Annual update sessions
- Boardroom meetings

Other CPAs

- Focus on practitioners who limit their practices
- Align with the Big Four
- Establish local network for sole practitioners

Insurance Agents, Sureties, and Stockbrokers

- Mutual seminars
- Send client newsletters

Real Estate Agents

- Send client newsletter
- Annual continuing education

Attorneys.   Lawyers are the best general source of referrals. Some people keep track of their lawyer contacts in their head, some keep a file folder, and some keep a business card file, Rolodex, or PDA. Still others haphazardly accumulate telephone messages, business cards, letterheads, scraps of paper, or names on cocktail napkins.

Most progressive accounting firms today are using a fast, efficient, and affordable contact management software package. Good programs will allow you to track all contacts with your current and potential referral sources, maintain a list of new clients generated by each referral source, remember when it is time to reward key referral sources, and generally maintain regular communications with all referral sources based on your needs.

For example, when you return from a meeting with a lawyer, you could log in all the key information and have it available for review weeks or months later. You could send "customized" form letters to selected groups of contacts or have the program remind you when it is time to contact a particular attorney.

One of the greatest benefits of such software is that it lets you know who has been sending you business. Any action that is rewarded is much more likely to be repeated. When an attorney sends you a referral, send a thank-you note the same day and follow up with a telephone call within 30 days. A small gift would be suitable, especially if the referral turns into a client. You may want to entertain your most prolific referral sources. Keep track of referrals, and keep in touch with your referral sources. The payoff is huge.

Summary

Referrals are your best source of new clients. But to achieve a consistent flow of referrals, you must take control of the process.

To be successful at developing a strong referral base, there are several key elements you should always employ in your practice:

- Track all contacts with your list of current and potential referral sources.
- Maintain a list of new clients generated by each referral source.
- Have a system for rewarding the referral sources.

Get Your Net Working

If everyone in your network is the same as you, it isn't a network, it's an anthill.

—Harvey Mackay[1]

Many accountants think that "networking" is a frill that they can ignore while they do the "important" technical work. In fact, networking—building contacts and relationships with people so that they like and trust you—is the most important thing you can do to develop yourself as a complete professional. Let's take just two examples.

In the 1980s, Bill and Joe graduated from the same top accounting school of a major university. They went to work for the same accounting firm. The two were the same age, had similar backgrounds, and had worked their ways through school with 3.5 averages. They seemed to have very similar prospects for advancement. But today Bill is earning about $80,000 per year as controller for a company and Joe, now a partner in a CPA firm, is earning over $200,000—more than twice as much as Joe.

What happened? Did Joe work harder? No. Was Joe smarter or did he get some lucky breaks? No, for the first five years, it was hard to tell them apart. They worked the same hours, had very similar assignments, took the same CPE courses, and performed excellent technical work. The major difference was how Joe spent about one-and-a-half hours per week. Bill ate three meals a day, at home, at his desk in the office, or with his buddies from the firm. Joe spent about one-and-a-half hours per week networking with young businesspeople outside his accounting firm, primarily during breakfast and lunch.

In a similar sort of situation, CPAs Sara and Melanie had been at a Big Four accounting firm together. Five years ago they decided to start their own separate practices in different sections of town. Five years later, Sara has two partners and a multimillion-dollar practice. Melanie is still a sole practitioner barely getting by. The only difference was that Sara focused some of her time on networking within the business community whereas Melanie just waited for business to come in the door.

Networking isn't just meeting people, although that's the first big step. Networking develops you as a professional in another big way. Being an accountant has a technical component. But what clients really want is an accountant who knows about their situation, cares about them, and can help them. The more you're out there meeting people from diverse businesses, the more you'll learn. Some of the networking will make you a more interesting person in general. Some of it will improve your knowledge that you use to understand and advise clients. Networking develops you socially and business-wise.

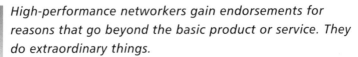

> *High-performance networkers gain endorsements for reasons that go beyond the basic product or service. They do extraordinary things.*
>
> —Thomas J. Stanley,
> *Networking with the Affluent and Their Advisors*[2]

Schedule Networking Time

Networking is one of the best business-building techniques in the public accounting profession, and yet less than 10 percent of CPAs are successful networkers. Networking is so powerful because it uses the principle of leverage, a concept that is powerful in investing and in marketing. Using leverage, you are able to invest a small amount of time and money, and, over time, you will reap a substantial return. Below, I'll show you how to create a $90,000 revenue stream from a $3,000 marketing investment using the principles of networking and leverage.

If networking is that powerful, why don't all CPAs invest in it? There are two basic reasons: (1) many CPAs do not understand how to network, and (2) many do not have the patience necessary to reap the rewards of a well-built network. That is why this Day 10 discussion is so important for every practicing CPA, whether you are in a large firm or practicing solo. If you will review the networking plan described here and implement what you learn, you will build one of the more successful accounting practices in your city.

You've probably heard that the best jobs are never advertised in the newspaper. That's because most people prefer to hire someone who has been personally recommended by someone they know and trust. The same is true for businesses and individuals wanting to change accountants. They rarely advertise for proposals. Let's get inside the heads of accounting service consumers for a few moments to try to understand the process they use in selecting CPAs.

PORTRAIT OF A SALES LEADER

JACK AMUNDSON has built a strong client and referral base because of his dedication to community service. Jack's mom was a legal secretary and taught him to type when he was 5. By age 10, he began working for a CPA in Glendive, Montana, typing tax returns during tax season. When he started high school, Jack worked at another CPA firm every afternoon for four years. At age 27, with 17 years of experience in public accounting, Jack had an opportunity to become managing partner of an office of a Minnesota CPA firm.

Amundson later became a named partner in the firm McMahon, Hartmann, Amundson & Co. Amundson's firm merged with Larson Allen Weisher a few years ago because of the availability of a wide variety of nontraditional services at Larson Allen Weisher (LAWCO).

Amundson has built his business with his personal-time investment in community activities.

"I always wanted to be a CPA. There was never any other profession in which I was interested. A CPA has such an opportunity to help people," says Amundson.

Amundson's former partners were much older than he. Those partners stressed the importance of getting involved in the community. He learned this lesson well. Amundson has been chairman or president of numerous foundations, including the Boy Scouts, the St. Cloud Area Chamber of Commerce, and the College of St. Benedict. Last year Amundson was recognized with the Professional Leadership Award by the Central Minnesota Community Foundation. He had helped his clients give over $10 million to various charities.

Jack has built a "pull marketing" system as a result of his community involvement. He says, "I want a client who also wants me. I will invest a great deal in building a relationship with a prospect. When that prospect develops a need, I want him to call upon me. When the prospect calls me, usually fee is not an issue." Getting involved in the community is a powerful way to build relationships with people who are making a difference. The movers and shakers in any community are usually highly visible in community activities and boards.

When a need for accounting services arises, most consumers contact a CPA they know personally. If they do not know one, they will ask someone in their family or their business or one of their other business advisors, such as a lawyer or banker, for a recommendation.

Up the proverbial creek? If you've got a network, you've always got a paddle.

— Harvey Mackay, *Dig Your Well Before You're Thirsty*[3]

Most individuals and small business owners hire the first CPA with whom they meet. Larger businesses usually interview three to five CPAs, or firms of CPAs, and then make a selection. Usually the CPA who is chosen from this process has had a personal acquaintance or friendship with a key decision maker in the client's business for an extended period of time.

Build Your Contacts

Edward D. Jones, the St. Louis–based stock brokerage, has one of the most successful sales training programs in the financial services business. One of the keys to the success of the training program is the requirement that all new brokers obtain the business cards of 1,000 people before they execute their first stock trade.

Once the brokers obtain the business cards, if they work those prospects, they will be successful. But the first step is to get the 1,000 cards.

The thought of having to develop a network of 1,000 people would frighten most CPAs. But, come to think of it, that is exactly what the successful young CPA who made partner did. He did it over a 10-year period, and the impact has been enormous for him.

And that is what Sara, the successful CPA in the earlier example, did as well. She had been networking in her Big Four firm, and for the first two years after starting her own firm, she really focused on networking within the business community.

The main thing to keep in mind is that marketing is a numbers game. For your numbers to work, you should keep prospects in the marketing pipeline at all times. And one of the best ways to obtain a continuous flow of prospects is through networking. Networking is a great prospecting tool. Even when economic times are soft, a good network will provide you a steady flow of new business.

Five Steps to Networking Success

There are five key ingredients to building a powerful network for your accounting practice:

1. *Set a target of obtaining 1,000 names in your personal prospect database.* You can do this over a 10-year period. In fact, if you are

beginning your accounting career with a firm, you may set a target of only 25 names during your first year. Then you may wish to expand the number each year. If you are beginning your accounting practice from scratch, you might want to gather between 200 and 250 prospect names right away. Terry Orr teaches younger CPAs to sell. Before he will invest any time with them, he requires each person to obtain 100 business cards to show that he or she is serious.

2. *Use a system to manage your names so that you can maintain the necessary information on them.* Certainly name, address, phone and fax numbers, and business affiliations are vital. As you improve your management of the system, you will accumulate additional relevant information on file. In Day 11, I discuss more ways to manage an effective system.

3. *Develop a sound communication plan for your prospects.* If you obtain 100 business cards and do not stay in touch, over half of them will be useless within a year. They will have changed businesses or moved, or will have forgotten who you are.

4. *Practice patience in the development and harvesting of your network.* Some seeds you plant in your network will germinate quickly. Others may take years. In fact, the best ones usually take years.

5. *Plan to allocate one to two hours per week to your network.* You work your network by meeting new people and adding new names. You work it by updating the information. You work it by communicating with your prospects.

Mackay's 66

Harvey Mackay, author of How to Swim with the Sharks . . . *and* Dig Your Well Before You're Thirsty, *is noted for his "Mackay's 66," a series of 66 questions detailing prospects' lives. You may not need to collect 66 items, but most people collect too little information about prospects. The more you know about prospects and their interests, the more ways you have to build relationships with them.*

Here are just a few categories of information you might want to collect: college attended, military service, hobbies, hometown, children's ages and interests, favorite restaurants, favorite foods, and spouse's occupation.

Power Networking

It's easy to set a target number, but you really need to know how to go about getting names that are of a quality that will one day benefit you.

Power networking is a skill much like playing tennis or golf. A few years ago I took up tennis. I was so enthusiastic that I wanted to play Jimmy Connors right away! After getting my brains beat in by several people, I decided to take a few lessons. The pro started by having me hit forehand shots in volume. In fact, after my first lesson, he assigned me to a ball machine and told me to work with the machine every day for a week, just on my forehand.

 Relationships determine success.

—Philip B. Crosby, *Quality Is Free*[4]

The same strategy is true for networking. Successful power networkers will go for a volume of networking contacts first, because they really don't know enough about the game yet to determine quality. Successful marketing focuses on the needs of prospects, and new acquaintances probably will not have a need at the time you meet them. In fact, over 90 percent of the businesspeople you meet will not have an awareness of any need for your services when you meet them. But, rest assured, almost all of them will have a need for accounting or tax services within the next ten years.

Build for the Future

When I first joined PriceWaterhouseCoopers, I became involved with the Junior Chamber of Commerce, commonly known as the Jaycees. Now, 20 years later, those young Jaycees are the leaders of our business community. One is the CEO of a $5 billion bank. One is the largest shareholder in another major bank. Several of them are in key commercial lending positions in our city's banks. One is a congressman. One is head of a large insurance brokerage. Several others are senior partners in accounting, law, engineering, real estate, and marketing firms.

The Junior Chamber had a membership of over 300 young businesspeople. When I joined, I received a directory that had the names, addresses, telephone numbers, business affiliations, and spouses' names of every member.

Over a two-year period, I met over 200 of those members just by attending the meetings and participating in a few interesting projects. You might think that it took a lot of time. Not really. The monthly membership meeting took about two hours. Normally I would sit at a table with 7 to 10 other people, and many of them would be new acquaintances to me each month. Then we sponsored a golf tournament and a high school football playoff game every year. I usually worked the events but could not afford to invest the time to be on the planning committee for the project. The real networking came between the meetings, when I followed up with people I had met and when some followed up with me. Over lunch or breakfast, friendships developed.

Mingling is like going fishing. You cast out your line, and if they aren't biting, you move to another spot.

—Don Gabor[5]

The really sad thing I find in too many CPA firms today is the lack of emphasis early in one's career on developing a network of acquaintances and friends. After a bright young person has been with a firm for five or six years, the partners say, "If you want to continue to advance with our firm and become an owner or partner, you must start bringing in some business." By this time, the task seems too overwhelming.

The same is true for the sole practitioner who hangs out a shingle to start providing services. Typically, enough clients come through the door to pay the rent and the receptionist, with very little left over for the professional.

I spoke to one sole practitioner who had been in business for a few years with very little growth in his revenue. He grossed a little over $70,000 and netted only half of that. Some con artist talked him into spending $10,000 on various advertising and marketing schemes that increased his revenue only slightly and didn't even pay for the programs. He found that he could be a lot more effective when he worked his network of acquaintances and friends.

Networking Techniques

During the 1990s, two of every three new businesses were owned by women. In the United States today, there are over 5 million women-owned businesses. The National Association of Women Business Owners (NAWBO) is one of the most beneficial organizations from which you can tap into this growth business segment. NAWBO is a great place for female CPAs to network with female decision makers and owners in business. It is also a good place for a male CPA to offer to give an annual tax update or write a column for their newsletter.

I have developed a lot of networking techniques through trial and error, but I also received some help from Terri Mandell's book *Power Schmoozing.*[6] I've found that there are ways to meet a lot of people really fast. First, on

---

The Odds Are Up for This "Bookie"

One accountant combines his love of reading with networking.

The accountant segmented his referral sources into A, B, and C. The dozen As are lawyers and bankers who refer to him regularly. He knows their interests well. One way he keeps in touch is by sending them books on topics that fit their individual interests. He puts a sticker in the books saying they are thank-yous from him.

Two or three times a year he sends the same book to his complete list of 50+ contacts. (He buys at a discount from the publisher.) Referral business increased almost 20 percent in six months.

—Rick Crandall, *1001 Ways to Market Your Services: Even If You Hate to Sell*[7]

---

joining a new organization, I would volunteer to be a host for the regular meeting. I would either stand or sit at the registration table and record the attendance of all the members as they came in. I would greet them and their guest on arrival, and many of them would want to get to know me. They would ask me questions, and within a few months, I would know all the regular attendees and they would know me. I developed the habit of dropping the nonattenders a note letting them know that we missed them, and I would call a few of them every month.

Resist the temptation to become your organization's treasurer. Most organizations recruit a CPA as treasurer. If pressed, agree to be treasurer for a short period only. Sometimes the treasurer's job becomes that of a bookkeeper. However, as treasurer, you do become well acquainted with the board of directors, the officers, and the paid executive director. You can utilize this position to gain professional respect if you can make some dramatic improvements in the accounting systems. But if it's just going to be a bookkeeping job, let someone else do it.

Small increases in the size of your network can double your odds of success, according to a Stanford study by Joe Podolny and James Baron. If your existing network is not producing many referrals, try to add 10 percent more quality contacts. That 10 percent can double your results.

Another great networking job is that of program chair. When I volunteered to be program chair for about 12 meetings, everyone came to know me. I also utilized my position to meet some of my target prospects within the community who were not members of my organization.

Typically, I would canvass the membership and ask for suggestions for speakers. Doing this would put me in touch with a number of the active members. Then I would prepare a list of potential speakers within the community who were on my prospect list and whom I had not met. I would write prospective speakers a letter on my letterhead and ask if they would speak to my club.

Most of them hadn't responded by the time I would call to see if they had received my letter. If you wait for people to respond in today's fast-paced world, you'll fail. So, about a week after the letter goes out, I call them. Invariably, 80 percent of the people I invite end up speaking. I make it a point to stop by and meet the person at least a month before the event. At this time I review with them the composition of our membership and answer any questions they may have as to our member interests. I also make it a point to pick them up a half hour to an hour before the meeting to see that they get to the meeting on time and that they don't have to hassle with directions, parking, and so forth. Doing this gives me some great time to get to know them on a personal basis in the car before and after the meeting.

Most chambers of commerce have business mixers for their members. I always come back from mixers with a few business cards. But I have found the best place for meeting new people is new member committees. When I was on the new member committee for the chamber, I had access to the new businesses coming to town before anyone else. That is particularly helpful for a CPA.

Susan RoAne's book, *How to Work a Room,*[8] is an excellent resource. It changed the way that I attend organization meetings. RoAne talks about "a host versus a guest" mentality. This advice to act like a host has been the best advice I've gotten. Whether I am an officer of the organization or not, I don't wait to be taken care of when I go to any event. I stand near the entrance and the traffic flows to see if there is something I can do to help out. I act like a host. I don't take over from the real hosts, but they always appreciate my helpfulness.

One of my goals is to meet two to four new people a month. I find that at least one of those new contacts will end up doing business with me within five years.

Another little technique is to approach people who are standing alone. I introduce myself and then introduce them to someone else in the room who may share one of their interests. Believe me, these folks will not forget you; they will remember you as being their positive link to your group.

Some people are really outgoing. It seems easy for them to meet people. Others are somewhat shy and reluctant to socialize. How can this networking advice apply to them? As I mentioned earlier, I believe that an *interested* introvert can be a better marketer than an *interesting* extrovert. Too often people who are the life of the party, the interesting extroverts, come away from networking opportunities with nothing. They have no information on the people they met. All they did was talk about themselves and their interests. Interested introverts are curious. Of course, they have to get up the nerve to approach or be approached. To help them, introverts should develop a list of questions that they can ask the people they meet. The answers to the questions should tell a lot about the people and their businesses.

Three Networking Tips

1. Don't spend time at an event talking to people you already know. It's easier, but you lose the value of new contacts.
2. Be positive—nobody wants to hear about your problems.
3. Stay as long as there are people you haven't met.

If you can maintain strong eye contact and ask good questions, you will make a great impression. Anyone can learn these techniques. They are not something that people are born with. An interested introvert can learn rapport building, questioning, and listening skills. That is why introverts are better networkers than extroverts.

Advanced Networking Techniques

Once you have become accomplished at meeting people and become comfortable with doing so, you can find ways to be more productive in networking. Trade associations are excellent places for accountants to network with prospects. Many trade associations charge an admission fee; this fee limits membership to only those who are serious about being a member of the association Also, every community has organizations that require participants to invest a major amount of time and money. For example, the Boy Scouts council, the arts council, and the symphony board may require members to contribute $5,000 to $25,000 to belong. Although the investment may be high, the other people on the board are also capable of investing this amount. This fact will work as a screening device for you.

Dr. Tom Stanley's excellent book *Networking with the Affluent and Their Advisors,*[9] is a classic in this regard. Dr. Stanley formed the Affluent Marketing

Institute in the 1980s. He has devoted his life to the study of marketing and selling to the affluent and has written a number of books, including *The Millionaire Next Door, Marketing to the Affluent, Selling to the Affluent,* and *The Mind of the Millionaire.*

Dr. Stanley has developed eight excellent and practical ways to network with the affluent. All of them apply to CPAs. As a matter of fact, one of Dr. Stanley's prime examples is a very successful Atlanta CPA, Art Gifford, partner of Gifford, Hillegass & Ingwersen, who uses all eight of the techniques.

One of the techniques that Stanley has observed is that of "purchasing agent." Your clients purchase many things. Every CPA can be knowledgeable in certain key areas, such as computers, software, communication systems, office furniture and equipment, and leasing. To the extent that you network with these suppliers and introduce them to your clients, you will build a strong network.

Another technique is that of "revenue enhancer." As a CPA, you can develop a list of 5 or 10 attorneys with different specialties to whom you will refer your clients. When you enhance the attorney's revenue, you have created a moral obligation for him or her to reciprocate. Make it a habit to always refer to three attorneys and send them each a letter. You will create a "due bill" even with those who do not actually get the work.

> The most powerful way to network is to enhance the revenue of opinion leaders. Realize that before receiving business-related endorsements, you must first "send business."
>
> —Thomas J. Stanley, *Networking with the Affluent and Their Advisors*[10]

A third technique is that of a "loan broker." As we all know, there are myriad financing vehicles in the market today. Sometimes they are bewildering even to sophisticated businesspeople. At a minimum, good CPAs will keep in touch with the key lending institutions in their areas—the mortgage brokers and bankers, the investment bankers—to always be in a position to provide their clients and prospects with a source of credit.

Some other techniques are those of "talent scout," "family advisor," "mentor," and "advocate." These techniques are self-descriptive and worth reading about in Stanley's book.

Summary

Many people put off networking as an optional activity they can take up after they establish their businesses. This is a mistake—networking is serious business. Most aggressive businesspeople attend networking events for the purpose of creating new business. I view networking as a very serious business game. My attitude is: "I've spent $25 to attend this function and I have one hour to find a good prospect. I didn't come to eat or drink or listen to the speaker. I came to find prospects for my business." Now, I try to work the room so smoothly that you would never know that's what I'm doing. I try to look like a lamb and sell like a lion. You can too.

11 Managing Your Network

*The greatest wisdom not applied to action is
meaningless data.*

— Peter Drucker[1]

Your first goal in networking is to meet new people or to stay in touch with existing contacts. Your second goal is to access the networks of your contacts. Even though you might stay in touch with a few hundred people, each of them is in touch with hundreds more. When you add up the networks of your contacts, it can be tens of thousands of people. The easiest way to build trust with your networking contacts is to take the initiative to stay in touch with them. The biggest waste in networking is when you meet people but don't have a system to follow up with them.

I learned this the hard way. After I attended a networking event, I had two choices: I could (1) hope that the interesting prospects to whom I gave my business card would call me or (2) plan a communication strategy for keeping in touch with them. I knew that I should be the one to keep in touch, but I selected option (1) because it was easier. What happened was, no one with whom I wanted to do business ever called me. A few people did call, but they were not the right types of client for me. So today I have a strategy to keep in touch with my network.

Managing all of the information about your network of clients, prospects, and other business contacts is absolutely critical to business success, but it also can be overwhelming. Many accounting firms are run like separate businesses sharing overhead. Each partner has her clients and network of contacts. Sharing your network with others in your firm is a strong indication that you have a vital business. You can add significant value to your practice when you and your colleagues manage your network of clients, prospects, and referral sources together.

Using a database, you can classify your contacts by their potential. Once you begin to classify your prospects, you will be able to manage your communications with people in your network.

The main reason for building a strong communication program with your network is to meet the needs of your prospects. Think about this question: How many prospects will you meet today who will have a need for your services? Probably not many. But of the prospects whom you meet today, what percentage may have a need for your services over the next one, two, three, four, or five years? The answer depends on the quality of the group with whom you are networking.

I would say that fewer than 1 in 20 people I meet has a need for my services the day that we meet. But over the next five years, if I meet them in a qualified context, over 50 percent may experience a need. A qualified context is a business setting. Certainly chambers of commerce and civic clubs count. Trade groups and specific interest groups often have an even higher percentage of qualified leads.

Terry Orr, whom you met in Chapter 5, describes his approach to network management in this way:, "A system that I developed during my early years was to go to the Dallas Chamber of Commerce. I would meet and listen to people from whom I really wasn't going to get business. But I learned how to network, how to meet people, and how to screen all of those cards. I wanted

PORTRAIT OF A SALES LEADER

GREG ANTON, partner with Anton, Collins & Mitchell, in Denver, Colorado, manages his network extremely well. Serious minded, goal oriented, and intense, Greg initially considered a career in selling. But a need for professionalism in his life, as well as building long-term relationships and loyalty, steered him into public accounting rather than sales. As audit partner, he is the Assurance and Business Line Leader and heads up his firm's SEC practice.

Anton said, "One thing that allowed me to become a partner at a relatively accelerated clip was not sales directly, but providing good technical advice to clients. The clients' satisfaction was crucial, and that has a lot to do with getting referrals or extended services."

Anton has a selling system that is unique in public accounting. Founded in strong technical skills and excellent relationships with SEC to learn which ones were prospects. Some of them were immediate and some were for later."

A qualified lead is a prospect who has a need for your service, can make or influence the decision to hire you, and has the money to pay for your services. Most groups eventually will produce a qualified prospect, but the pickings are much slimmer in some groups than others. You must evaluate every group you attend as to its quantity of qualified prospects. Give a group at least two tries, but if it isn't producing qualified prospects, move on to another group. The important thing is to make a commitment to gather a certain number of leads every year.

Setting Up a Communications Program

Now we are going to review a communications program for CPAs to follow with a qualified lead.

Say that you met someone at the state manufacturers association meeting who told you that she was the CFO of a medium-size business in a community about 50 miles from your office. You swap cards. Immediately after the event, make as many notes as possible about your prospect's needs, role, size of the business, products, names of any others in a decision-making capacity, and so forth.

experts around the country, Anton attracts companies that are public or that are considering raising funds from the public. He teaches a course on SEC matters for the Colorado Society of CPAs. "From that course, I come in contact with many accountants in industry who are charged with the responsibility of helping take their companies public," explains Anton. Meeting prospects in a professional environment is important to help him qualify his leads. He knows if someone is taking his course, he or she is serious about matters of the SEC.

During the class, Anton offers his students additional information not found in the class materials. If participants ask for additional material, he sends it to them. Anton enters each participant into a database of contacts. Doing this allows Anton to communicate with the group periodically, and they continue to provide him information, additional leads, and referrals.

First thing the next morning, send a nice-to-meet-you letter that is very short and to the point. I'd say something like this:

Dear Carol,

Thank you for spending a few moments with me at the state manufacturers association meeting last evening. I enjoyed meeting you and learning more about your successes at Rutherford Enterprises. As I mentioned, I focus much of my practice serving many businesses just like yours. Keeping that in mind, I have taken the liberty of adding you to my mailing list and from time to time will keep in touch with you. Best wishes for a successful year.

Warmest regards,
Troy Waugh

Also send along a small written article on your firm. You may want to have as many as 10 to 20 written items to select from when sending out marketing material, so you can match the material to the prospect.

It is very important *not* to send a package of information at this time. Most people who receive a package of material in the mail, even if they ordered it, tend to set it aside for future consumption. Then it gets buried. By sending a package, you are also demonstrating your lack of marketing savvy and may even irritate the prospect. All you want to do at this point is to make another impression. A short note with or without a brief article on your firm is perfect for this.

This is the time to evaluate the type of prospect and put him or her in line for an appropriate communications program. For example, you'll place most prospects you meet into category C (based on the letter-grade ranking of A, B, or C we discussed in Day 10). In this program, they will receive 30 communications over a five-year period, most through the mail and over the phone. Some prospects deserve to be placed in category B, the communications program which is a little more intense and should result in closure within two years. And, of course, category A prospects have an immediate need; jump on these quickly.

Build for the Long Term

Thirty or more communications with a prospect may seem like a lot of contact and a lot of money for a "shot in the dark" with an uncertain five-year payoff.

Think about it this way. What would it cost you to take someone to lunch? Depending, of course, on where you go, the cost will vary. You certainly want it to be a memorable occasion. Realistically, you might spend $60 out of pocket.

Now calculate how much it would cost to send a letter and a copy of an article. About a dollar? How much would it cost to send a brochure? Not much if you have them printed in quantity. (They aren't doing you any good in your storage room—send them out!) How much would it cost to add someone to your newsletter mailing list, assuming that you send out a newsletter? Adding one more newsletter would cost only the postage and the incremental printing charge—probably less than $1 for each calendar quarter.

So, for $5 a year per prospect, you can stay in touch with many prospects through your newsletter. For about the cost of one lunch, you can send your newsletter and a variety of other communications during a five-year period. And although any one of these communications will not have the impact of a luncheon, together they will keep your prospects from forgetting who you are. The cumulative effect will definitely add up. What you are trying to do is increase your odds of being in front of your prospect when the need for your services arises.

For C prospects, you might call them once a year, send a quarterly newsletter, and send another relevant piece of information (a brochure or article), so that over a period of five years they will have had numerous opportunities to interact with you.

Bob Gaida, whom you'll meet in Day 15, manages his 2,479 prospects using a similar method. He describes it this way: "Prospects are separated into subcategories of gold, silver, and bronze, so that I know out of that 2,479, the gold ones are definitely being managed. The bronze ones may not need to be managed. A gold prospect is a person who had given us business, that we want, that met our profile—and can give us more. It could be a client. It could be a referral source. It could be a person who is the gatekeeper to the prospect or referral source. A law firm may give me the kind of work I want only because of the political environment that is represented between us. So I make sure that the gatekeeper is the one I'm focusing on, because he can open that door."

Rate Your Prospects

Let's look at the qualifiers that differentiate C prospects from Bs. If prospects were decision influencers and expressed no immediate dissatisfaction with their current accounting services, they would be rated Cs. If the potential fees from the account would be under a certain size, they would be rated Cs. Read the Day 10 chapter for more information on qualifying prospects. Using the 10-point scale from that chapter, some people will classify 8 to 10s as As, 6 to 7s as Bs, 4 to 5s as Cs, and 1 to 3s as Fs.

If prospects were over a certain size in annual billings, were the decision makers, or expressed any dissatisfaction with their current accounting provider, they would be classified as B prospects. With Bs, you want to move the process along a little faster, but you do not want to be pushy—assertive, yes, not pushy. With B prospects, your letter might be a little meatier; for example, you might mention that you focus your practice in their industry or that you have dealt extensively with the problem they had discussed with you.

Your second correspondence might include a brochure, newsletter article, or reprint of something that you have written or read on the subject discussed. In that letter, you may want to request a meeting or mention that you will call for a meeting. A category B prospect will be one with whom you want to develop a relationship. Call the prospect and, during your chat, determine that the information mailed had been received and whether you can set up a meeting. A breakfast or lunch would be appropriate in this situation. Don't wait until a lunch date opens up; you can just have coffee and see the prospect's operations, offices, or plant. At this point, early in the relationship, often just a 20- to 30-minute meeting is all you need to stay in touch and improve your visibility with the prospect. Typically it's not appropriate to ask a B prospect if you can present a proposal until you have laid a solid foundation of interest over a period of a few months, maybe even as long as 18 months. Out of every 20 prospects you meet, one may be an A, two or three may be Bs, and all the rest will be Cs.

Sam Sommerville, partner in Simpson & Osborne in Charleston, West Virginia, recently captured an A account that was a C just a few years ago. A $1,000 tax-return client has grown into a six-figure client. This poses the question: How do you efficiently stay in touch with Cs and Bs who might turn into As? If you design a solid communications program to all of your prospects, over time you will experience a dramatic increase in your new business. In most cases, the real impact will not be felt for two to three years. That is when the C prospects start turning into Bs and As.

Systems Simplify Marketing

You may be thinking, "This long-term marketing business sounds expensive and complicated." But if the system is well planned, an administrative assistant can run it. And there are numerous resources to help you with the material. PDI in Chicago, Newkirk in Albany, New York, and Mostad & Christensen in Washington state have numerous industry- and service-specific newsletters that can make you look as if you are an industry expert in your region. All of these newsletters can be printed with your logo and letterhead. You can purchase these newsletters with geographical protection at very reasonable rates. You could not publish these materials yourself for the small prices you'd pay one of these good firms.

> *If you will use some of the available resources, it will make your job much easier.*
>
> *Method goes far to prevent trouble in business; for it makes the task easy, hinders confusion, saves abundance of time, and instructs those who have business depending, what to do and what to hope.*
>
> —William Penn[2]

Now, let's look at your investment. If you maintain communications with 500 prospects, you can purchase and mail quarterly newsletters to them for less than $4,000 per year. You can send them two pieces of mail each for about another $800 annually. Begin with 500 prospects and move up to 1,000 over a period of time, say one to five years. As you increase your number of contacts each year, you might even delete a few on a very selective basis. But evaluate the potential return: If out of 20 prospects, 1 is an A prospect who you are able to convert into immediate business, 2 are B prospects who produce business within two years, and 17 are C prospects, only half of whom develop a need and only half of those are converted, your new client return will be six times greater than if you only converted the one hot prospect. If you will work this system, the system will work for you.

The revenue impact will be different for every practice. A practice that focuses on executive tax returns, for example, at $1,500 each would be an ideal candidate for this program Say you convert 5 As, 10 Bs, and 21 Cs for a total of 36 new clients at $1,500 each, or $54,000 in recurring annual fees (that's $250,000 of revenue over five years). Your acquisition cost is less than $5,000 invested over five years. If your average sale is larger, say for consulting engagements, audits, installing computer systems, or monthly write-up work, the profit potential grows. The leverage is great for CPAs because you are very likely to keep the client year after year and also are likely to add services along the way.

You may have heard CPAs say that newsletters and brochures don't work. One CPA told me he sent out 200 newsletters last year and didn't get one client. He probably didn't. Newsletters and brochures don't work by themselves. To be effective, they must be a part of a coordinated marketing and sales program. What typically happens is that the marketing material is filed away in the storeroom—or it is sent to nonqualified lists—or it is not used in conjunction with a coordinated networking program.

Newsletters and brochures are tools that give you credibility, add impact to your sales message, sell for you when you are not there, and allow your prospect to carry your message to an associate or a family member. But, like any tools, to be effective, they must be used properly.

Make Mondays and Fridays your days to call prospects. Starting and ending your week strong gives you momentum.

Patience, Patience, Patience

The person who networks regularly will have good success just by picking off the A prospects. But if you are really going to respond to the needs of the marketplace and get some leverage working for you, you must have the patience to correspond with non-A prospects until either a need arises or you can create a need.

Marketing expert Jay Conrad Levinson says that a large number of businesspeople network for a few weeks or months, then stand back so as not to be stampeded by their new clients. When nothing happens, they change their tactics. Again, nothing happens.

All of the research I've seen indicates that consumers of accounting or any other service require about nine positive marketing interactions, including about five personal meetings, in order to move from apathy to a readiness to engage you. In fact, over 80 percent of all sales in this country are made after the fifth sales call. Working through this communications program will keep your prospects moving positively along the path from encounter to engagement.

Contact Management Software

Put what you've learned into practice. Networking is a contact sport. You can't learn it by reading a book or listening to an audiotape.

Do you wake up at 4 A.M. with this frightening thought: "When was I supposed to call Bill about that proposal?" Do you have sticky notes all over your files? Do you have difficulty keeping up with all the clients, prospects, and referral sources who are in your network? Do you always have a scary feeling that you have missed something that you promised or should have done? Do you manage your network or does your network manage you?

Contact management software (CMS) is a powerful solution to these common problems. CMS enables you to maintain a database, history, to-do list, contact plan, marketing strategy, word processor, and tickler file all in one system.

If you are new to contact management, buy a single-user version of ACT, Goldmine, or Telemagic and start using it. It may cost you $200 at the software dealer, but it will be one of the most helpful items you have ever used. Then, a year from now, investigate an upgrade to a network or more sophisticated version.

An extra payoff will come when you are able to leverage your experience by installing the system in your clients' businesses. The consulting, installation, training, and support you can learn to provide will make CMS a profit center for you. Consider how many of your clients have sales organizations or contact networks they want to manage. CMS can enable you to be a *value-added* advisor.

Summary

Meeting people is only the starting point of networking. The most important thing you can do to achieve the benefits of networking is to develop a system to keep in touch with your contacts. Allocate a certain amount of time every week to working your network. Find the groups that work for you, and keep in regular contact with people you meet through those groups. It may take many contacts before people trust you or have a need for your services. The key is to not stop. Allocate at least one hour every week to contacting your network. If you do, you can be assured that your business will increase more every year.

12 Co-opetition: Partnering for Better Business

When spider webs unite, they can tie up a lion.

—Ethiopian proverb

When you combine the words "cooperation" and "competition," a new word emerges: co-opetition. Co-opetition works when normally competing organizations come together cooperatively to serve a client. Competition for the best clients and staff members has never been fiercer. Today's clients are demanding more value at less cost. Technology is turning many traditional services into commodities. The national and global economy brings competitors you never heard of and don't know how to compete against. A new graduate can command a signing bonus, a new car, and rapid advancement. Banks and insurance companies are giving away tax advice to get our clients. Business consulting firms are offering our clients technology planning, strategic planning, mergers and valuations, expert testimony, and many other services that compete directly with services traditionally provided by CPAs.

The emergence of companies that offer clients a range of financial resources, such as business credit, travel, employee benefits, and more, will only become more prevalent. These firms, including American Express, are organizing around a multidisciplinary approach to become one-stop shops.

Many CPA firms lack an approach that will enable them to prosper from these challenges rather than being victimized by them. The big secret is joining with others to serve your client in innovative ways. Working with your clients' other service providers is the key to serving the highly evolved client of the future. Partnering approaches let you create a continuing stream of opportunities. The result is a true win-win-win situation for you, your partner, and your client.

A competitive world has two possibilities for you. You can lose.
Or, if you want to win, you can change.

—Paul Thurow[1]

Examples of Partnering

Partnering can be as simple as sharing office space with other CPAs, or it can be a multifaceted approach, such as sharing offices and clients with other professionals. Partnering can be low tech or high tech. It also can be joint venturing with your clients. It can be among separate CPA firms or among different types of professional services firms.

Partnering with your clients can be as simple as thinking as if you were their in-house accountants, or as complex as taking an equity interest in a new entity or joint venture.

Creating the best perception to your end client is a challenge every firm faces, with or without partners—but partners add a level of complexity. The way your service is promoted and supported influences how the end client views and experiences the service.

Kevin Poppen, president of Enterprise Network, an alliance of leading CPA firms in the United States, says, "Strategic partnering is one of the foundation stones of the Enterprise vision. CPA firms are challenged to meet the many needs of their clients today. Enterprise members (CPA firms with $1 to $12 million in annual revenue) cooperate with each other to provide client services they could not provide on their own. Cooperation actually strengthens our member firms' competitiveness. The opportunities for financial planning, technology consulting, international assistance, M&A capabilities, and many other services are impossible for the small firm to develop on its own."

That is where the new associations are having such an impact. Partnering helps firms overcome a lack of skills and capital. It permits forward-thinking owners to be highly successful in the new marketplace.

Enterprise Network has developed an alliance with an international association of CPA firms that provides members access to several hundred office locations around the world. "Now, when one of our member's clients needs help in London or Hong Kong, we have a great relationship in those places," says Poppen. Another example of an innovative partnering is the Enterprise Network Financial Services Solution. Enterprise partnered with Oppenheimer & Company and its broker dealer to provide money management, investments, insurance, financial and estate planning, and employee benefits to their clients. "We competed with the life insurance guys for years for financial and estate planning engagements. Now we can compete and cooperate at the same time."

Accounting firm clients often consider selling their businesses; heretofore we could only make limited contacts on behalf of our clients. Now, with the Enterprise Network–Duff & Phelps investment banking partnership agreement, the two groups are working together to offer clients an international outlet for selling those businesses.

Partnering for Profit

The best partnerships between companies come when these conditions exist:

- **True mutual need**. *This is more important than control in an alliance.*
- **Shared objectives**. *Rather than just buying and selling to each other, partners should have objectives that they hope to accomplish by working together.*
- **Shared risk**.
- **Building relationships and trust**. *It's not enough to just be partners on paper; people have to feel comfortable with each other.*
- **Handling disputes**. *Partners should have an agreement at the beginning to bring up tough issues to each other.*
- **Exit strategies**. *Ways of dissolving your contract should be defined at the start.*

—Jordan Lewis, *Partnerships for Profit*[2]

Enterprise Network is working with other CPA firms and associations to provide their members' clients a broad array of services. The international alliance mentioned above is being used by member firms in the larger cities right now, but we are becoming a global economy, and I believe the smaller firms in smaller markets will need international help. Enterprise is cooperating with RSM McGladrey for the latest in practice management improvements for firms with large audit practices. Enterprise members are cooperating with smaller (mostly sole practitioners) accounting firms through the CPA Link program.

Enterprise offers its member firms cutting-edge partners' conferences, a client newsletter, and a Web page hyperlinked to each member. The mission of Enterprise is to challenge its members to think about their futures and to help them adopt strategies that empower members to improve their lifestyles and profits.

Partnering Is All Around Us

All you have to do is look around to see cooperative ventures in other businesses. American Airlines has numerous travel partners from whom passengers can earn frequent flyer miles. Frequent flyer miles have become a strong travel currency, good at hundreds of hotels, restaurants, auto rental agencies, and airlines. Food establishments, once stand-alone franchisees, are banding together in food courts, interstate stops, and convenience markets, and cooperating to serve the customer. Microsoft and IBM cooperated around software. Microsoft and Intel cooperated around the computer chip. These cooperative ventures helped both the companies and their customers.

I remember snickering at a sole practitioner a few years ago, when he talked about competing with the Big Four accounting firms. Concerned that one of the Big Four firms was going to take his largest client, he was like a gnat competing with an elephant. But when CPAs are too focused on competition, they fail to see the possibilities in cooperation, and that usually ends up hurting both the CPA and the client.

Coopers & Lybrand, now PricewaterhouseCoopers, reported in 1995 that strategic alliances were becoming increasingly important to business growth. At that time, 55 percent of the nation's fastest-growing companies were involved in an average of three alliances.

Here is an example of how cooperation can work to everyone's advantage. A client of Jim Belew, whom we met in Day 3, went public a few years ago. He says, "They were one of our largest clients, and we knew they were going public at some point. We could face up to reality and help our client, or we could bury our heads in the sand. We chose to work with our client on their IPO plans. We introduced them to one of our Big Four friends and began to facilitate a relationship. The IPO was delayed about a year, and we kept all the work. When the IPO finally occurred, we assisted and received larger fees than ever during the registration process. We ultimately lost the audit work, but we still do a substantial amount of work for the client today, and they are still one of our top 10 clients. We could have been shortsighted and lost the client. I believe that our partnering type of relationship with the Big Four firm really helped our client and helped us."

Kevin Poppen says, "If the CPA firm is not primarily interested in serving the client's best interests, we cannot work together well. We partner with

CPA firms of the Enterprise Network through an alliance. Oppenheimer and Enterprise make certain that the client's best interests are at the heart of every service we provide."

Consultant Bill Reeb says, "Mid-sized CPA firms do not have the capital to develop skills and deliver the range of services that larger-sized clients need and want. The only way is to collaborate with other CPAs or other professionals to serve the client."

Produce Results for Clients

CPAs must be able to drive financial results for clients now. Doing this takes a much higher level of competence than filling out a tax return. To drive financial results, you will be called on to provide assistance to your clients in areas in which you are not competent. I witnessed this situation several years ago when one of my clients decided to get into the financial services business. One of the client's partners was recruited to get his securities and insurance license, which he very diligently did. He affiliated with a well-known broker dealer with a line of financial products. Twelve months later, however, he had sold very little. Even his partners wouldn't invest with him. They certainly wouldn't recommend him to their clients. Only when this firm partnered with a financial services professional did it begin to prosper in the financial services business.

Larry Wilson, author with Hersch Wilson of *Stop Selling, Start Partnering,* says, "Creating significant advantage for customers is the only game played by the individuals and organizations that are serious about keeping customers." Wilson describes the need for firms to become customer-keeping organizations. To do this, a firm must organize around client needs rather than around the hierarchy of the firm.

RSM McGladrey, a national CPA firm, has been operating an alliance of CPA firms for years. Dan Brooks, president of the 80-member RSM McGladrey Network, says, "Clients of our member firms are the real beneficiaries of the partnering relationships we have with our firms. A local 50-person firm cannot possibly provide the range of services their best clients want and need. Cooperating with McGladrey & Pullen and the local firms has been win-win-win. In fact, most of our members can point to a handful of their best clients which they have obtained or retained specifically because they have McGladrey Network resources available."

With the McGladrey Network, members can access the global resources of the national and international offices. This adds great credibility to the CPA for larger clients of smaller firms. I once interviewed an accounting

Benefits of Belonging to a Network

Some of the benefits of associating with CPAs from across the nation and around the world include:

- *Marketing*
- *Conferences*
- *Cooperative advertising*
- *Information technology ideas*
- *International staff exchanges*
- *Member databases*
- *Niche and specialty services*
- *Peer review*
- *Public relations*
- *Referrals*
- *Seminars and CPE*
- *Special projects*
- *Vendor discounts*
- *Joint Web site*

—Richard Glickman[3]

firm's client whose revenue had grown to over $300 million. The CEO said, "We were considering changing to a Big Four accounting firm because of our size relative to our local CPA firm. But when the local firm introduced us to their worldwide resources through RSM McGladrey Network, we felt we had the best of both worlds—great local service with people we knew and trusted, and access to deep tax research and international connections."

Members of a major alliance were convened. Here is what they reported as very important in their relationships:

- Training at CPE courses
- Staff sharing
- Access to national and industry technical experts.
- Assurance—including SEC
- Tax
- Technology

- Specialized services such as business valuation, litigation and financial recovery
- Ability to jointly compete for larger engagements
- Marketing assistance
- Recruiting
- Access to proprietary software
- Online access to other firms

In addition, the members listed ways they have profited from the relationship:

- Involvement with the firm's financial services partner
- Access to specialized tax solutions
- Referrals to and from each other
- Management of accounting practice information sharing
- Group buying power for tax software, office furniture and supplies, accounting and tax manuals, and practice aids
- Greater fee realization on joint engagements
- A revenue-sharing arrangement with each other for general consulting and other services

Form Your Own Network

A number of midsize firms have developed networks of smaller practitioners. Joint-client projects, CPE sharing, technical research, and ideas are all part of such a network. Many informal organizations of competing CPA firms work together to help clients prosper.

International services is a growing sector throughout the United States. Most CPAs are not prepared to help a client with a tax problem in California, much less Canada or Chile. International affiliations of CPA firms are preparing CPAs to help clients throughout the world. Consultant Gary Boomer uses an analogy when he asks audiences, "When did you first buy a fax machine? Most people respond when my client wanted to fax me something and I didn't have one." The same will be true with international services unless CPAs connect with an international alliance. A client will have an international need; if you cannot supply it, the client may change CPAs.

Creating synergistic partnerships with other professionals to serve your clients' needs is a way to improve. This is true everywhere you have a wide array of services. David Morgan says, "The key for us winning many new accounts is the wide array of nontraditional services our firm can provide a client. And yet, with almost 200 employees, we can't do it all. We belong to the Leading Edge Alliance and Kreston International to give us ideas and support in better serving our clients globally."

Summary

True synergy can be had through an alliance. True synergy is where the whole is greater than the sum of its parts. When you quarterback a team of professionals to drive business results for your clients, you provide better service and retain your clients longer. Competing is usually a zero-sum game. But with cooperation, done right, there is more of a win-win-win situation. In cooperating, everyone gets a larger piece of the pie—and the pie grows.

When you are providing services to a client through a cooperative relationship with other professionals, you make it easier for clients to use you as a one-stop shop—and you make it harder for them to switch CPAs.

Some of the most effective sellers in the accounting industry today use cooperative alliances to attract better clients. Cooperation is the spirit of the new economy. It is the way in which we will master change and make the future work for us.

PART

THREE

Better Selling Helps Your Clients

13 Opportunity in the New Rules

In crisis there is danger and opportunity.
—Chinese proverb

You've heard people call the tax code "the lawyers' and accountants' full employment act." And of course there's some truth in that cynical analysis. Each time there are new tax, auditing, or reporting requirements, there is more opportunity for us. The Sarbanes-Oxley Act is the latest example of new regulations that create new demands for CPA services. To handle this and other new regulations well, you need to see them in the overall context of your role as a most trusted business advisor.

For those of you working for public companies, the Sarbanes-Oxley Act is the latest example of new regulations that create new demands for internal controls and financial reporting. Many of the early reactions to Sarbanes-Oxley were negative and extreme. I'll take this Act as an example of the general case of new (and old) laws and regulations and show how it applies to your sales and later ongoing client relationships.

Fear and Loathing of Sarbanes-Oxley

A great example of overreaction to Sarbanes-Oxley is provided by a report written by a lawyer, Jack Myers, in late 2003. He opens with statements about how regulatory issues have replaced management focus on management, sales, innovation, and customer loyalty. For instance, "demands for Sarbanes-Oxley compliance have replaced traditional corporate goals of long-term revenue growth and shareholder value." Myers goes on to say that "executives are forced to concentrate on daily, *even hourly,* compliance issues" (italics added).

Myers seems to be prone to exaggeration and alarmism. He summarizes the high-tech bubble years before the crash of 2000 as lacking long-term

PORTRAIT OF A SALES LEADER

TONY ZECCA, partner in charge of consulting at J.H. Cohn in New York, has supervised a large amount of audit, audit-related, and consulting work for public companies in the last three years. He is intimately familiar with the opportunities and the pitfalls of the new SEC and Sarbanes-Oxley rules.

Tom Marino, managing partner of J.H. Cohn, says, "Tony has probably attracted more business to our firm, since the new rules have been adopted, than any one else. He has a unique ability to help clients play by the rules while not becoming adversarial with his clients."

Tony learned to keep clients happy and keep them from breaking the rules at a very early age. He worked with his father in the family business when he was young and learned you could do both. Growing up in a large first-generation American family, Tony was one of 13 children. Tony learned firsthand the value of a dedicated work ethic.

J.H. Cohn is the largest regional firm in the northeastern part of the United States. Its clientele is owner-managed companies, but it has a large public practice as well. Zecca believes that the demand for high-level accounting services will continue to grow, as governments, not-for-profit organizations, and large private companies deal with the inherent risks in allowing a CEO or CFO to be responsible for hiring and managing the audit firm.

Tony joined the audit staff of J.H. Cohn right out of Fairleigh Dickenson University. He has a keen interest in computer technology and has found that his computer and audit skills have been a powerful resource for him during his career.

investment, when "a pervasive contempt that marks the relationship between corporations and customers began to destroy the fabric of society," including intellectual property rights.

Applying this alarmism to Sarbanes-Oxley, Myers goes on to say: "It is time for regulators to free companies from those binds and restriction that have been imposed as an overreaction to the corporate malfeasance on Enron, WorldCom, Arthur Anderson . . . [etc.]. Sarbanes-Oxley was intended to cleanse corporate America, not to drag it down. . . . Corporate strategies are being determined by regulatory compliance rather than shareholder and consumer interests."

It's true that regulations add costs to corporations and may sometimes change business strategy to exploit the easiest available economic options. However, Sarbanes-Oxley simply reinforces regulations that were already in place and try to create an informed marketplace for all participants. "It appears that the regulatory agencies and the public are demanding lower scopes and more detailed audit procedures than what was expected in the pre-Enron era," says Jeff Everly, whom we met in Day 4. It's hardly the end of capitalism as we know it!

New Regulations Are an Old Case

Any new reporting and record-keeping requirements can cause fear and loathing because of the uncertainty they engender. Just as the stock market hates uncertainty, so do public companies. When new regulations create new demands in the corporate community, it is your role to bring solutions and a calming influence. Accountants are trained to point out problems and often forget that their real job is to *handle* and *avoid* problems for clients.

The financial nucleus of Sarbanes-Oxley is better records retention for audits, corporate responsibility, auditor independence, clear financial disclosure, and avoidance of conflict of interests in financial analysts. Public corporations should have been dealing with all these issues for many years. But the negative events that stimulated passage of the Sarbanes-Oxley Act caused more negative reactions in the corporate—and even accounting—communities than new regulations usually do.

The financial scandals of WorldCom and Enron led to passage of the Sarbanes-Oxley Act. Either through outright fraud, auditor malfeasance, or lack of clarity, major transactions slipped by investors and destroyed the integrity of balance sheets and stock market values. But again, the intent of the Sarbanes-Oxley standards is nothing new. Public companies have always been required to report in ways that allow investors to make accurate judgments.

Be a Source of Calm Confidence for Clients

Jeff Everly says, "I think more emphasis is placed on firm integrity and differentiation from the large firms in the proposal process. In addition, the proposal process has moved more from management to the audit committee. These individuals seem more focused on the quality of the product and have a lesser interest in obtaining the absolute lowest fees."

When your clients or prospects are inclined to panic about any new regulations that may affect them, the first thing you need to offer is a sense of surety and control. Too often accountants spend all their time pointing out problems and not enough time assuring clients and prospects that they know how to take care of things. Even though a number of unknowns exist regarding applying Sarbanes-Oxley in the future, you still can help clients *now*.

"Our firm used to focus almost exclusively on privately owned businesses and their owners with some nonprofit work. Since SOX, we have increasingly focused on public companies. We are positioning our firm to be the second firm that a public company works with. Although we registered with the PCAOB [Public Companies Audit Oversight Board], we do not intend to audit public companies; however, all the other services that used to automatically go to the company's auditor are now potential services that we can provide. We continue to focus on the middle market as well and have seen significant growth since the Big Four must focus most of their energy on their public company clients, causing them to shed nonpublic clients," says David Morgan, whom we met in Day 1.

The general intent of the act is to avoid earnings surprises and stock manipulation. Although it is impossible to guarantee complete predictability, the overly negative reactions to the act are also unrealistic. In general, the act requires procedures that are beneficial to any company as well as to investors. For instance, real-time access to company data is valuable to managers; many companies have looked at summary statistics daily to see if sales or expenses were in line. And there already exist software programs that meet the Sarbanes-Oxley requirements.

The Sarbanes-Oxley Act will be phased in through 2005 for smaller companies. The long-range implications of the act may be delayed further until court cases are decided about specific provisions and how they apply. For instance, outside of core financial issues, full disclosure is required of off–balance-sheet transactions or other agreements that may have a material effect on financial statements. Conceptually, this is nothing new. Investors have read footnotes in annual reports for years to dig out these "hidden" factors.

Deborah Bailey Browne, whom we met in Day 2, says, "In New York state, the attorney general Elliott Spitzer has proposed regulations that would be similar to Sarbanes Oxley for nonprofit agencies. One possibility is the rotation of the auditor. Another is not allowing auditors to do any kind of consulting or extended services; they couldn't even draft clients' financial statements. It's going to increase the fees of nonprofits. If I'm bidding and know I'm only going to have it for three years . . . I'm going to bid it a different way. In the past, we started making money in the third year. We lose the first year. If we know we're not going to keep it past three years, we're going to price it differently. I also think we are learning the job the first year. Just when you get to the point when you can really help the client a lot, really getting some deep insights, you have to rotate off."

For example, when a company acquires another company, or even raw land, there may be "hidden" liabilities. Sarbanes-Oxley simply makes more pointed the requirement to fairly report and account for these potential liabilities. Clearly accountants cannot estimate environmental clean-up liabilities themselves. However, there are experts available to do so, and their analyses can be used in accounting for liabilities. Even if there is uncertainty in such estimates, by complying with ISO 14001 or other accepted standards, your use of these estimates will accrue no liability.

In other words, despite accountants' deep training to never be wrong, the CPA is not always liable for mistakes in financial estimates as long as you made good-faith efforts and did the proper due diligence to make those estimates.

The General Case

Due to the complexity of government regulations, miscalculations of the tax code will always be made. News of the mistakes will create new fears in the minds of your clients and prospects. The Sarbanes-Oxley Act is the latest, but is only one case of many. Whether your clients are public companies or not, your job is to help them deal with the constant flood of financial and tax regulations. "A thin line separates the types of services an auditor can provide to those affected companies. A 'due diligence/quality control' attitude as to governmental rules is a part of the marketing strategy as we direct efforts to such companies. You cannot violate these new rules," says Jim Belew, whom we met in Day 3.

You need more than technical competence regarding new laws that impinge on your clients. Many of your clients and prospects don't care about the details of any regulations. What they want is reassurance that you will take care of details the best way for their situations. Establishing yourself as the most trusted business advisor is as important as your proper handling of the details. Unless clients trust you, they won't let you implement solutions. Thus, the communication that is at the heart of the sales process applies far more broadly than merely convincing people to hire you.

Tony Zecca says, "We are targeting companies that need an internal audit department. Most of the companies are totally unprepared for Sarbanes. They don't have poor internal controls. They have a lot of controlled gaps and have not paid attention to proper controls. And so we're getting contracts where they outsource their entire Sarbanes-Oxley compliance program. We will actually function as their internal auditors.

"Sarbanes has a recommended framework. So the risk analysis is the first stage. There is really nothing the company gets that is helpful in pointing out and fixing deficiencies. Basically, what it requires is that the company be well controlled and that those controls be documented. Then management, either through outsourcing it to another firm or through an internal audit, will test controls every time they file 10Qs. So we're going in like that three-and-one-half-million-dollar contract I told you about, two and one-half million of it is just the first year getting them ready for Sarbanes-Oxley compliance so that when the external audits come in they can issue their certified report on the controls. And then the other million dollars is the ongoing internal audit outsource that they're going to give us. It's a nice market because it also creates some annuity work for us."

Once they have their clients, too many accountants focus on the delivery of technically correct paperwork. But what clients need as much is ongoing communication that reassures them that you are on top of the details. Clients generally take your technical competence for granted. Once they've hired you, what they judge you by is how you communicate with them. And it is the establishment of a trusting relationship that causes them to hire you in the first place.

Summary

Will Sarbanes-Oxley come and go like Y2K? Tony Zecca doesn't think so. He says, "Most people are saying that, and that's why I think we are just so much better positioned, 'cause I don't believe that at all and we're not operating that way.

"And I think the firms that are thinking this is a blip are missing the boat. Even some on our management committee said, 'We don't think that you can compete with the Big Four.'

"I think we read the market right. I think a lot of people—and I'm using it to our advantage—a lot of people are looking at this like a Y2K thing, it's going to come and go. And so it's affecting their pricing. I don't want to say they're gouging. I don't mean it that way, but their pricing is more—it's higher because they think it is a one-shot deal. I'm going in with a little bit lower pricing because I think that they have to have the ongoing internal audit work and if we do the Sarbanes-Oxley work right in the beginning, they will give us the ongoing internal audit work so it'll be annuity work.

"I also think that other people are going to be affected by Sarbanes. I think that not-for-profits are going to have to comply with Sarbanes-Oxley, 'cause the board members are going to require it. I also think larger private companies who offer financing, like banks, are going to start requiring compliance. I think it's going to become a base factor, so I think the people that are looking at this as a Y2K-type thing are just missing the boat completely."

There will always be new regulations coming down the pike. Sometimes old laws become newly relevant, like 1031 exchanges. Clients don't care about regulations until they have that particular need. It's up to you to be proactive rather than reactive—to do more than keep up on rule changes. You need to build trust and communication both in the sales process and throughout the relationship. Then you are in a unique position of trust where you can both help clients with the regulations that apply to their situation *and* receive premium fees.

14 Marketing and Sales Work Together

We are all salesmen every day of our lives. We are selling our ideas, our plans, our enthusiasms to those with whom we come in contact.
—Charles M. Schwab[1]

Perhaps the biggest distinction often made between marketing and sales is that marketing makes people aware of you, brings them to you, and builds the relationship. A sale is when they sign on the dotted line. Often a managing partner of an accounting firm will say, "I'm tired of this marketing malarkey—I want to sell something." This sentiment expresses those of many partners who are frustrated with the lack of marketing results. In fact, sometimes good marketing does close the sale. When people receive a great marketing piece, perhaps they make an appointment and are ready to buy. Or your low-key networking efforts build trust so that when a need comes up, they call you to help them.

Marketing directors are often given the job of taking care of your marketing material, Web site, seminars, newsletters, and so on. They can create awareness of your firm. They can generate leads. They can keep in touch with existing clients. But seldom can they close the sale. When people hire an accountant, they want to talk with the accountant. It may be an easy sale to close, or it may be hard, but all accountants need to be able to sign up clients for work.

Because so many CPAs are marketing reluctant, it is easy for them to leave marketing to others. We CPAs love the marketing director who does a good job getting our names out. (Although we may complain that the director doesn't close the sale for us.) Often I witness a different frustration. A partner who worked his way through college selling books door-to-door attacks today's marketplace in the same manner. He is knocking on many doors and dragging clients into his accounting firm—whether their needs are compatible with the firm's skills set or not. His attitude is: "Get a small bank this week, a construction firm next week," and "Oh yeah, high tech is hot, let's get an Internet start-up." This approach to dragging them in produces clients, but not the right mix of clients where you have advantages in retaining them. To have a strong accounting practice, you need to enjoy the kinds of clients you work with and the issues involved.

Marketing and Sales Work Together

This book is devoted to helping you improve your profits *and* your lifestyle with the right clients. I've built a practice, and I've worked for a Big Four firm. Now I work with CPA firms, helping them build their businesses. All of the things I've learned have come from other people who have used them successfully. I've pulled together the information for you to use.

Marketing Communications

All communications is marketing. Public relations, advertising, selling, networking, and public speaking are each a type of marketing. The manner in which your phone is answered is marketing. The look of your report covers and the reports themselves are marketing. The subtle oral, written, and non-verbal communications that you have with people are all part of marketing, as is your personal grooming.

The object of marketing and selling is to create opportunities for increased business and to convert those opportunities into revenue.

Good marketing is further defined as a communication of the truth, made in an interesting manner, with the expectation of a positive result.

Benefits of Marketing and Selling

In much of this book I use the terms "marketing" and "selling" interchangeably since both create more business for you. Successful marketing and selling impact the revenue stream of a CPA firm in six basic ways. They help you:

1. Manage client attrition
2. Attract new clients
3. Sell additional services
4. Increase your rates

5. Improve your realization rate

6. Control and enjoy your practice more by attracting better clients and dropping less profitable ones

Marketing and selling are what allow you to have a practice. Increasing your control over your practice will heighten your enjoyment of your work.

Experts in marketing and selling often compare the fields to warfare, gamesmanship, or even gardening. Marketing and selling work together to attract and retain highly profitable clients who will help you attract and retain the best team members. In warfare, the artillery (marketing) and infantry (selling) work together to win a war. In gamesmanship, the principles of focus, offense, and defense help win the match.

I like the gardening metaphor best. Selecting the right ground—good dirt, a location not too shaded or too sunny, and easy to tend—is like the strategic marketing planning the consultants at Waugh & Co. help our clients perform. Marketing is tilling the soil, planting the seeds, fertilizing, watering, and nurturing the young plants. Selling is harvesting the plants. Marketing supports selling. and selling works with marketing. If marketing is not done well, the plants (prospects) will not grow and will be difficult to harvest. If you market in one field and sell in another, your resources will not be used effectively.

Two Kinds of Clients You Want

To maximize client value and profits, CPAs should focus on attracting clients who meet two basic criteria: They are both highly qualified and highly interested.

Highly Qualified Clients

In the cases described in the opening paragraphs of this chapter, the marketing department was getting the word out—but indiscriminately—and the word was attracting clients who were not highly qualified. Likewise, the partner was bringing in clients who were not ideal.

A highly qualified client is one who hits your "sweet spot." Just as when you hit the sweet spot on your tennis racquet or golf club and send the ball off well, a client who hits your sweet spot is one who will obtain maximum value from you and from whom you will obtain maximum profits. Whether you are providing compliance or consulting services or both, you probably have specific in-depth skills for serving a particular type of client.

When you accept a client who doesn't fit your sweet spot, you may only have surface skills, which are not strong enough to serve the client's real needs.

When an unqualified client is very interested in doing business with you, he or she is often quite ignorant about the depth of your skill set. Many times the result is a bad deal for both of you.

Highly Interested Clients

To maximize client value and your profits, clients must be highly interested in working with you. When you go after clients who are not highly interested, it is tempting to raise their interest in a way that is not beneficial to you, such as by reducing your fee. Highly interested prospects will be willing to pay a premium to work with you.

One objective of good marketing is to raise the interest level of highly qualified prospects. Novice sellers often attempt to close the sale before the prospect is highly interested. This is a mistake. To the prospect, this either comes across as high pressure or a cheapened business exchange.

Yet some prospects or clients may be highly interested in doing business with you, and even willing to pay a premium, but may not be qualified. When I worked at Price Waterhouse (now PriceWaterhouseCoopers), my mom often referred relatives to me to do their individual tax returns. She would say, "He works at this big accounting firm and he is cheap—he does my tax return for free." These relatives were very interested in doing business with me; even if they had been willing to pay a premium instead of looking for a cut-rate deal, neither Price Waterhouse nor I were set up to serve this type of client very well.

Consider Exhibit 14.1 on the following page. You might say that effective marketing is a process whereby you direct your communications resources at a particular market, a market that would be rated as an 8, 9, or 10 on both dimensions. Then, as a result of a focused communications effort, prospects rated as 5s, 6s, or 7s would be attracted to you because they might see or hear your communications. You could decide whether to take the client or not. And you would definitely reject any prospect rated a 4 or below.

The Demand for Financial Help Is Greater than Ever

Personal and business economics are becoming decidedly more complex. Each time Congress "simplifies" the tax code, it becomes even more complex. World trade and competition, exchange rates, fluctuating currencies, and rapid technological advances are complicating our financial lives.

The basic economics we once studied focused on accumulating and managing scarce resources. But now we are learning that technology, intelligently applied to resources, can create virtually unlimited resources. The

Exhibit 14.1

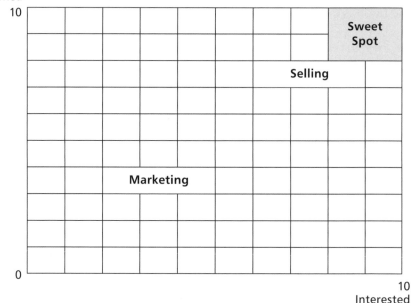

dynamics of this change complicate people's personal and business lives. We once believed that successful companies needed to be profitable from quarter to quarter. Now we are dealing with a dot-com generation of companies that can be valued based on market-share potential, not profits.

Business is becoming decidedly more complex. Information is more plentiful than ever before. Competition for services is intense. Your required knowledge base is expanding. I believe that you, the practicing accountant, can be the most successful businessperson in your community. I believe your future is bright. You can add real value for your clients.

"What we have here is a failure to communicate" is a famous line from the movie *Cool Hand Luke*. This exasperated lament is played out every day in executive suites across the world when businesspeople become infuriated with their accountants. In a landmark 1994 study by professors Lon Adams and Brian Davis of Weber State University, good communications were at the heart of the reasons why CEOs choose accountants. Failure to communicate was related to four of the top five reasons why CEOs switched accountants.

In our profession, no longer can we just be number crunchers; now we must be number communicators. For the most part, technology has assumed the role of number cruncher.

The Market Is Open for You

Until recently, clients rarely changed CPAs. Not only was there limited competition, but also the accounting guilds kept information from consumers. With the exception of the financial statement audit, today accountants no longer have a monopoly on accounting services. Bankers, software developers, insurance brokers, credit card companies, lawyers, financial planners, investment brokers, and many others compete with you. Not only are you faced with stiff competition, but the level of personal service is dramatically improving in all financial service businesses.

Today's consumers are looking for fulfillment of their needs from specialists who will save them both time and money. If you cannot provide the needed service at a convenient time and at a fair price, then consumers will search for a better way.

In today's Information Age, businesspeople are overwhelmed with choices. If you are willing to help them make decisions, the demand for your advice and services could well grow at an exponential rate. Today, more than ever, wisdom—not knowledge or information—is power.

No longer can the accounting guilds keep consumers of services in the dark. In the United States, we accountants allowed our societies and boards to bend our constitutional rights. Many state society leaders have restrained free speech and free trade long enough. They are losing their protectionist battles only to find that other service providers who were willing to engage in free and open communication have taken away much of the profession they were trying to protect.

Until recently, businesspeople placed high value on an accountant's past performance. The primary focus was: "What did you do for me last year?" Today, however, many businesspeople are less concerned with past performance and are asking, "What have you done for me lately, and what will you do for me tomorrow?" Client loyalty to accountants exists only when the accountants are creating value. Clients are saying, "Give me results, not reports."

Summary

The practicing accountant will always be the best-educated, the best-trained, and the best-suited professional to help clients make financial decisions. I have a vision that you will maintain your practical, honest approach in a changing and challenging world. I have a vision that businesspeople will always rate you as their most-trusted business advisor.

For you to capture this vision, you must focus on building your existing clients. For you to build your practice, you must first focus on growing your clients' businesses. And you must communicate this focus to your clients and your prospects. Marketing and sales allows you to serve clients while you improve your practice.

Selling Services *Is* Different

Marketing your personal services is different from marketing cars, appliances, or retail goods . . . with services, people are buying YOU.

—Rick Crandall[1]

Selling accounting services is very different from selling products. And, in many ways, an accounting sale is unlike any other service provider's sale. Bob Gaida, partner of BDO Seidman, LLP, had experience selling tangible products before moving to public accounting. He says, "With products, the buyer is not buying you. Many times you will buy a product and loathe the salesman. With public accounting, the buyer must trust you, have chemistry with you, be able to communicate with you, and not fear you."

To make your sale, you must build rapport with prospects or clients, you must understand their situation, and you must create a custom approach to meet their needs. And you must communicate this in a way that causes them to take action because of the picture of benefits you've created in their minds.

Let's look at some of the ways accounting services are different.

More Trust

Selling accounting services requires more trust in the service provider than in a product seller. When you purchase a product, the product itself does a great deal of the selling. You can see the product. Do you like its color and design? You can touch the product. Do you like its feel? Does it fit? Sometimes you can taste or smell or hear the product. When buying accounting services from you, a person or committee cannot see, touch, smell, taste, or hear your final product. Even when they see the final work product, they generally can't judge its quality. They must trust *you* to deliver what you say you will deliver for their benefit.

More Communication

Because people cannot use their senses to test-drive accounting services, much more communication between the customer and the seller is necessary. The seller must convince the prospect that the seller's accounting services will benefit the potential client. Often great sellers will offer a small service first, so the prospect can be persuaded that great service can be had. Mike Kruse, managing partner of Kruse & Associates, in Nashville, Tennessee, who is profiled in Day 6, began offering a "business physical" that has helped skyrocket his business. He said, "Once potential clients experience our kind of service and the quality of our results, very few will not do business with us. It has been a differentiator for us."

In his book *Trust in the Balance*, Robert Bruce Shaw points out that integrity and concern alone are not enough to establish trust. Results must be produced for genuine trust to be established between people or organizations.

PORTRAIT OF A SALES LEADER

BOB GAIDA could have been a CEO in many types of businesses. He possesses a unique combination of drive and compassion, intelligence and judgment, and an eye for detail and creativity. Gaida is deeply involved in the operations of his clients as well as the operations of his accounting firm. During the last few years he has advanced from a partner in the New York office to office managing director of the Woodbridge, New Jersey, office.

Gaida is the "dean" of the BDO Sales College, a two-year intensive sales training program for the professionals in the firm. He has led numerous successful firm-wide efforts. Gaida said, "Seidman & Seidman began its practice 80 years ago helping small- and medium-size businesses keep the tax bill low. Seidman grew to become a national firm on its reputed tax prowess. I am glad to lead us back into a strong emphasis on tax. For most businesses, tax is the largest bill paid. If we can help them keep taxes as low as possible, we can make a huge contribution to their bottom line.

"I started in public accounting in July of 1968 directly out of college," Gaida said. "Uncle Tony, my godfather, was an entrepreneur and had his own business. In the circumstances under which I grew up, most of the men that I had as role models were employees. But Uncle Tony was his own boss, and he had a nice shop. He did well and lived well,

Making a sales presentation to a prospect can suggest integrity and concern. But to establish a strong bond of trust, the prospect must also see results.

> *Quality in a service or product is not what you put into it.*
> *It is what the client or customer gets out of it.*
>
> —Peter F. Drucker[2]

More communication is necessary because the accounting seller is attempting to paint a picture in the mind of the prospect. Whether it's verbalized or not, prospects have their own picture of what they want. If you ask the right questions and listen well, you will be able to "see" this picture. The initial communication of taking the order usually involves asking many probing questions. In some cases, prospects are not exactly sure what they want. In others, prospects may not tell the seller everything.

and I liked his spirit and his philosophy on life. He seemed like a much freer person than other men who were employed. So he was very much a role model who inspired me to want to do something that would be in business and entrepreneurial in its nature."

Gaida worked in a bakery during his youth. He said, " Part of my job there was to not only bake the pastries but also be out in the front selling them." He became the manager of one of the stores while in high school. So early on Gaida had to deal with all of the aspects of running his business. He went on to say, "I just found it natural to talk to people. I moved on to jobs selling magazines and Tupperware in college. The regional guy wanted me to give up college and sell Tupperware full time.

"I got into public accounting from observing people in business. So when I went to college, I studied accounting and liked it. Accounting seemed to be a good sounding board for whatever else I might do. I joined Seidman thinking that I would not necessarily do that for the rest of my life," Gaida says.

Gaida thought accounting would teach him things about running a business. Today he proclaims, "Helping our clients succeed in their businesses is one of the highest callings a young person can have. Serving medium-size companies and families and helping my partners succeed are very important to me. I really enjoy the differences that public accounting brings to a person's career."

Prospects Are Fearful

More communication is also necessary because prospects often have many fears about buying accounting services from a new provider. "Will the tax advice I receive from these new accountants be as aggressive (or conservative) as I want?" many prospects are wondering. "When the accounting systems get installed, will the reports be timely and will they help me make better decisions?" People usually can tell right away when a product stops working. For example, the car stops running or makes a strange noise. When accounting, tax, or consulting services do not work, it may take years to find out.

A purchase decision is not a decision to buy an item . . . but a decision to enter a bonded relationship. . . . This requires of the would-be seller a new orientation and a new strategy.

—Tom Peters

The Selling Cycle Is Longer

The selling cycle for accounting services is quite long compared to many other services and products. People attending my training classes estimate that, on average, businesses change accounting firms every 12 years. (Some CPAs estimate that businesses change accountants every 5 years.) Neil Rackham, in his book *SPIN Selling*, demonstrates how businesses go through a predictable cycle of making decisions to change service providers. Rackham points out that needs usually begin with some small imperfection in service and over time "become wants, desires or intentions to act."[3]

Accounting Is an Intangible Service

Accounting is an intangible service, not an intangible product. Intangible products are insurance policies or investments. Although they are intangible, these products are created, and then sold. Accounting services are sold, then "manufactured" to order. In our training course *Five-Star Customer Service*, accountants learn how to take the order from a prospect. Taking the order progresses through a four-step process:

1. Prepare.
2. Ask and listen.
3. Write it up.
4. Restate and confirm.

In the preparation step, you must begin to anticipate the client's goals and attitudes. Then, in step 2, you must put the preparation on hold while you listen to your client's—stated and unstated—needs and wants. Writing it up in step 3 engages another sense for both you and your client. And, of course, restating and confirming in step 4 compares the picture in your mind with the picture in your client's mind.

Terry Orr, the sales leader you met in the Day 5 chapter, says, "I think selling accounting and consulting services is really about deeply understanding a client's situation. It is about finding solutions to problems. If you take that attitude, then what you are selling is the ability to solve business issues. Everyone is seeking various answers and the skill is being able to listen with your ears and see with your eyes, to really uncover their true needs. True needs are wants or desires. I might think that a client should have a particular need. But unless the client really wants to address the need, it is not a true need. I don't know that crunching numbers has a lot to do with selling, but solving people's problems has a lot to do with selling."

Harry Beckwith, author of *Selling the Invisible,* says, "The most compelling selling message you can deliver is not that you have something wonderful to sell. It is: 'I understand what you need.' When you can listen with your ears and your eyes, you really begin to understand your client."[4]

 The most important thing in communication is to hear what isn't being said.

—Peter F. Drucker

The Professional Makes the Sale

Professional salespeople often have difficulty selling accounting services because so much of the sale has to do with the trust, communication, skill set, and chemistry between the prospect and the CPA. In most cases, the CPA who is going to do most of the work makes the sale. For this reason, many CPAs are hesitant to sell more services because it will be they who must do the work.

Bob Gaida says that many professionals are afraid of selling at first. "There is deep fear of selling because people know it's an important attribute today to be successful and they don't know how to do it. Very few firms provide ample training in this area. So it's difficult for an achievement-oriented person. This type of individual gets very anxious wondering, 'How will I master this?' There is not enough guidance and training being given there."

In more sophisticated selling systems in accounting firms, highly skilled sellers are called relationship brokers. These people generally are CPAs or highly trained consultants who can "talk the talk" of the service and build a relationship with the client. Jim Heller, a CPA in Milwaukee, says, "I have become expert at selling that which I do not do." One of the real keys to strong profits in today's accounting firm is to appropriately leverage your resources. In firms where partners are responsible for $1 to $5 million in billing, partners spend very little of their time actually doing the work. These types of partners are the relationship managers, relationship brokers, or client service partners.

Understanding how selling accounting services differs from other types of sales is crucial to being successful in the accounting business. When you understand the challenges, you are better able to prepare for the test of selling: seeking out a qualified prospect and persuading him or her to hire you.

Don't Wing It

If you agree that selling accounting services is more difficult, does it make sense to just "wing it," as so many CPAs do? To sell well, you must study and train to be successful in accounting sales. Taking a one-day CPE class or reading one book on selling will not make you an expert.

The mark of good salespeople is that customers don't regard them as salespeople at all, but as trusted and indispensable advisors, auxiliary employees, who, fortunately, are on someone else's payroll.

—Harvey Mackay[5]

Mike Kruse says, "I think selling can be learned. Mostly it's just having a perspective and a determination that selling is important. If somebody feels that it's important, he or she can learn it."

Perhaps many CPAs are lulled to sleep as a result of the "ringing of the telephone." When you perform excellent work for clients, they refer you to others. Bankers and attorneys witness your work and refer you. When that new prospect calls as a result of a referral from one of these sources, it feels like you are selling. But really, the prospect is presold. Now your job is to determine if this is a client for whom you can produce real value. In a good selling system, many call-ins should be turned down. Think of it this way: If the only clients you get are the ones who call you first, then you may be getting the clients no one else wanted. Selling involves seeking out prospects of the types you want who are both qualified and interested in doing business with you.

Summary

Selling accounting services is different from selling most other products and services. People are buying you and may not be able to judge the quality of your actual services. You must focus on increasing communications and building trust. Prospects may be fearful and the selling cycle may be long. Don't be lulled by repeat and walk-in business. Active selling allows you to develop the type of client base you want.

16 It's All About Communication

If I went back to college again, I'd concentrate on two areas: learning to write and to speak before an audience. Nothing is more important than the ability to communicate.

—Gerald D. Ford[1]

Have you ever found your unopened reports in your client's files and heard your client ask, "Well, how did we do?" Speaking at the famous Missouri MAP (Management of an Accounting Practice) Conference, CPA Bill Reeb likened poor-communicating accountants to radiologists who send their patients the MRI film of their tests with a note that says, "Look these over; if you have any questions, call me." His remarks drew a knowing chuckle around the room, because all too many accountants send clients financial statements, tax returns, or other reports with a similar type of note.

Compare the differences in your reaction to a radiologist who simply hands you the film and says, "Look these over and if you have questions, give me a call" to one who spends 30 minutes talking with you and interpreting the film. To which doctor are you willing to pay a higher fee, and to whom will you listen when another test is suggested? Which doctor would you drop the soonest, and which doctor will you recommend to your friends?

Communication Is Your Most Profitable Activity

Calculate what would happen to your profits if you added 20 percent to your revenue next year. Would you add any more overhead? Would you add more staff members? When established accountants answer these questions, they usually conclude that extra revenues produce a very high incremental margin of profit.

Recently I referred a friend to an accountant for tax assistance. My friend was just starting a new business and needed someone to help with structuring

PORTRAIT OF A SALES LEADER

MARK KALAND, member in charge of the Milwaukee, Wisconsin, office of Clifton Gunderson, LLC, is a different kind of communicator. Kaland believes that he must communicate in the language of the client. And since each client communicates somewhat differently, Kaland must be more versatile in the manner in which he communicates.

Kaland joined Clifton Gunderson (CG) in Macomb, Illinois, right out of the University of Wisconsin. He says that during his early years with the firm, he was fortunate to work for two of the Clifton Gunderson future chairmen, Curt Mingle and Carl George.

Curt Mingle had a habit of taking young people to client and prospect meetings. Kaland was impressed with Mingle's ability to listen for client needs and then articulate a CG solution. Over the years Kaland began to take some personal responsibility for meeting with prospects and clients to help solve their needs.

"It was so helpful, watching Curt Mingle perform. We got the jobs. He always amazed me at how articulate and smooth he was, especially under fire. You really couldn't rattle him. It was a good experience for me to learn from him," says Kaland.

Kaland does not like the word "selling" because he feels it connotes pushing a product on people. Kaland is a major business developer for CG because he approaches his clients and prospects as a servant. He says, "If a prospect has a tiny glimmer of dissatisfaction with their present CPA, we can almost always get a new client.

"Carl George taught me to be very client focused. If I can convey my intense interest in helping, the prospect will be convinced to hire us. Carl George had a profound effect on me. He really helped me to mature. Carl would help me set goals and action plans to attain those goals," said Kaland. George helped him set goals for getting involved in the community. Getting involved helped Kaland build confidence, and, as a result, he began to establish his own relationships. "Meeting with people who you don't know, improving communication skills, and George taking me out on proposals was how I learned to market myself," says Kaland of his early training. Going to client meetings and getting involved in the proposal process early helped him learn what clients wanted.

his business and saving taxes. For the first three months of his business, my friend actually lost money. And although he was optimistic, the second quarter didn't look all that promising.

I was horrified to learn that the accountant delivered tax forms that required my friend to pay $4,000 a quarter to the IRS based on a hoped-for $50,000 income in his first year in business. There were no verbal communications about alternative estimated deposit options. My friend had one meeting with the accountant, dropped off his prior year information, and picked up his completed tax forms.

Marketing is communication. All communication is marketing. Without communication, the accountant's value is decreased. My friend will never recommend this accountant to others.

Your MBA in Marketing

When I ask people in my training classes "What is marketing?" they usually respond with one of the elements of marketing: advertising, selling, or printed materials (i.e., brochures). Yes, these are all parts of a larger process of communication.

Prospects make decisions to engage your services on an emotional, subconscious level. They may go through a fact-finding proposal process, but ultimately prospects will say, "I *felt* ABC firm was my best choice" or "I *felt* like we had the best chemistry." Effective marketing should be designed to tap into prospects' minds and influence their thought processes.

Take Control

Left to their own schedules, prospects may meander through the marketplace of accounting providers until they hit a problem. Then they will rush to find comfort with someone who can solve that problem. The most successful marketing program will lead prospects to your door—and to your door only. Accomplishing this requires you to be communicating with your prospects before they encounter problems.

Sometimes your communications create demand for services for which customers have not yet perceived a need. The Chrysler minivan, the Sony Walkman, and the Macintosh computer were all created before customers demanded them.

The process described on the following pages depicts a framework for the marketing process to help you see how marketing works.

The Buying and Marketing Process

The best way to develop a complete marketing program is to understand the manner in which people make significant purchases. We aren't talking about a small $1 purchase, but a significant commitment.

Suspects Become Aware of You

The first event potential customers experience is *awareness*. People must be aware of you to consider a purchase. But with only awareness, they do not have enough information to purchase. Awareness often comes long before a need develops. Marketing research has shown a strong correlation between brand awareness, or top-of-the-mind awareness, and eventual purchase.

In marketing lingo, "suspects" is the name potential clients before you know whether they have need of your services. Suspects become prospects when they are qualified. You create awareness in potential clients most efficiently by advertising and public relations. Advertising can be paid, as in the television ads of Arthur Andersen and Ernst & Young. Public relations can be word-of-mouth testimonials, speaking appearances, print coverage, or myriad other alternatives.

An accountant told me, "Well, I ran an ad and didn't get one client, so I quit marketing." Awareness building through advertising is important in creating receptivity and helpful in reinforcing a buying decision. But you can't rely on advertising to close sales.

Mark Kaland says, "Marketing is everything the firm does to put its members in front of potential clients. I also look at it as ways that we become more familiar with our clients' needs. You have to communicate with them as to where we can help or where we can get them help. I guess it includes everything from projecting an image in the community to getting your people in tune with putting themselves in organizations in positions where they will come in contact with new prospects. This includes speaking engagements and everything else that you can do in an organized way to consistently be visible. We do a lot of analysis of our existing clients as to who their key advisors are and what their needs are. We caucus as a team. This is all part of the process in being able to serve the client in the best possible way. Whatever puts me in front of a prospect or a client with a new product or service that is going to solve a problem for them, I view that as part of the marketing effort."

Familiarity Develops

The second general event in buying is developing familiarity. Think about your last vehicle purchase. You were aware of a brand that created your initial interest. When you began investigating options, simple awareness made you more receptive to a test drive. But the test drive or the tryout enabled you to become familiar with the product.

Accountants develop familiarity in prospects through networking, seminars, and one-on-one meetings with potential buyers. Sometimes prospects do not aggressively seek familiarity until they begin to perceive a need. But marketing research shows a strong correlation between the familiarity level and final buying decision. Familiarity is really a deeper level of awareness.

When I perform postproposal follow-up for my accounting clients, I find a strong correlation between the amount of time prospects invest with the bidder and winning the bid. In over 70 percent of the winning proposals that I have tracked over the last five years, a decision maker in the buying entity knew one of the accountants for well over two years. Most of the losing proposals were from accountants who were not as well known to the client.

Greg Anton, who was introduced in the Day 11 chapter, says, "I compare my marketing activity to that of a funnel. For example, when I teach a class, I regard all the participants as flowing into the wide opening of the top of the funnel. Some of those participants will flow out of the bottom, and those are the ones with whom I can have a mutually beneficial relationship. It's like a dating process. It involves a series of questions, answers, meetings, greetings, and socializing opportunities that naturally occur as the participant-prospect moves through the funnel to eventually become a client."

From a prospect's point of view, developing familiarity begins in earnest after a need arises. From a seller's perspective, waiting until a need arises to begin developing familiarity is risky.

Need Develops: Suspect Becomes "Live" Prospect

The third event that occurs in a typical buying cycle is that when a need arises, the potential customer begins to sort through available options, seeking a solution to a specific problem. From a seller's perspective, differentiation is the appropriate marketing response. Sellers must demonstrate how their services are different from the competition and how their services more precisely fit the prospect's perceived or real needs.

Sellers can improve their odds of success by creating differentiation in the potential client's mind long before a need arises. For example, assume that a CEO develops a need for an improved technology system for her business. If she is familiar with your capabilities to help, she will call you first. Your firm may be the only one considered.

Differentiation occurs when you become a specialist in a service category or an industry. Prospects typically ask questions like these in the early portion of interviews: "How many other businesses like mine have you worked on?" or "How many other problems like mine have you solved?"

Before prospects decide to commit, they must develop positive perceptions about the winning seller. David Maister, in his landmark book *Managing the*

Professional Services Firm, says, "Excellent capabilities are essential to get you into the final set to be considered, but it is other things that get you hired."

Usually, after all the technical screening is complete, the intangible qualities are considered. Do the prospects' executives like you? How do they judge your commitment to their problems? How do they perceive your willingness to stand behind your services when you err? When they err? What about your other professional relationships? What about any other benefits from a relationship with you?

Awareness building, familiarity development, and differentiation can all occur, but if the buying influencers develop negative perceptions about you, they will not engage you. A CEO recently told me, "We just didn't like the partner even though he was probably the most technically qualified of the four we interviewed. We needed someone we could relate to and work with."

 You make the sale when the prospect understands that it will cost more to do nothing about the problem than to do something about it.

—Ben Feldman[2]

Conversion from Prospect to Client

Many books have been written on closing the sale. Many speakers extol artful phrases designed to close the sale. Most commission plans pay on closing the sale. Although it is the one climactic event, emphasis on closing the sale is overdone. I have found that the sellers who emphasize the elements leading up to closing the sale succeed more often.

Think of the Olympic athlete who focuses all of his attention on winning the event, with very little time spent on preparation. Without cross-training, endurance training, strength training, and nutritional training, most world-class athletes would not win. When an athlete mixes God-given talent with solid training and strong desire, he is prepared to win.

Converting a prospect into a client is an exciting event. It should be celebrated and rewarded. But the high success rates will go to those of you who lay a foundation through advertising, networking, specializing, and generally creating an environment whereby you will be the obvious and sometimes the only choice.

Building Client Loyalty

Very few businesses have clients with as strong a recurring need as do accountants. People outside our profession call it "evergreen revenue." Most other businesses must sell their clients on every purchase. Largely because of this phenomenon, many accountants are lulled to sleep when it comes to marketing to clients.

Those accountants who continue to market to their clients as if those clients were their best prospects tend to experience the most profitable growth. In today's economic environment, customers and clients are more demanding than ever. Pressure to improve the quality of service is being applied from many directions. In today's marketplace, it is crucial for you to aggressively build client loyalty.

Client loyalty means a great deal more than satisfaction. Loyalty is clients who come back because you are the best choice. Loyalty is clients who tell others about you because you provide them great service. Clients who are merely satisfied can, and often do, find a better alternative.

After the sale is closed, you must continue to market to your clients by listening, talking, and writing. You must find ways to reinforce their decisions to hire you.

A lot of accountants pay lip service by marketing to clients, but few follow through. For some reason, many accountants don't feel the immediate need, so they fail to communicate with their clients well.

Business is built on the loyal customer, one who comes back and brings a friend.

—W. Edwards Deming[3]

In the Adams and Davis study mentioned in the Day 14 chapter, clients who had left their accountants cited "The accountant was not proactive in delivering services" as the top reason. Accountants have a wonderful opportunity, similar to that of the phone company, to create new services and deliver them across a client base. What are you doing to deliver new services to your clients every year?

Clients who are grappling with today's complex business environment are demanding new and more services. Financial technology is exploding and is confusing for most businesspeople. The winning accounting firms are up-to-date on providing solutions in this high-tech world.

The highest order of marketing is the successful promotion of word-of-mouth advertising. When you create a steady referral marketing program, you are creating a whirlwind of clients. Clients who refer you are loyal and are likely to be using several of your services. Prospects who arrive at your door referred by a delighted client are ready to engage your services.

So there you have it, almost 30 years of marketing study and practice boiled down into one small chapter. Everything you will learn about marketing throughout this book and others will fit neatly into the structure described in this chapter.

Summary

Your best marketing step is to improve communication with your clients and prospects. The marketing and buying process includes initial awareness of you, increasing familiarity, need development, conversion from prospect to client, and building client loyalty. This process, done right, will generate the repeat business and referrals that will enable you to build a strong and successful business.

17 Power Sellers in the Accounting Industry

If it works, copy it.

—Will Rogers

Selling accounting services is a relatively new art form. Until a few years ago, people in our industry wouldn't even say the word "marketing." The terms "business building" and "practice development" often were used to describe sales and marketing activities. But now in the accounting profession as well as in all other businesses, selling has taken a front seat. Even though the federal laws regarding sales and marketing changed in 1977, accounting firms did not begin to seriously address the practice of marketing until the late 1980s.

Since that time, most of the large accounting firms have developed training programs to help professionals learn how to sell. Ernst & Young led the way in 1988 with comprehensive sales training for most senior professionals and a dedicated team of salespeople. BDO Seidman created a sales college for those at the manager level and above. Even the venerable PricewaterhouseCoopers has a telemarketing center to attract leads for its salespeople and professionals. Some of their sales training programs have caused firms significant problems. The primary reason for these difficulties stems from the aggressive change in culture that has resulted from the institution of such programs. Firms that have established themselves as relationship-oriented businesses will always find it treacherous to try to convert to selling products.

A few years ago, here at Waugh & Co., we began to notice the shift from requests for marketing training to an increased demand for sales training. As a result, we developed The Rainmaker Academy, a three-year intensive training and coaching program to help professional CPAs learn how to sell.

Through a process of live training courses, personal marketing plans, personal coaching, accountability, participant teaching of the material, and many more techniques, students learn to sell by learning and doing.

Great sellers are not born; great sellers are trained. Andre Agassi was not born a tennis star; Tiger Woods was not born a golf professional; a brain surgeon was not born as such. Certainly we are all born with varying degrees of intelligence, athletic abilities, and other traits. The truly great in any field have a combination of inborn gifts and developed gifts. I believe that over 90 percent of all CPAs I have met can be trained to become good sellers of accounting services.

In our training programs, we classify people in three basic categories:

- **Mistmakers** focus on building existing clients and may attract up to $50,000 per year in expanded services and new clients.
- **Rainmakers** have developed skills in selling and may attract up to $500,000 per year.
- **Stormmakers** are those amazing few who regularly attract millions of dollars of new business to their firms.

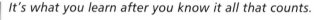

It's what you learn after you know it all that counts.

—Earl Weaver, former manager of the Baltimore Orioles

Selling Is Profitable

If you were to provide consulting to two businesses, both $100 million in sales, you would not necessarily approach each of the businesses the same way. Assume that one of the businesses has a 2 percent gross margin on sales and the other a 30 percent gross margin. To get the most leverage, where would you focus most of your attention: cost cutting or business building? In a business with thin margins, a good consultant will focus on cost-cutting strategies. Reduce the cost structure by 1 percent in a business with a 2 percent gross margin, and the impact on gross profits will be 50 percent. But in a business with a 30 percent gross margin, a 1 percent reduction in costs has less than a 2 percent impact on gross profits.

The business of accounting is a high-margin business. Properly priced, new business in an accounting firm can mean between 30 and 100 percent incremental profits on the sale. Yet most accountants approach the business of accounting the same way they would a thin-margin business. Many accountants focus on cost cutting rather than business building. The power sellers

PORTRAIT OF A SALES LEADER

RICHARD ("DICK") RECK, a retired partner at KPMG in Chicago, is still a stormmaker for his firm. He is bigger than life and regularly attracts several million dollars of new business to KPMG.

Today, Dick Reck combines his unique background with extraordinary selling skills to lead his Chicago-based information technology practice. During the last 10 years, Reck's team has grown from 7 professionals to over 200. He distinguishes himself as a businessperson first and a CPA second. Reck says, "A businessperson works in the marketplace. I think most accountants could become good businesspeople if they wanted to. Trouble is, many of them don't want to make the transition."

Jeff Weaver, the KPMG director of marketing who is responsible for supporting the Sales Partner Program, says, "Dick Reck has always been a sales leader within our firm. He was a highly developed sales leader before we started this program. We learned how valuable selling can be to KPMG, so we wanted to bring in more partners." The Sales Partner

in our profession are rapidly learning that selling—not cost cutting—is the way to make profits in an accounting business.

 Gather as much information as you can about customers, then tailor the entire enterprise to customers' very personalized needs.

—Tom Peters[1]

Power Sellers—Coach and Mentor

During my years at PWC, the business developers provided a complete role model for me. Fred Frick, partner in charge of the Nashville, Tennessee, office was quiet but very effective. Frick focused on building his clients, serving clients with great dignity, and responding to opportunities aggressively when they arose.

In contrast, Maurie Dahlem, partner in charge of the Los Angeles office, was bigger than life. He was extremely active in the community, he engineered the firm's leadership in the entertainment industry, and he was a power seller. These two different approaches to selling became models from which younger managers and seniors could learn.

Program at KPMG has attracted the firm's line partners who move away from billable time and focus exclusively on selling. The average new business goal for each partner in the program is between $2 and $3 million per year. Reck says, "The real success of any firm comes when the owners are businesspeople first and foremost."

After graduating from DePauw University, Reck obtained his MBA from the University of Michigan. He studied math and computers and wanted to be an information technology consultant when he joined the audit staff of Peat, Marwick & Mitchell (now KPMG) in 1973.

Reck learned his persuasive skills at the dinner table from his mom and dad. He says, "You don't learn much about communication skills in college or graduate school. You reflect your environment. The formative years are crucial: It's mom and dad. My mom was a teacher and my dad a highly educated research chemist. That's how you learn things in this world, always being pushed by those around you. That's why folks do or don't communicate well. It's because mom and dad communicated well."

Fred Frick used a low-key, cross-selling philosophy with his clients. Today I would call the approach he used in the 1970s and 1980s cycle selling. If you are like most accountants, many of your clients utilize only a few of your services. Too often, a client engages another kind of professional to perform services that you could provide.

To ensure that you are providing all the services possible, take advantage of a client-marketing tool called cycle selling. Maintain a listing of all the services that you provide for each client. Frick taught me to keep this listing in the front of a permanent file. Then, over a period of two to five years, systematically present each service to your client. Keep notes of your actual conversations with the client and what resulted from your exchange. This cycle-selling concept is not a one-time-only proposition: Keep updating your list of services, and keep reviewing your capabilities with your clients, year after year. Your bottom-line strategy is to make sure that all of your clients are aware of all of your service capabilities.

Don't overlook the services that fall into the category of "He (or she) will never need this." Instead, say something like: "Mr. Jones, you may never have a need for the service I want to tell you about, but I would be remiss if you weren't aware of all of our capabilities." If the client doesn't use the service, she might still refer you to others.

Present only two new services at a time. Most people are unable to absorb and retain much information at once. Depending on many factors, you could present two services every three or six months.

By adopting the cycle-selling method, you can be proactive in delivering services to your clients.

Cycle Selling Works with Prospects, Too

One of the reasons it is so challenging to sell CPA services to a new client is that the average client changes CPAs only every 5 to 12 years. Yet, in spite of this fact, most CPAs only make one or two sales calls, then move on to the next prospect. When you are trying to woo a prospect away from another firm, patience isn't just a virtue, it's a necessity.

Don't ever be disappointed when your first visit fails to pay immediate dividends. Apply the cycle-selling process to prospective clients by planning a five-call program. On each sales call, provide new information about your firm that is relevant to the prospect's current interests.

Terry Orr says, "I have courted target clients for several years before bringing them into our firm. In order to do this, I must have a reason to call back until they buy or they die!"

To make this strategy work, you must keep excellent call records. Keep track of which services you talked about and when.

Maurie Dahlem focused more on leading a selling effort in the Southern California marketplace, much like Dick Reck does today in Chicago. Lunching at the California club with Dahlem was almost like networking at the White House. The movers and shakers of the Southern California business community dined at the club. On any given day, Dahlem would engage the top captains of industry in business conversation, by just going to lunch at the right place. Dahlem developed his reputation and could get into most corporate headquarters in the Los Angeles area.

It doesn't matter which approach you take; you can be effective using either the quiet approach or the highly visible approach.

The great sellers will create a training program to coach others in the fine art of selling. As you design your training sessions, you may become aware that your staff's objections to selling do not change. To avoid this kind of scenario, you must help your staff members do two things:

1. Develop positive attitudes rather than skeptical attitudes.
2. Develop relationships with clients and prospects.

Teaching your younger staff members to establish relationships may be the most important aspect of your sales training. What you need is a way to sell your staff on selling your services.

Setting Up a Training Program

While your training program cannot extend over the same 10 to 20 years that you have taken to learn to sell, you can take your staff through the same steps. Just follow the steps listed next.

A Step-by-Step Training Process

1. Discard any idea you might have that your staff cares about the additional billings that will accrue to your firm. Forget that you may even be able to bill 125 percent of standard.

2. Throw out your mechanical, one-way, classroom-style lecture in which you explain how you sell.

3. Assess the learning needs of the group. Because selling is not widely understood, every person will need to know it inside and out. All your trainees need to believe in your firm so strongly that they cannot wait to tell a prospective client about it. And they will need to get over their fears of dealing with client objections.

4. Design exciting and fun activities to accomplish the learning objectives. The activities should include practice sessions in describing the features, advantages, and benefits of your firm and its services. A feature is a physical description of the service. Each feature may have several advantages. The client can only describe the benefits as they affect him or her. In the training sessions, brainstorm at least three advantages for each feature and then rehearse them in breakout groups. This will provide your firm with the basics of a good selling program.

5. Teach group members how to ask the right questions that reveal the benefits to their clients. Not all advantages will translate into the same benefits for everyone. Telling all your clients all the features you offer and the advantages of each without speaking to their real concerns may bore them.

Role Playing Is Helpful

Don't be lured into thinking that a staff accountant or even a partner really knows something just because it has been explained to him or her. In your training sessions, be sure to set aside at least one hour for practice role-plays. Divide into groups of three, where one person plays the CPA, one is the client, and one is an observer/coach. You can help things along by writing up a three-paragraph scenario in advance.

Set Expectations

After training, you are ready to set realistic expectations for selling your services throughout your community. Within 48 hours of a training session, every attendee should be able to forecast his or her presentation of the service during the next 30 days. Schedule a follow-up meeting 30 days hence and review briefly how each person succeeded in using the selling methods you taught. You will get good results when you train, set expectations, then follow-up.

F-A-B-ulous Benefits

Another way of summarizing the features versus benefits distinction is FAB, or fabulous. You want what you do to be fabulous. Your features give you advantages that provide benefits for your clients. Therefore, your service is fabulous.

Coach in the Field

Demanding 30-day performance reports is not enough. Set up a system to give hands-on coaching at client and prospect meetings. And don't forget to positively reinforce staff members when they do produce. Bill Jenkins says, "Many of our younger staff members are somewhat reluctant to sell services at first. But I learned many years ago that the way you teach a dog to hunt is to take him hunting. And that's what we do with our people. We take them hunting with the partners who praise them for success. Once a young person gets the taste of selling success, he wants more of it. It feels good."

Summary

You may be both a role model and a student when it comes to selling accounting services. If your career is relatively young, learning to sell will make the biggest contribution to your and your firm's future. If you are a partner, you are a role model to your staff members. Take time to educate them on the importance of selling. Explain how it benefits clients. Regularly train members of your team on selling. Reinforce good selling techniques and results with rewards. One worthwhile tool in any selling situation is to keep careful records of work done for new and existing clients so you can systematically inform them of all of your services.

Power Tools for Better Selling

18 Newsletters Communicate to Sell

Forget information overload. All people crave information and, even more, being "in the loop."
—Tom Peters[1]

To keep in touch with prospects and clients, you need tools that communicate professionally. Newsletters are ideal for this purpose. They allow you to show off your knowledge and give something to readers, and they keep you in front of people. They can be elaborate multipage, multicolor creations or brief e-mails.

As mentioned elsewhere, a newsletter is ideal to offer when you're starting to communicate with prospects. It allows them to show their interest and gives you permission to stay in touch.

Newsletters are one of the best marketing tools that accountants can use. From a marketer's point of view, the newsletter is a tool that enables you to promote yourself and demonstrate your expertise at the same time.

Newsletters can be used throughout the marketing process:

- Prospecting
- Networking
- Differentiating
- Helping close sales
- Building client loyalty and the relationship
- Selling additional services
- Stimulating referrals

Few marketing tools provide this range of uses. Of course, newsletters must be editorially and graphically interesting to be effective. A dull newsletter may work against you.

Newsletters come in all shapes and forms. They don't even have to be called newsletters. You could call them trendletters, financial notes, money makers, reports, tax notes, financial memos, or many other titles. You can mail them, fax them, or e-mail them. But the fact remains, direct mail correspondence is one of the most versatile and efficient tools a CPA can use to enter the world of marketing. Too many clients leave CPA firms because of a communication deficit. Don't let yours.

Because you can never predict when prospects will want to talk to you, don't leave it to chance that they'll remember your name. Stay in front of them with a newsletter. When you buy advertising in newspapers or journals, there is an enormous waste factor. Newsletters promote you in a much more focused way. With a newsletter, you can target the specific prospects you wish to attract with a low-key professional document.

David Morgan, whom we met in Day 1, says, "We have used several niche newsletters for years that have kept our name in front of our clients, referral

Increase the Odds that Your Newsletter Won't Be Thrown Away

If you use a printed newsletter, you can encourage people to keep it as a reference.

- Three-hole punch it. That gives the subtle message that it's meant to be kept.

- Provide imprinted binders for your clients and top prospects. Then, instead of your newsletter getting buried under other papers, your company name on the spine of the binder will remain in sight on your prospect's or client's bookshelf.

- Include features such as calendars of events and deadlines, how-to articles and tips, and news items that impact your prospects and clients.

If you use an e-mail newsletter (e-zine), speed and flexibility can work for you.

- You can send topical notices out at a moment's notice.

- You can remind people of deadlines.

- You can provide links to more in-depth information, including your own Web site.

- You make it easier for people to respond to you.

sources, and good prospects. We want to stay on top of our clients' minds and our newsletters have helped."

Debra Skolnick, director of marketing and communications of Goldenberg Rosenthal in Pittsburgh, Pennsylvania, uses many newsletters from different sources. She says, "Our goal is for name recognition, and the newsletter we use must be the best available. We send very targeted materials. In addition to purchasing several newsletters, we write three of them ourselves."

Prospecting with Newsletters

When you regularly publish a newsletter, sending a copy to each of your target prospects will create name recognition for you. Name recognition is important. Remember the last time you met a person who was familiar with your firm's name? Their response to you was smiling receptivity. Meeting someone who has never heard of you creates an opposite response and, usually, very low receptivity.

A newsletter should be only one tool in a communications program. Although simply sending a newsletter may obtain some response from prospects, the best way to create business is to actively follow-up your newsletters with phone calls, visits, fax-backs, and invitations to seminars or your office. A 1 percent response rate per year from a passive newsletter program is normal and can in itself be profitable, but active programs can attain 5 to 10 percent prospect response.

Take a Reader Poll

Include a poll in each issue—anonymous, of course. Here are some ideas about what to ask your readers:

- Has their staff increased, decreased, or remained the same over the last year?
- Has turnover increased, decreased, or remained the same over the last year?
- Are accounts receivables are being paid faster or slower than last year?
- Who's going to win the big local football game or political race?
- What do they use their Web sites for?

Reader polls offer these benefits:

- The results give you a ready-made story for the next issue.
- Polls are involvement devices for your readers.

- Readers can benchmark themselves against a local market.
- Other media are likely to pick up your poll results.

Greg Anton uses various tools provided by his firm. He explains his use of newsletters this way: "I'll bring three or four pieces of our firm's materials that would benefit the participants. For example, I might bring our *Guide to Going Public* and a few of our topic newsletters. I'll say, 'If you want to receive some of these materials, write your request on the back of your business card and I will make sure you receive them.' I also add their names to the national list to receive quarterly newsletters, such as *SEC Insights*. They're always seeing our logo. Periodically, I'll do a follow-up with some of these individuals to make sure they are indeed receiving our materials and to see if they have any questions. It gives me a chance to do a little 'scratch 'n sniff' test to see who their current service provider is and how satisfied they might be with them."

RISE above the Competition

Newsletters function at four different marketing levels to help you rise above the competition:

Recognition. *Your prospects need to know who you are, where to find you, and what you do before they do business with you.*

Image. *You create an image for yourself in print.*

Specifics. *Tell readers exactly what you can do for them.*

Enactment. *Show and tell readers what you want them to do (like contact you).*

—Elaine Floyd, *Marketing with Newsletters*[2]

As discussed in the Day 10 chapter, personal networking is one marketing tool that every accountant or consultant should learn to use well. Whether you are networking at a chamber event or at a trade organization, a newsletter gives you a written tool to send to your contacts. If, after you have met someone, you send an article you have published on the subject you discussed, your meeting will be strongly reinforced.

When you meet someone who has been receiving your newsletter, he or she will have increased receptivity to you and recognition of you. That's why you should include photos of key partners in newsletters. Photos personalize your intangible service. They add interest and increase recognition dramatically.

Debra Skolnick says, "We prospect with our newsletters by sending them to qualified leads. The qualification measures are different in each industry category. But we will not send them to the tiny nor the mega-prospect."

Differentiating with Newsletters

A newsletter communicates that you are knowledgeable because you can write interestingly about financial and business matters. When two CPAs compete for an assignment and all other things are equal, the one who is considered to be a good communicator will win the engagement.

Industry newsletters can help position you as an expert. Most CEOs report that they want their accountant to understand their businesses. What better way to differentiate yourself than to have published a series of industry-specific articles? For example, a construction contractor interviewing prospective CPAs will assume that the CPA who publishes a construction newsletter has greater industry knowledge than another CPA.

If your newsletter articles have been published in industry trade magazines, you have even more credibility in the industry that you are trying to penetrate. Once written, newsletter articles make excellent grist for speeches and other articles. For instance, some of our newsletter articles are reprinted in dozens of other accounting publications.

Put appropriate local media and trade publications on your newsletter mailing list. When you call them, they'll know you. And, they might get a story idea from your newsletter.

You can interview media people for a story. For instance, if your clients are high-tech companies, interview reporters and editors of those trade publications on what forces they see impacting the industry over the next year. Your readers will appreciate the information, and interviewees might very well refer to your article in their publications.

You can also target your letter to specific needs of a group, such as women business owners, large employers, and companies with pension plans. Sally Glick, director of marketing for Polaris International, calls these types of newsletters "functional specialty letters."

Newsletters Help Close Sales

Many accounting firms that regularly publish newsletters report that often they are the only firm interviewed for an engagement. Many new clients report that receiving regular communications from the accounting firm was a key factor in their decision to contact only that firm.

You'll need to close sales in person. But the more professionally published material you have to establish credibility, the better your chances of closing more sales.

Newsletters Build Client Loyalty

Have you noticed that competition for your clients is getting tougher? Competition is not coming only from other accountants, but from credit card companies, banks, insurance houses, and business consultants. Many are hammering your clients with regular marketing messages about services that you could provide. Phil Scissors, managing partner of Hochschild Bloom in St. Louis, says, "We have assembled our newsletter from various sources. We write some of the articles and we borrow some of the articles from other firms with whom we share newsletter resources. Our clients comment regularly about the personalized look and feel. They seem to be glad that we go to the trouble."

> A newsletter does more than just remind clients you're here and build your expertise in their eyes. It gives you a reason to contact them for ideas for the newsletter. As a "reporter-researcher" you will also tend to uncover new needs in a subtle way.
> —Rick Crandall, *Marketing Magic*[3]

Certainly, you communicate regularly with your biggest and best clients. But what about the hundreds of others whom you see only once a year? A bimonthly or quarterly newsletter program can help make all those smaller clients feel welcome. And with a newsletter program, you can keep your name in front of these clients for as little as $4 a year.

Jim Belew, whom we met in Day 3, says, "Our *Tax Notes* program is written by our own people and edited by a professional writer. We believe in delivering solid information to our clients. Many of the lawyers and bankers who refer business to us do so because they appreciate the solid content we deliver in our newsletters and in our work."

Even your biggest and best clients will be more loyal when they read an interesting article that you wrote. They are reading *Money*, or *Forbes*, *Barrons*, or *The Wall Street Journal*, or their industry's trade publications. They expect to read material from you too. These best clients want to know that you are on top of the relevant information for them. There is no better way to reinforce their loyalty than with regular written and oral communications.

Newsletters Sell Extended Services

How many of your clients use you for only one service? How many for two? If most of your clients are not using at least three services from your arsenal, then you have tremendous opportunities to cross-sell and up-sell your clients.

How to Keep Your Readers Reading

The first rule of success is for a company newsletter to include information valuable to the recipient. Here are other tips to keep your customers reading:

- *Keep stories short (less than a page each).*
- *Write in a personal style so that clients feel that they are hearing from a person.*
- *Give clients a name to call for more information about any story or your company in general.*

Most accountants I know can help clients in a wide array of potential ways. What better way to keep these services in front of your clients (and referral sources) than to write about them in your newsletter? For example, telling how a client improved his decision making and profits by installing a budgeting and tracking system will create definite interest in this service.

Highlighting service specialists and constantly talking about the many services your firm offers will help your firm overcome the tendency of many partners to protect their clients. Too often partners fail to mention services that other partners or staff can perform. Writing about all of your services in your newsletter can keep your clients aware that they are available.

One of the best ways to write articles that pique the interest of your readers is to tell stories about successful clients who have used your services. Clients enjoy being involved with your newsletter. In some cases, your clients will actually get business from being mentioned in your letter. This increases their loyalty to you.

Buy or Build?

CPAs everywhere wonder, "Is my newsletter worth all the effort and cost? How do I know if my newsletter is effective? Should I do a newsletter? Should

I do my own newsletter, or should I purchase one? If I purchase one, which is the best for me?"

Of course, once you decide to add a newsletter to your marketing mix, your first decision is among three options: You could write your own newsletter. You could purchase a newsletter. Or you could write part of the letter and purchase part of the material.

Your Best Alternative

Only you and your partners can decide what is best for you and your clients. Here are the pros and cons for each.

Publish Your Own Newsletter

The best of the three options is to publish your own newsletter if:

- You are willing to allot sufficient time to the project.
- You have quality writers on staff.
- You will commit to the rigors of the publishing business.

Not many accounting firms can or should select this alternative. With a less formal e-mail newsletter, clients don't expect as much length or expensive production. So e-mail is an easy way to test newsletters. Your ezine can be as brief as a paragraph if it has useful information or reminders. It can be customized easily to small groups of similar clients, and each accountant can do his or her own simple ezine, if desired.

Purchase a Newsletter

The best of the three options is to purchase a newsletter if:

- Your time is more valuably spent serving your clients.
- You want to retain the best writers in the country.
- You do not want the hassle of being a publisher.

Write Part of the Newsletter and Purchase Part

The best of the three options is to write part of the letter and purchase part if:

- You want your newsletter to be very specific to your clients and your region.
- You want the newsletter to sell something.
- You want to combine the best aspects of the first two alternatives for your practice.

Self-Publishing for Success

If you decide to self-publish, you must follow four basic rules.

1. *Write the newsletter to the interest level of your recipient clients and prospects.* Do not write the newsletter for other CPAs.

   Debra Skolnick says, "We are writing a very targeted letter especially for women entrepreneurs. This is a very powerful group of new entrepreneurs that have special interests and we want to capture the attention of the movers and shakers in that group. This letter is not written for any other audience than women business owners."

2. *Write so that an eighth grader can read it.* Your audience has developed wisdom from experience, and they appreciate your recognition of that sophistication. However, people want a quick, easy read. You should hire a non-CPA editor. Sometimes your marketing director can perform this function, but often he or she may not possess the skill or the distance from the profession to edit well. A good editor is often a business writer for your local newspaper or a freelance business writer in your community. The extra press coverage that your firm could receive from this relationship will often pay for itself.

3. *Set a schedule and budget for the publishing process.* Your schedule should insure that the newsletter is in the hands of recipients before the publication date. In other words, your January newsletter should be received by December 31. Allocate time for writing in each contributor's monthly or weekly time budget. If you ask people to do the work on their own time, you are setting yourself up for failure.

4. *Hold quarterly editorial planning meetings to plan future articles.* Articles should be assigned far enough in advance so the writers can meet the editor's deadline and the editor can make the printer's deadline. An annual editorial calendar is also a good idea so that you stay ahead of the game.

Cost and Sources

Usually you should allocate no more than 5 to 10 percent of your marketing budget to the newsletter. A firm grossing $3 million and spending 3 percent of firm revenue on marketing would allocate $5,000 to $9,000. Start-up costs may make the first year's expenses somewhat higher.

Newsletters that ignore design issues miss at least half the intended audience. Because we CPAs are so factually oriented, we tend to forget to communicate with people who are motivated through design, color, and layout.

Horne CPA Group shareholder Joel Bobo says, "Our firm uses four pre-packaged newsletters from PDI and Mostad & Christensen. We are not publishers and these letters allow us to bring timely information to our clients in an attractive format." Working from the firm's headquarters in Jackson, Mississippi, Bobo is director of the firm's Construction Services Group. He and his owners have developed a web of marketing activities that the newsletters support. "In addition to our newsletters, we send annual letters to all our readership with updates on our specific services and staff, as well as pertinent industry/service news. Our Construction Newsletter (Pencor) is featured on our Web site and in industry ads to reach potential subscribers. Our Employee Benefits Update (PDI) offers a great fax-back response form to receive more information. All of our newsletters are distributed with brochures to prospects and referral sources," says Bobo.

Sources of Prepackaged Newsletters

In recent years, several excellent sources of newsletters have developed. Three excellent sources of prepackaged newsletters are listed. All of them have many options for you to make your newsletter effort manageable.

> Mostad & Christensen
> Oak Harbor, WA
> 800-654-1654
>
> Newkirk, Inc.
> Albany, NY
> 800-525-4237
>
> PDI
> Chicago, IL
> 800-227-0498

Summary

Newsletters make tangible your intangible services. Clients cannot touch, feel, or see your knowledge. But they can examine your materials. Impressive newsletters really help.

Newsletters are great communication tools. Remember, by itself, a newsletter will not sell much business. Debra Skolnick combines her firm's newsletter programs with a variety of other marketing tools. She sends a cover letter and a response vehicle with each one. A newsletter is part of a total marketing program wherein all the elements support the total effort. Skolnick says, "A newsletter is a good way to develop awareness with prospects and to keep in touch with your best clients."

Newsletters help you differentiate yourself from your competition, give added value, and provide a vehicle from which you can cross-sell services. There are many good resources available. The discipline necessary to produce a regular newsletter is worth the effort.

19 Speaking Attracts More Clients and Referrals

Speaking brings you instant credibility. You may get business even from people who didn't hear you speak.
—Miriam Otte, *Marketing with Speeches and Seminars*[1]

Speaking on topics of interest to your audience can be a great marketing technique. The only drawback to it is that many people rate fear of public speaking *above* fear of death! The benefits of speaking can be terrific. You establish yourself as an expert. You test topics for audience interest. You give people a sample of your services. You gather feedback. You obtain referrals. People come to you. These benefits can be yours if you're willing to risk "death by speaking." Actually, it's possible to use seminars to promote your firm and get *other people* to do most of the talking. For instance, you can do a joint seminar with an attorney and a business consultant who are referral sources. And your "talk" can be a question-and-answer session where you don't have to give a speech at all.

Seminars enable you to communicate your knowledge, demonstrate your creativity, and generate chemistry between you and a prospect. A carefully planned program can enable you to leverage your "selling" time and use group dynamics to motivate potential clients to hire you. Jeff Everly, whom we met in Day 4, says, "The speeches that David Frazier or I give to banking organizations position us as experts in a particular field. We both believe this has been one of the most important activities we have used to attract clients to our firm."

Speaking can vary from the local Rotary Club, to seminars in your office, to industry meetings. You'll want to do most of your speaking to audiences who could be clients or referral sources. That means talking less to other accountants and talking more to client-related groups. If the Lions or other local groups are appropriate for you, you're in luck. Usually there are dozens of such groups in any urban or suburban area. You can start with your personal contacts and the local phone book and contact Pilots, Soroptimists, Moose, Chambers, and many more such groups.

Greg Anton tells about his speaking experiences: "Sales training has taught me that becoming a 'famous' person is valuable. I mapped out a methodology to use to become famous within an area of expertise. I really set out to become a knowledgeable SEC and assurance expert within our local office.

PORTRAIT OF A SALES LEADER

DEBORAH BAILEY BROWNE graduated from The Rainmaker Academy in 2003. She has always been interested in developing new business for her firm, but she felt like she needed more tools and better skills to grow to her full potential.

Browne just opened her own accounting firm after many years as a partner with a major New York accounting firm. For many years, she was the leading business developing partner for her firm, so she decided to start her own business. "Blonde and smart" is how one of her fellow Rainmakers described her. She holds an MBA from Fordham University in New York and a BA from Pace University. She graduated summa cum laude and received Beta Gamma Sigma honors.

Browne grew up in a very competitive family. Many of her relatives were involved in accounting, so the influence of finance was overwhelming. She considered becoming a professional dancer, but her mother convinced her to pursue a career in business. This decision was very wise, as Browne has become a very sought after public speaker on important business topics. Her performance training has enabled her to better connect with her audiences.

In her first year, Browne expects to bill over $1 million in gross volume to clients. She is building her firm as a full-service firm, offering audit, tax, and business consulting services.

I began teaching SEC-related courses for the AICPA [American Institute of Certified Public Accountants]. I teach an SEC course twice a year, and the majority of the public companies send their controllers and accountants to these courses. This gives me an opportunity twice a year to be in front of good prospects as a 'somebody.' People naturally gravitate to me to talk about their issues, problems, and opportunities."

Six Steps to Speaking Success

When you speak before an audience, even a small one, the attendees perceive you as having a high level of expertise. Positioning yourself as an easygoing, articulate advisor is a great way to attract prospects to your accounting practice. I have found that there are six keys to success in becoming successful in seminars and speaking engagements:

1. Select the right target audience.
2. Select a topic that communicates benefits.
3. Select a topic that interests you.
4. Cover all of the logistics early.
5. Remember the element of theater.
6. Follow up with every invited guest.

Bill Fingland, managing partner of BKD, says, "I think doing presentations and then following up with audience members is a good use of people time. Any time you prioritize a list, people involvement is number one. The key thing in presentations is the follow-up. Don't just go give a speech and then walk away. Give a speech and make sure that you interact with the group either during the breaks or after the speech. Collect business cards and follow up with phone calls. I want to know who's asking questions, and then I follow up to make sure that I explained it well in the seminar. 'I'm going to be out in your area—why don't I stop by and talk to you about it?' Do those kinds of things.

"Any marketing activity that involves people that's well done has a higher priority in my mind than just the written kinds of brochures and newsletters and advertising."

Select the Right Target Audience

To make your investment in seminars worthwhile, you should target an audience that has the potential to produce profitable business for you. A good way to focus your selection process is to invite or solicit those prospects with the same characteristics as your best clients.

Of course, some CPA firms use seminars to attract prospects from a new market segment. A seminar is a good way for you to acquire visibility and establish expertise. Last year a California CPA firm developed its manufacturing practice in spite of intense competition. Utilizing a seminar program as the centerpiece of its marketing efforts, this firm added over 10 new clients in one year.

Mike Kruse's office specializes in construction clients and gives seminars for them. He says, "When one of my partners appears before a construction trade group, we almost always come away with prospects. Most of our business comes from serving construction businesses and being in front of a group of construction firms is the right audience for us. We have developed a semiannual program for insurance companies and surety agencies. This is where we get most of our referrals. It is very important that you speak to groups that can help you."

Bill Jenkins on the Value of Educational Programs

Bill Jenkins is a big believer in educational programs. He says, "Several things happen in a good education program. One, the people within your firm are being trained—they increase their knowledge and become more sophisticated. Invariably the person who learns the most in any kind of educational setting is the person who is delivering the education, not the person in the audience. The educators not only learn more about the subject, they learn more about how to talk about it, how to express themselves—so it's a great learning experience for the people in the organization.

"From a marketing standpoint, it creates the opportunity for you to show off your knowledge. And, if you do it the right way and people feel like they are learning something from you, then they respect you and your firm. Heck, we all want to learn, and when we learn something from somebody, we hold that person in a higher regard. Educational programs are a natural way to open up doors for people to seek your advice. I still run into people every so often who will refer to something that they heard me say at a seminar several years ago. I want to keep an environment within our client base of 'We need to go to that Kennedy and Co. seminar because we learned something when we went to the last one.' That's the kind of high-level relationship we would like to have with our clients."

In targeting an audience, you'll want to consider the demographic profile of the participants—age, sex, income level, and so forth. It is important for you to know that you are talking to eligible prospects. It is important to know the occupation and industry affiliation of the attendees to insure your topic is relevant—medical professionals and medical administrators are interested in very different issues. Participants' residence could be very important. If you are serving a local or regional client base, you may want to avoid national speaking opportunities. However, even when you don't want to attract clients from a broader geographical base, speaking to regional, state, or national groups is often worthwhile because of the publicity. Your image is enhanced when your clients read in their trade magazines or local papers that you are a featured speaker or seminar giver at the state convention.

Early in your career, you may want to join Toastmasters International. There is a chapter in almost every city in the United States. Toastmasters will help you hone your speaking skills so you are interesting and on point.

Deborah Bailey Browne says, "I think that almost any speaking engagement is a good speaking engagement. Anytime you are able to get in front of a crowd, it gets your name out, it gets you known and people are impressed by people who can speak in front of people. One of the things I've done is chair some nonprofit meetings. Usually nonprofits attract good potential clients. So they have been good for my business."

The Body Language of Public Speaking

If you want to become a good public speaker, watch others to see what they do and how they carry their bodies. For example, I've observed that good public speakers walk with their shoulders back, their heads high, and use a lot of hand and arm gestures. If you are nervous, hold your head up and your shoulders back and say, "I am feeling really good." Silly as this may seem, it actually works. Think of a time when you were feeling very confident and productive in some area in your life. How did you act? How did you walk? How did you talk? It's pretty hard to feel inadequate if you walk and act like you know what you are doing.

—Ken Blanchard[2]

Select a Topic that Communicates One or More Benefits

Have you ever prepared a good seminar, sent out hundreds of invitations, and had almost no one show up? If so, then the problem may have been the attractiveness of your seminar topic.

A person who decides to attend your seminar must believe that his or her investment of time and effort will pay off. And the expected return must be proportional to the investment. Therefore, your seminar must offer real benefits to your target audience.

For example, your topic could be "Section 125 Cafeteria Plans"—but that title, while descriptive, won't even attract your mother! If, instead, you called the seminar "Increase Your Profits Now by Giving Your Employees a Raise," the title spells out two possible benefits.

Advertising whiz Leo Burnett once said, "Don't tell them how good you make the goods, tell them how good the goods will make them." Before you finalize the topic for your seminar, ask yourself, "What benefits could my clients receive?"

Maximize the Effectiveness of Overheads and Slides

Here are a few suggestions to get the most out of overheads and slides:

- *Don't begin or end a talk with overheads unless it's a dazzling montage to get people's attention.*
- *Make one point per slide.*
- *Use as few words as possible in the graphic. This allows you to do the narration to explain it.*
- *Never hand out copies of your presentation in advance. People will read them and not listen to you. Instead, hand them out after it's over as a wrap-up.*
- *Tell people the essence of what's covered on a slide before you show it to them. This puts you more in control as a speaker, not simply someone reading slides.*

—Granville N. Toogood, The Articulate Executive [3]

Bill Jenkins says, "The more our clients know about a particular subject, the more open they are to understanding the need for a consulting service. As a simple example, the more clients know about how the federal estate tax rules work, the more anxious they are to apply what they know and use more of your knowledge to help address that issue. And that is true over and over again, whether it's estate planning or income tax planning. The other thing that education does prior to consulting is substantially shorten the individual sales cycle that is required with a particular client. If they can come to an educational program that Kennedy and Co. does and gain a basic understanding of concepts or some area of our practice, when we want to consult with them we don't have to go back to ground zero each time. It reduces the amount of time it takes to explain to clients why they might benefit from that particular consulting service. The more educated people are, the more consulting services they will buy."

Select a Topic that Interests You

People respond extremely well to an enthusiastic speaker, no matter what the content. Your passion about the subject must come through. No one will enjoy your speech unless you do. Giving a speech on a topic that doesn't interest you will do you more harm than good. Even though you may be tempted to accept the offer of a speech because you will get the exposure, turn it down if you cannot get passionate about the topic.

Terry Orr has had great success in coaching people on how to make presentations to owners of companies seeking financing. It is a subject in which he is extremely knowledgeable and passionate. Mike Kruse speaks to surety agencies on construction industry trends. Greg Anton speaks on SEC issues. These individuals are good business developers because they are knowledgeable and passionate about their topics.

Cover All of the Logistics Early

The myriad of details that come with planning a seminar can be quite extensive, so make sure you use a checklist. Otherwise, you may overlook seemingly trivial but ultimately important details. Consider location and timing early in your seminar planning. Although you want to avoid holidays and any significant local events, you might want to plan your seminar around another event. For example, a Friday afternoon–Saturday morning annual seminar before a major college football rivalry may be a great time to sponsor your industry event.

Timing for your audience is quite important. Bankers generally like breakfast seminars in their own large conference rooms. But attorneys seem to prefer late-afternoon programs that allow them to be in court in the morning.

Almost as important as the subject matter of your talk is the comfort of the room. You must consider temperature, lighting, sound, and potential distractions. I once did a seminar at a beautiful yacht club. Everything went great until about noon, when scantily clad bodies began parading by our windows!

Room temperature is very important. When people are too cold or too hot, they will not pay attention to you. Try to have the room's temperature at exactly 72 degrees if possible.

One of the worst things you can do is dim the lights for a slide presentation. When you do that, the focus goes off of you. Also, dim light tends to make people sleepy. You should be the focus of the program, so keep the lights up. If you are speaking to more than 20 people, or if the ceilings in your room are high, always use a microphone.

Before you begin speaking, make sure that all service personnel are out of the room. Clanging dishes and glasses, and people moving around the room, are distracting for you and your attendees.

If you are going to bring your partners or other personnel, have them prepped on all aspects of your speech. This group makes a great dress-rehearsal audience for you. Coach each person on how to answer different questions that may arise. And have each person from your firm sit with a different segment of the audience. Don't allow your people to sit together.

Bob Gaida recognizes the importance of being in the audience when another firm member is speaking. He says, "I'd rather not be giving the speech; I'd rather be in the room working it and have somebody else giving the speech. When you give a speech or sponsor a seminar, you ought to do your homework. First of all, there are so many opportunities to find out who's going to be there, at least by category. Is it going to be all CPAs? I don't need to go to meetings of CPAs. Shortly before you attend, you can get details on who signed up. Compare the names to your database. For those you don't know, research them. Identify those you think you want to meet. Go in with a team and say, 'Okay, you're going to meet these five people and I'm going to meet these five people tonight.' Keep your focus and get to those five people."

Listen to Yourself

Most people talk in more of a monotone than they realize. Grab a tape recorder and recite something into it. Get crazy with your intonation! Then play the tape back. You might find that it sounds pretty good.

—Art Sobczak, *Telephone Selling Report*[4]

Remember the Element of Theater

In his book *Selling to a Group,* Paul LeRoux[5] says, "Successful seminars walk a fine line between advice and entertainment." Many accounting firms forget this important rule. All too often, a parade of knowledgeable but dull presenters plods to the lectern and reads the latest tax rulings. That's a waste of everyone's time—yours and the attendees. Remember, your audience is conditioned by years of movies and television and expects to be entertained. If you let them down, it will hurt you.

If you are not a showman, give interesting case studies or tell stories. People relate well to stories about situations like theirs. Also, it is much more interesting to tell a story about a client who survived an IRS audit than it is to list the seven tactics for surviving an audit.

Here's another tip: The more you can involve the audience, the more they will like your presentation. Get your audience to stand up, ask questions, or role-play—your audience will stay awake and will be "tuned in" to you. There are wonderful books available to help you select some audience involvement techniques. Games and quizzes are fun. *Games Trainers Play* by John Newstrom and Edward Scannell[6] has hundreds of ideas. Setting up case studies so that your audience gets involved with each other is a great way to keep the session interesting and moving.

Another technique that adds credibility to your presentation is to show that your advice is timely and of national importance. For example, hold up a copy of *The Wall Street Journal* when you quote it. Audiovisuals, presentation technology, and handouts can also be helpful, but just be careful that they don't overpower your presentation.

Another way to keep your audience involved is to talk with them the way you would with your best friend when you are discussing something that really interests you. If there is a gap between the formal way you present to an audience and the way you talk to your friends, use extensive rehearsal to close that gap.

When a show opens on Broadway, there are at least 60 hours of rehearsal behind every performance hour. Your preparation time is the most important aspect of your presentation.

Go for Involvement

Plan to get your audience involved. Give them ways to respond and react. Ask questions and ask for a show of hands. Have them shout out what's important to them about your topic. Gather responses or questions from them.

—Richard L. Hudson, *70 Steps to Speaking Success*[7]

Follow Up with Every Invited Guest

Allan Koltin, president of PDI Global, says, "The purpose of seminars is to create new business, so don't be like the doctor who said the operation was a success, but the patient died." The most important element in making your seminar a sales success is in how you plan to follow up with your new contacts.

At the seminar itself, make sure that every member of your firm's team has an ample supply of business cards and is prepared to schedule follow-up appointments when the opportunity avails itself. You can also follow up with new contacts after the seminar is over. And your efforts need not be "high pressure." For instance, you could call and ask the attendees what they enjoyed about the program. If the contact has some interest in the subject matter—or in your firm—you should be able to detect it.

When you think about how you are going to follow up with your target audience, don't overlook those who did not accept your invitation. After all, your goal isn't to have people come to your seminar—it's to have a marketing interaction with them. So send them a copy of the handouts with a cover note saying you missed them and will be calling soon.

Summary

Those CPAs who only hold a seminar every year or two will have a low marketing return. Like compound interest, as they increase in frequency, seminars have an increasing rate of return. Not only do you become more adept in the organization and presentation of seminars, but your audience will respond to you better.

Some of the most successful seminars my clients have held are those with 5 to 20 participants, held every week or twice a month. Develop a catchy topic, such as "Power Up Your Profits," and invite a small assortment of clients, referral sources, and prospects so that you can meet the attendees personally. Over time, you will be surprised at how good you become in presenting your material.

The other key reason for an increasing success rate from a frequent seminar program is that you capture a share of the mind of your potential clients before their need develops. If a prospect thinks of you first when the need for your service develops, then you have created a competitive advantage.

The CPA who commits to a regular seminar program will become known as a communicator. As our complex business world changes, those who communicate on their feet will have a distinct competitive advantage.

20 Advertising, Publicity, and Brochures

Early to bed, early to rise, work real hard and advertise.
—Advertising slogan

You can spend a lot of money on your marketing and advertising. Often, advertising is the first culprit in eating up your budget. You can advertise online, in newspapers, on TV, in magazines, and so on. Advertising is defined as *paid* mass media exposure; publicity, however, is *free* exposure in the same places. However, it can cost you a lot to arrange, especially if you hire a PR firm. Brochures are another costly sales tool. They mainly demonstrate that you are established, but seldom do they actively sell for you.

Is spending money on advertising, publicity, and brochures worth the cost? Sometimes yes; often no (compared to your personal sales efforts). To prove the power of advertising, a magazine salesperson said, "If you don't believe that people read your ads, then give away $10 to everyone who brings in your ad." During the years I spent in the advertising business, our sales team wasn't able to convince any of our clients to do this. However, a fine clothing store did agree to give away a man's tie to everyone who brought in its ad. Result: over 2,000 ties given away from a magazine with 25,000 circulation, an 8 percent "pull rate." An 8 percent response rate on any type of ad campaign is extraordinary. Usually, a pull rate of over 2 percent is very good. Many campaigns are successful with less than one-tenth of 1 percent response rate.

Advertising and public relations can be helpful in the promotion of a CPA firm's services. But rarely will you want to give away a free tax return to all responders to your advertising. Some accountants are uncomfortable with the idea of advertising—but for the wrong reasons. They are uncomfortable because they don't like sales and marketing in general. The real reason to be uncomfortable with advertising is that you pay first and only later find out if you will get results. It is easy to squander large sums of money in advertising campaigns that miss the mark.

The reason some firms use advertising regularly is because it is easier to write a check than to think out their marketing. Salespeople are constantly calling on you to advertise in the local paper, the trade magazines, radio, charity events, and so on. It's all deductible and they design the ad for you for "free," so why not? Because you not only waste money, but you generally don't track and repeat successful ads. When you don't know how effective each ad is, you're wasting your money. Even more, most firms don't know what their prime sales message is or whom they are trying to reach. Another problem with advertising is the popularity of "image advertising" over the last 20 years and "branding" during the last decade.

I am very skeptical about the results accounting firms will achieve with branding. Hundreds of millions of dollars are being spent annually to brand professional services firms. I believe that the senior management at many accounting firms has put too much faith in image advertising. Don't get me wrong: Some advertising is useful. But, for accountants, most marketing and sales budgets should focus on personal one-on-one involvement with clients and prospects. Blasting hyperbole about yourself through advertising doesn't build trust.

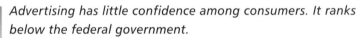

Advertising has little confidence among consumers. It ranks below the federal government.

—Hal Quinley of Yankelovich Partners, discussing the results of a consumer survey about advertising

Dick Reck[1] says, "The national firms are investing in advertising that is a total waste of money—and you can quote me on that. Not one person will buy one hour of service from them because of the advertising campaigns. I mean, these people are making decisions on idiotic stuff. When I walk out of the airport in Reno to go skiing, there are three of these airport signs sitting there—one of them is a casino, the next one is a Big Five firm, and the third is some local whorehouse. That's what greeted me on the wall. I just sit there and shake my head."

Use Advertising to Build Awareness

Although there are many who will disagree with me, I believe the primary purpose of advertising and public relations is to allow people to become aware that you exist. If prospects are aware that you exist, there is a small chance they will call you. The best situation occurs when you or one of your partners meets a person for the first time, and that person says, "Oh, yeah, I've heard of your firm."

Jack Amundson[2] says, "You need to have community awareness of who you are. Some level of advertising or public relations will be helpful for any significant accounting firm." Awareness makes people much more receptive to you.

Marketing expert Seth Godin says, "For ninety years, marketers have relied on one form of advertising almost exclusively. I call it Interruption Marketing. Interruption, because the key to each and every ad is to interrupt what the viewers are doing in order to get them to think about something else." In his Internet work, Godin advocates "permission marketing" in which you ask potential respondents if they want to hear from you. It's a very professional way to start a relationship using any medium. (For more details, see the Day 8 chapter on permission marketing.)

Seven Reasons Why You Need Free Publicity

1 Publicity establishes credibility about you and your products or services.

2 It enhances customer retention.

3 It makes it easier for you to enter new markets.

4 It creates a competitive advantage.

5 It helps to position your products or services in your target markets.

6 It helps you sell more.

7 The price is right. It's practically free!

—Adapted from Rick Crandall, *Celebrate Marketing: Secrets of Success*[3]

Public Relations

Public relations (PR) activities are a bit more subtle than advertising. Public relations activities, such as sending out press releases and writing articles, result in free media exposure for you. Examples of PR are a mention in the newspaper that you have become a partner in your firm; a local radio station interviewing you as an expert for an end-of-year story on ways to save on taxes; or a column that you write that is published in a trade magazine.

Most PR is through the print media, so I'll refer to the recipients of your PR as readers, although they could also be online users or radio listeners or television viewers. With PR, readers are pulled into your article in the natural course of their reading a newspaper or magazine, so they don't experience the feeling of being interrupted as they do with advertising. Readers perceive articles placed by a PR activity as more believable than advertising and will stay with those articles longer than the same articles run as ads.

Even though you don't pay for print space or radio or TV time with PR, PR does have a cost. In many cases, companies spend a great deal more on specialized PR agents than they would on advertising. However, you can obtain effective, low-cost PR yourself by writing articles, giving talks, and participating in community activities.

Advertising, public relations, and other marketing materials are often thought of as ways to attract new clients to your firm. In many cases, they have a much greater impact. Advertising and PR can favorably impact current clients by reinforcing their decision to hire your firm in the first place. Both advertising and PR also can build morale for your employees.

Brochures

Brochures, flyers, and other sales materials are important sales aids. These materials help imprint your message in the mind of your employees, clients, and prospects. Good sales materials enable you to reinforce your personal sales message. They demonstrate to your prospects that you have a well-organized service offering. They also give you confidence during a presentation.

Note, however, that brochures and similar sales literature seldom close the sale for you. Although they are useful tools for personal sales, they should not become "excuse crutches." Many times prospects ask you to send them something or to leave a brochure for them to study. Often this is just an excuse to not talk with you and give your service serious consideration. Many accountants who are uncomfortable with selling end up merely passing out brochures without making a serious sales effort. Don't use your sales literature this way.

Preparing an effective brochure is a task for a good marketing person. You must insure the brochure appeals to both the creative and the logical side of the brain. Therefore, you must insist there is a balance between design and copy. All your materials should be designed around a consistent theme, typeface, and color scheme.

Too often, accountants fill their brochures with heavy copy detailing all the features of their service offerings. I have found a good rule to follow in writing copy is to lead with possible client benefits, then follow with the detailed features. (See the example below.)

Sample Feature-Oriented Text for a Brochure

Providing our clients peace of mind, convenience, and assurance

Clients of ABC CPAs receive peace of mind knowing that the professionals who are preparing your returns are highly trained in all aspects of the tax law, rules and regulations. Many times, we have found that our partners have more knowledge of and training in the tax law than do the auditors from the IRS. You will gain peace of mind by knowing that you are not just another number with us. Each client receives highly personalized attention.

We know that many of our clients have the intellectual capability to prepare a tax return. But in today's competitive and fast-paced business world, it just doesn't make sense for you to spend an inordinate amount of time doing something we could accomplish much more quickly. While we are preparing your return, you can focus on your business. This creates a win-win situation for everyone.

Knowing you are receiving expert tax advice from CPAs will give you the assurance you need to know it is done right. You will also have the confidence of knowing that if the IRS does audit your return, we will be by your side.

When preparing brochures, follow a well-tested budgeting process: Allocate about 40 percent of your resources to design, about 40 percent to copy, and about 20 percent to printing.

Your Budget for Advertising, PR, and Marketing Tools

Generally, I recommend that no more than 20 percent of a firm's marketing budget be invested in advertising, public relations, and marketing tools. As mentioned in the Day 1 chapter, advertising alone should be less than 10 percent. Bill Fingland says, "I would place people involvement as the most important marketing tool and advertisements of a general nature at the bottom. But we do a little bit of all of it." So, a $5 million accounting practice that invests 4 percent in marketing ($200,000) should spend no more than about $40,000 in these tools. (See the Day 29 chapter for more on developing the marketing budget.)

An advertising budget of $40,000 will not make much of an impact in any market. Therefore, smart CPAs invest very carefully and wisely in advertising.

Waugh's 11 Rules of CPA Advertising

1 Never run just one ad.

2 Beware of special advertising promotions.

3 Use cost per prospect as your evaluation tool.

4 Focus on targeted advertising and public relations media.

5 Limit yellow pages advertising.

6 Use a professional design firm.

7 Use evidence.

8 Focus on benefits.

9 Seek electronic over print media.

10 Seek public relations over advertising.

11 Once your PR story comes out, send reprints to clients and prospects.

Never Run Just One Ad

People are influenced by advertising mostly through repetition. Running an ad just one time will not provide you the compound effect of repetition. If you plan to advertise in a magazine, your return will be greater if you run a smaller ad more times than if you run a larger ad once. Rather than a one-time full-page ad, consider running a quarter-page ad 4 times or a classified ad 12 times. The same holds true for radio and television advertising.

Beware of Special Advertising Promotions

CPAs and other business owners are easy prey for advertising salespeople. The pitch goes something like this: "Our newspaper is running an annual spotlight on CPAs next month and you will be listed in the Top 50 accounting firms in your market. Let's design you an ad for the facing page." The problem with these types of promotions is that only CPAs and people who want to sell stuff to CPAs read these special inserts. Schools and charities are notorious for hitting you up for once-a-year ads. If you want to make a contribution, okay. But don't think you are advertising.

Use Cost Per Prospect as Your Evaluation Tool

Good advertising salespeople will supply you with demographics for their audiences. Generally they will calculate the cost per thousand (cpm) or cost per reader. Some media salespeople will impress you with their "pass along" (how many people read the publication in addition to the subscribers). When evaluating these investments, you must be very careful. Say a magazine has a circulation of 30,000 and a two-to-one pass-along factor, the salesperson might tell you that for a $3,000 ad, you can reach 90,000 people. He might show you a calculation that shows you can reach his readership for 3.3 cents each. That is an excellent price for advertising directly to clients and prospects of your firm. But you need to take into account that most advertising media are being viewed by people who are not prospects or clients. If 29,000 of the subscribers in this example are not prospects, you may be paying from $1 to $3 per prospect. That is an extremely high rate. For $1 to $3 per person, you can use direct mail or other forms of communication.

Focus on Targeted Advertising and PR Media

If you focus your practice on medical professionals, doesn't it make sense to advertise primarily in medical newsletters and magazines in your community? Invest your advertising and promotion in activities that are most likely to reach your potential prospects and clients. If you are active in a trade association, placing advertisements in the organization's monthly newsletter is an excellent method to promote your involvement.

David Morgan says, "I can't say that we got a client because they saw our ad in the *Nashville Business Journal*. I do believe we have higher name recognition because we consistently advertise in the *Business Journal*. We did get a client because we ran an ad in a medical newsletter. Because it was a focused industry for us, we wanted to get in it. That got us recognition, which got us in the door, and we got a client."

Some CPA firms have developed radio and television advertising programs. These work very well when they are focused on your prospective clients. Programs like *MoneyLine* on CNN or *Marketplace* on NPR may target the audience you want. For many of these national shows, you can buy ads that are transmitted only to your local area.

Limit Yellow Pages Advertising

In recent years, yellow pages and directory advertising has exploded. Sometimes a single community has three or four yellow pages opportunities. Ask yourself, "Will the prospect I get from the yellow pages really be a choice client for me?" In most cases, your answer will be no. The yellow pages are important so people can find your phone number, but they are poor for finding prospects whom you'd consider to be 10s. Most CPAs are very dissatisfied with the high cost and low effectiveness of yellow pages advertising. That is because yellow pages advertising doesn't create desire on the part of the client.

Never direct people to look you up in the yellow pages. When you do so, people will check out your competitors at the same time. Instead, have your phone number and address on every ad, brochure, and article you write.

Use a Professional Design Firm

"Art is in the eye of the beholder." Whenever you are advertising, it is crucial that you don't come across as "low class." A professional design firm may not know your services and may not be able to write copy, but it usually knows the latest in graphic design and has the skills to execute it.

Some people who could become your clients are left-brained—very logical and factual. These people are impressed with lots of strong words, facts, and support. Other prospects are more right-brained—creative and emotional. To make your advertising effective, it is crucial to appeal to both sides of the brain. A professional design firm can help tap into your viewers' emotions.

Focus on Benefits

Remember, your prospective client is purchasing a set of benefits from you: tax savings, peace of mind, financing, convenience, status, and so forth. For your ads and publicity to be most effective, they must stress the potential benefits. Ads that stress features (i.e., number of partners, staff, and offices) are the least effective.

Use Evidence

Testimonials or stories of clients receiving benefits are some of the most successful advertising and publicity messages. They are almost as powerful as a third-party personal referral. Bob Gaida says, "Third-party testimonials are like a nuclear blast while generic advertising is like a hand grenade."

Seek Electronic over Print Media

Most people are receiving information electronically today. It is crucial for you to seek to use electronics for your advertising and PR as much as possible. Some possibilities are: your own Web page (see the Day 21 chapter for more on this), "telephone on hold," audiotapes, videotapes, and radio and television. Television advertising can be very effective and at lower cost than you might think. You can purchase TV spots on selected cable networks for less than 5 percent of what you would spend on a local channel.

Seek Public Relations over Advertising

Bill Fingland says, "I think advertisements, as far as newspaper ads and radio ads and those kinds of things, are not very effective in selling professional services. That doesn't mean you are not going to sell something. That just means there are better ways to spend your resources. We send press releases and advertise for name recognition in industry specialty journals. But the purpose of that is not to try to sell a service, but to get the new logo exposed and get name recognition."

There are a number of very creative ways to obtain public relations. One of the most powerful ways is to network with the business press in your market. In most markets, the business press is a very small group of people. If you network with the people who cover the business community, you will get mentioned and interviewed in their pieces. Suggest that the press do a story on one of your interesting clients. Invite the press to your seminars or presentations. Keep them informed of national trends in the accounting industry.

Regular press releases can be cost effective. Potential clients learn of your firm. Existing clients may be favorably impressed. You can develop your image and credibility in the community. They may also improve staff morale.

An effective press release might include a relevant event that is newsworthy. Such events might include staff promotions or new hires, merger of firm, a new client, a clever interpretation of a particular rule, your trade show or industry attendance, or your CPE attendance.

Always keep press releases simple and to the point. If possible, include a black-and-white photo of a person. Photos add interest. Don't send color photos to publications that are printed in black and white, because color photos do not reprint well. (However, do send color photos to those publications that use them.)

Many editors are constantly seeking articles for their publications. Editors hire writers for most of the articles, and often the writers are not well versed in business subjects. Thus, editors may prefer to use a well-known and respected professional. If you are not well known, write a few articles in the business press and you will become famous.

When you get a good story, send a thank-you note to the reporter and the reporter's editor. This happens so seldom that reporters won't forget.

—Lorraine Kingdon, *Take the Mystery Out of Media*

Articles for publication can be difficult to write. If you have a staff member who is a great writer, ask him or her to cowrite an article with you quarterly or monthly. If you have developed a good network of business writers, ask one of them for help in writing. You may be referred to an excellent freelance writer who can talk with you and write the article. Have non-CPAs (your spouse, your receptionist, a friend) read your articles. What is a simple concept to you is not simple to a layperson.

If you utilize any of the geographically protected newsletter programs from Pencor or PDI, you may be able to arrange for publication rights in your market. Arranging for publication rights will allow you to submit the article with your byline to publications within your protected territory.

Once Your PR Story Comes Out, Send Reprints to Clients and Prospects

You can benefit more from printed PR after it comes out than immediately. When you send a clipping about you or by you out to prospects and clients, it builds your credibility and name recognition.

Summary

Marketing authority David Maister says "I think the branding that is going on among professional services firms is b.s. I think it's a complete waste of money. Branding should distinguish two things: brand recognition and brand value. All this advertising crap they are doing will help brand recognition, I'll concede that, but not a lot. The real question is, 'Does anybody value the stuff? Will anybody pay more?' Your brand is not what you claim. Your brand is what you enforce."

Advertising and public relations use the media to transmit your message to prospects and clients. Whether online or in the newspaper, exposure will benefit your marketing program. Be careful of the many opportunities to advertise that are "sold at" you. Don't place an ad just because someone makes it easy for you. Free publicity takes more time to get, but is much more effective.

21 Online Marketing and Technology Consulting

The Internet allows information to be distributed worldwide at basically zero cost.

—Bill Gates[1]

The Internet as a marketing tool is now mainstream as large companies utilize its capabilities to grow their businesses. As far back as 2000, Dell Computer sold $45 million of its products and services *each day* online.

Many CPA firms have tried Internet marketing strategies. Electronic commerce will continue to grow in importance, and savvy CPAs will learn to use online tools to build and promote their businesses. This chapter will help you develop a sensible framework for online marketing and will lead you to deeper resources for further thought and action.

A good electronic-commerce selling strategy has the same strengths as any other good marketing strategy. You must first focus on serving your clients in better, more meaningful ways. Your Web site allows you to provide everything from staff bios to white papers as references for prospects and resources for clients. Communicating with clients via e-mail is a powerful tool. Transmitting files, general ledgers, check runs, and analyses online is a smart and efficient way to work with clients in the new electronic-media world. If you meet with a prospect and cannot discuss your ability to do this, you will be at a major disadvantage.

Client Services Online

There are an endless number of ways to serve your clients more thoroughly using the Internet. For example, a search on google.com on "reminder system" will provide free and other software that will remind you of important dates. You could set up a similar system for your clients, where you would remind them of important tax deposit and filing deadlines. This system could be the basis for a personalized e-mail newsletter. Such a reminder system would be a way to have additional interactions with your clients. Via such a system, you could also keep your clients updated on relevant products and services that you want to cross-sell.

Jim Belew, whom we met in Day 3, has been using the Internet for some time, along with the rest of his firm. He says, "We work internationally through many of our Horwath affiliates. The Internet has helped us serve our clients by putting them directly in touch with someone in Europe, Asia, or Australia who may be able to help. Most of those areas are in significantly different time zones. We can communicate during our working hours and they can respond during theirs. Also, being able to check tax and financial information available through our worldwide organization has been powerful to many of our clients."

David Morgan, whom we met in Day 1, uses his Web site to work with clients. He says, "I'm real excited about our Web strategy. For one thing, we've pulled all the affiliates together on the front page to make it easy to get to all of our different businesses. One of our differentiators is our broad range of services. We are going to an electronic newsletter. Sending out what we call our 'e-alerts' is a little teaser to come to our Web site. The main information will be on the Web site. There are also links to other information that our clients will find interesting, so we're moving rapidly to the Internet to disperse information to our clients."

You can also have client financial statements, tax returns, and other data online so the CPA and client can view the documents together, real time and online.

 The consensus is strong that relationship marketing will thrive on the Net thanks to its speed, low cost, and convenience.

—*Direct* magazine

Your primary goal in any online strategy is to make it easy for your clients to work with you. In their book *Customers.Com*, Patricia Seybold and Ronni Marshak recommend that you invest "at least 50% of your IT [information technology] dollars in making it easy for customers to do business with you." Seybold and Marshak cite five customer fundamentals:

1. Don't waste our time.
2. Remember who we are.
3. Make it easy for us to order and obtain service.

4. Make sure your service delights us.

5. Customize your products and services for me.

How do you obtain full value from your online strategy? The only way I know is to meet with your most important clients and representatives from your other clients and quiz them on ways you could design your Web and Internet strategy to make it easier for them to do business with you.

Bill Fingland is guiding his firm to use the Internet more: "Let me give you an example. Not having e-mail would show a lack of technological capability which would be a disadvantage in the marketing process. But most everybody now has e-mail. Now look at our small business service clients—they want us to have the capability of downloading checks over the Internet so they don't have to send us their checks and have us re-enter them. Then go one further step—which we do, by the way. We are interacting with our clients over the Internet relative to 401(k) and other employee benefit plans we administer. The clients' employees can log onto the Web site and get their account balances, after going through certain security measures."

Industries and businesses that must operate in the marketplace of free choice know that they must change, they must adapt, they must accommodate to changes in public attitudes—or they will surely die.

—William D. Ruckelshaus[2]

David Morgan says that his firm has been able to assist on major litigation or other analysis matters by working with firms on the other side of the globe. He says, "We can scan documents or FedEx them. Very good accountants in India can analyze the information during our nighttime. Then we can present the product to our client the next morning. This is awesome client service."

Great businesses have been built during the last few decades by using technology to serve clients better. H&R Block used technology to capture nearly a billion dollars of tax return business on which CPAs were losing money. ADP, Paychex, and others have some of the most rapidly growing businesses processing routine payroll transactions. You can be sure that some of the major players are readying a strategy to reach the heart of your business—the owner-managed business, with sales of $1 million to $100 million.

Internet researchers are thinking about how to attract your clients to their firms and provide services you can provide. Can they involve your clients in frequent user clubs? Can they disconnect clients from you and reconnect those clients into their communities? Who knows if the players on the scene will be the successful ones? But, count on it, there are online experts lusting after your clients.

> *Too often technology is perceived as the problem rather than the solution; as something to be avoided rather than embraced. This is about as logical as my daughter's observing, while our family was driving through an unfamiliar city: "Trying to read a map while driving causes all the traffic lights to turn green."*
>
> —Norman Augustine[3]

Recruiting Online

Some of the most important marketing a CPA firm does is recruiting. Obtaining the best resources to provide your clients with high-level, uninterrupted service is crucial to any firm staying in business today. Low-tech firms that are not using the Internet will be at an increasing disadvantage as more experienced people become techno-savvy.

College students have used the Internet for many years to search for employment and to research prospective employers. Have you had a serious candidate interview you in the last few years who hasn't seen your Web site? Have you seen theirs? Most candidates have personal Web sites, and you can learn a great deal about them by reviewing their Web sites before the visit. Most of all, you will impress the students that you took the time to check them out.

Bill Fingland believes in the power of the Internet for recruiting. He said, "I think the most important marketing that we do on the Internet is recruiting. And I think recruiting is marketing and selling. Using your farming analogy, the only difference between recruiting for people and recruiting for clients is growing beans or corn. They are both the same processes. For us to get the best clients, we must have the best people. The Internet is a critical ingredient of our recruiting process."

Developing Community with Your Referral Sources and End Users

Some of the best referral sources for CPA firms are end users of your products. End users might be investment bankers, surety agents, or commercial bankers. An online strategy for your referral sources will encourage them to refer you more. For example, online financial statements will allow you to richly communicate with clients and bankers when all three of you may be in different cities. Bankers who experience such an event will rave to other bankers and prospects about your capability.

Prospecting and Selling Online

Success in the online marketplace isn't a sure thing . . . [but] nothing we've seen so far comes close to its potential.

— *Guerrilla Marketing on the Internet*[4]

Just as people do not want junk mail, they seem to hate junk e-mail—"spam"—as well. Spam is uninvited e-mail. Many people have told me that they hate all that spam littering their e-mail systems. Yet it is tempting to e-mail prospects your solicitation or newsletter. After all, it doesn't cost you anything more to send 10,000 e-mails than it does to send 10. Anything that inexpensive is attractive to a good business marketer.

As discussed in the Day 8 chapter, in his book Permission Marketing, Seth Godin describes how to develop good online relationships. Just as in face-to-face relationship building, you must be willing to invest to get something in return. Godin recommends that you give something away free to prospects who meet your criteria and will provide you with some information about themselves. In your case, it could be a free subscription to your firm's newsletter. It could be a special report you have prepared. The concept of permission marketing basically is an ever-increasing give-and-get relationship with a prospect until the prospect "holds up his hand," Godin says. Two advantages to any online marketing strategy are that it is both customizable and interactive. You can provide your clients with custom date reminders, custom newsletters, and custom services. Then the clients or prospects can interact with you in a much richer environment of collaboration and communication. You can communicate with clients 24 hours a day, in a way that is convenient for both of you.

Building a beautiful Web site and then not marketing it properly is like building an incredibly elaborate billboard and putting it in your basement.

—John Audette[5]

Technology Consulting

CPA firms throughout the world are facing opportunities in technology consulting. Some of the opportunities are overwhelming, a bit like trying to take a sip of water from a fire hydrant. The market for high-tech services offered by CPAs is unlimited. But the challenge is in making a profit for both you and your clients.

Only a few firms are creating significant profits from technology services. Some firms are creating high revenue, but still earning low or negative margins. Many firms have yet to try their hands at helping clients with technology. Other firms are losing big bucks in high-tech endeavors. Some badly burned CPAs say, "Never again." No matter what type of firm you represent, this section will help you align your services package for maximum impact for your clients and profitability for you.

CPA firms are naturals for technology consulting. CPAs are the most-trusted business advisors. CPAs understand the financial transaction side of business and how business owners make decisions. "Techies" understand the hardware and software but may struggle with business applications.

With high tech such an overwhelming market and with the unique positioning of CPAs, why do so many firms make low or no profits from technology consulting? Having consulted with dozens of CPA firms experiencing these challenges, I have learned some dos and don'ts. They can help you be more successful.

Six Do's for Successful Technology Consulting

1. Decide on your business strategy.

Do you tell your clients that you are in the relationship business, then come across like a used computer salesperson? Naturally, there will be a "disconnect" with you, your staff, and your clients when you use two or more business strategies. Most accounting firms are relationship oriented. When you are relationship oriented, you will not be able to lead the competition on price or product quality.

If customer intimacy (relationships) is your business strategy, then you must say to your client: "We may not have the lowest price and we may not have the latest doodad, but we will serve more of your needs in a more effective manner." Service packages that fit this strategy might include technology assessments, tech plans, request-for-proposal design, disaster recovery planning, software compliance, accounting and cost system design, financial and stakeholder information systems designs, EDI (Electronic Data Interchange), security, and technology utilization studies. Pick areas you are already strong in. Don't try to do everything.

And remember, since relationships are your business, don't let your computer experts talk you into one-time engagements. Relationships are ongoing, not hit and run.

2. Develop a team approach and have people with consulting and business savvy lead and manage the effort.

Gary Boomer of Boomer Consulting says, "To run a successful computer consulting business, you need four mentalities: a business consultant, a salesperson, a teacher, and a strong computer expert." Perhaps a couple of these mind-sets can be resident in one person, but usually one person cannot be all of the things you need to have a fully functioning consulting business.

Be wary of computer people who cannot communicate with you in layman's terms. They will not communicate with your clients any better!

Boomer goes on to recommend that you build a team of individuals with outstanding and unique abilities. Team members with the leadership and relationship skills should come from inside your firm, but other team members can be either on your payroll or on someone else's.

The team member who fulfills the business consultant role is crucial to the interface with the client and the leadership of the consulting team. Usually, sending your business consultant to perform teaching or technical work is not effective. Rarely do the consultants or the salespeople devote the time to deep technical proficiency.

The technical experts are the ones who will assure that applications perform as promised. But technical experts rarely have the business acumen or personal communication skills to help clients strategize or the patience to teach clients how to use systems and software. Without good teachers, clients' utilization of new systems will be difficult at best, or will fail. Teachers have the step-by-step knowledge and patience to help clients learn systems and software at each client's own pace.

When starting a technology consulting practice, many CPA firms try to use the in-house network administrator to lead the consulting practice for clients. This is a big mistake. Begin the consulting practice with a business consultant with technology knowledge. This leader should develop alliances with specific technology experts both inside and outside your firm. As the technology practice grows, you can be selective as to whom and what applications you bring into your firm.

3. Hire people with integrity.

Someone once said, "To err is human, to really foul things up, you need a computer person." *Trust* is at the heart of your client relationships. Many computer people are prone to overpromise and underdeliver. Most of us have heard or experienced horror stories of great client relationships being ripped apart when a firm tries to "help" with a client's computer installation.

By the same token, the CPA must understand and be willing to accept the fact that computer hardware and software are always "under construction." Systems and software will not be error free. Therefore, you must manage expectations and be prepared for the normal debugging process.

The computer industry has its share of technical geniuses who lack basic integrity. Many of them think nothing of cost overruns, delays, and inoperative systems. Some will even "infect" clients' systems with secret codes that will prevent other technicians from working on the computers. We have all heard the stories of entire computer departments leaving in the middle of the night to open their own shops in competition with the CPA firm that helped them start. Also, the industry has its share of hobbyists who sometimes try to appear as businesspeople. So, be very careful when selecting the people who work in your computer-consulting department: Look for basic integrity.

4. Develop standardized processes and systems.

To become an expert in anything, one must focus. Installing MAS 90 today, Medical Manager tomorrow, and Peachtree the next day is a sure road to poor performance. The firms that select a high-demand service to apply throughout the client base are the ones that most often succeed. This is why deciding on your business strategy is the first step.

Performing independent computer assessments and helping with technology planning, for instance, are compatible and similar services to auditing, accounting, and tax planning. These services can be standardized, render great client value, let you profit, and help you avoid many of the pitfalls of hardware and software installation and service.

5. Become a model in the use of technology and invest in training.

Training, not CPE, is crucial. The acronym PEBKAC stands for Problem Exists between Keyboard and Chair. If your firm is full of PEBKACs, you cannot model the use of good technology.

Ron Eagle, former managing director of the MCS department of Olive, a large Indianapolis accounting firm, says, "A firm that promotes the effective use of technology must itself use the technology." If your partners and staff members are lagging in the use of technology, you will not have credibility with your clients. You will be better off developing a strategic alliance with another firm that can model the use of the systems you recommend than trying to implement systems you do not use.

6. Focus on progress, not perfection.

Computer experts agree that the perfect system has yet to be invented. If you wait for all the bugs to be worked out before you attempt to make progress, you will fall farther behind. Gary Boomer has coined the phrase, "Let's focus on progress, not perfection." CPAs need to heed this savvy rule.

Four Don'ts of Technology Consulting

1. Don't select a business strategy for technology consulting that is incongruent with your firm.

You must operate to help your clients succeed first. If you profit as a result of clients' successes, then you have the right formula for long-term success.

If your primary motive is profit, you can easily be attracted to a business strategy that will pull and tug at the very fabric of your firm. Oftentimes incongruent business strategies will lead to firm breakups, lost and unhappy clients, broken trust, and bad publicity. This can happen in the largest and the smallest situations.

Some firms have developed a business strategy for technology that will attract different clients from those the CPA firm can serve. Unless your firm markets to upgrade the client list to include the new technology customers, the one-shot engagements will be high cost and low (or no) profits.

The best implementation strategy will develop deep communication and trust among your accounting and tax partners and senior management and the technology consultants. Separating the consultants from your accounting firm (to do their "own thing") may not be in the best interests of your clients' success. When you violate the principle of "clients' success creates profits for us," you are entering a high-risk and low-payoff arena.

2. Don't bill by the hour.

Focus on the value your client is receiving from your services, and you will be able to deliver higher value for the client and more profit for your firm. CPA firms that bill technology services by the hour must produce hours to be profitable. Those that focus on value-billing will produce value for the client and for themselves. Ron Baker, CPA and consultant, says, "When CPAs focus on effort rather than value, both the client and the CPA lose. Technology consulting offers CPAs a tremendous opportunity to add value. Why ignore the opportunity by focusing on effort?"

3. Don't forget to manage the consulting process.

Technology consulting requires a different management style from that used by traditional CPA firms. Charge hours per year are usually less because of the enormous training and selling time required. Good technology consultants command premium salaries. When you combine training expenses, lower charge hours, and higher salaries, you face the need for premium billing rates and management's attention to downtime and cost overruns. Due to the fact that many computer experts are hobbyists, management must continually help refocus team members' efforts on the business. Without careful management, losses can mount in a technology consulting practice very quickly.

Know Your Customer's Techno-Rating

Dell Computer classifies customers so that they know better how to deal with them:

- **Techno-Wizard:** *Most interested in being on the leading edge of all new technology.*

- **Techno-to-Go:** *Just wants the computer to come out of the box and work without any hassles; they worry about not having enough hand-holding from technical support.*

- **Techno-Boomer:** *Wants to be and look intelligent; they do a lot of research before purchasing, sometimes putting off the purchase because they worry about making the right decision.*

- **Techno-Teamer:** *Is going to be plugged into the office network, so the biggest concerns involve network failure.*

- **Techno-Critical:** *Uses the computer as the lifeblood of the business. Biggest fear is system failure.*

- **Techno-Phobe:** *Rejects technology altogether. It would be hard to sell techno-phobes a computer.*

---

4. Don't become the low-margin sales force for a high-margin manufacturer.

Some of the VAR (value-added reseller) contracts offered to CPAs are downright laughable. Manufacturers can make up to 90 percent marginal profit on a new software sale. Some of them will leave it up to you to explain to your client why it costs $5,000 to properly install and customize the $600 software package. This is a tough sale. In addition, many manufacturers charge premium prices for training and for firms to become certified to sell their products. You will be better off refusing to represent manufacturers and software developers who use your client-trust bond to gain access to your clients. Seek out developers who will treat you fairly.

Hardware manufacturers give the best prices to volume buyers. If you are a boutique, superstores' retail prices will be lower than your wholesale price.

CPA firms that clear 8 to 12 percent gross margin find it very difficult to have profits show on the bottom line.

Summary

To stay competitive, you need to use technology in your marketing and practice. Although technology has a cost, it also gives you new services to sell.

Technology options are flooding the world. Many of your clients are bewildered by all the choices, opportunities, and dynamics offered by their computer systems. Many clients have a hodgepodge of software and hardware and are using only a fraction of the power at their fingertips. These forces are creating an environment for the most trusted business advisor, the CPA, to bring credibility and reason to an industry that is exploding. Inefficient utilization, business applications, new accounting systems, and good planning and execution are all fabulous opportunities for the CPA to participate in the ever-expanding technology revolution.

22 Working with the Professionals

People who truly are effective have the humility to recognize their own perceptual limitations and to appreciate the rich resources available through interaction with the hearts and minds of other human beings.

—Stephen R. Covey[1]

If the CPAs in your firm don't particularly like marketing and sales, it's logical to hire marketing help. After all, if other people can bring in a wide variety of work, you can spend more time selecting and doing the type of work you like. Unfortunately, most CPA firms don't use marketing and salespeople very well.

Marketing and salespeople tend to be creative, outgoing, aggressive, persuasive, and quick to act. CPAs are usually more deliberative, cautious, and introverted. Although these personality types complement each other's weaknesses, they often cause conflict. These differences, and the difficulties they cause, are natural and should be planned for as part of engaging a marketing person for your firm.

The conservative CPA and the creative marketing director are prone to frequent and volatile collisions. In the best of cases, smoldering beneath the surface are the doubts and fears that accountants and marketing support personnel have about each other.

A veteran marketing director lamented: "My managing partner is not a leader. How am I going to get my ideas implemented if I can't get a decision out of him? He always seems suspicious of my recommendations. When we finally do start a program, he wants a payback next week. If the payback doesn't come, he wants to pull the plug and rethink our marketing approach."

On the other side, a managing partner said of his marketing director: "I don't know what she does all day. My partners are glad she is here, but she hasn't brought in any business yet. She turns her time sheet in late and she is always wanting to spend money."

It is clear that both of these people need to gain some understanding of the other. It is pretty difficult to value the differences in business style when they aren't clearly understood.

Anecdotal evidence bantered around the Association for Accounting Marketing is that the average life of a marketing coordinator or director is about 13 months. For both the CPA and the marketing professional, this is a tremendous waste of investment. Marketing support personnel are excellent resources for accounting firms, as they are for any business. According to Art Bowman, firms that utilize the services of marketing personnel grow faster than ones who do not. In his *1999 Special Report on the Bowman Top 100* firms, Bowman reported that firms who use marketing professionals grew 14.5 percent, compared to 11.2 percent growth at firms with no marketing specialist on staff.

Clarify and Agree on Roles

One reason why accountants and marketing/sales people don't always get along is the lack of clarity about what marketing people can do. Generally they *cannot* sell your services. People who want to hire you want to have a relationship with *you*. You would not have your secretary hire a lawyer for you; why do you think anyone would hire you by proxy?

Marketing and sales people can produce marketing collateral. They can handle the logistics of seminars and newsletters. They can produce leads— prospects. They can research possible clients. They can edit articles for you. They can develop ads and obtain publicity. They can manage your Web site. They may even be able to train you and your staff on customer service or sales. *But they aren't you!*

Ultimately, your prospects and customers want to judge you and how you'll work with them. They want to know that you are informed about their industry and issues and can communicate with them. They even want to know that you care about them! For instance, one big firm in California decided to do a seminar for prospects. The firm arranged a two-day golf outing at Pebble Beach and lodging at a five-star hotel. The seminar was aimed at top high-tech CEOs and cost several thousand dollars. Because the accountants didn't want to take the time to invite their contacts personally, they decided to leave it up to the marketing people, who mailed invitations to lists of people, such as subscribers to *Forbes* magazine.

Although the idea was interesting, not one of the several thousand executives who received the mailing signed up. If you're going to commit a weekend to a new firm, you generally want to talk to a *person*, even if the golf and accommodations are great. The event flopped, costing tens of thousands of dollars even though it wasn't run. The professionals abdicated responsibility and never should have run the event unless they were sure they could personally obtain enough people to make it work.

 People don't care how much you know until they know how much you care.

— Ken Blanchard, *The One Minute Manager*[2]

Using marketing and salespeople properly takes awareness and planning. You wouldn't buy a computer and program and deliver them without training to someone who'd never used that system. You need to train yourself to use marketing help effectively, and you need to make sure you have the right person who can work with you.

Lou Mills, whom we met in Day 9, began hiring solid marketing support personnel a few years ago. He says, "When I originally hired our marketing manager, it was for outside sales to generate leads. But I think our marketing manager has developed as more of an internal resource. What this person will do from a marketing standpoint is that he will help our younger people: coach them, develop them, help them generate leads, help them generate a process for them to attack a certain target list, for example. We also have another individual up in Everett, which is part of the Puget Sound region, who focuses on financial institutions, not-for-profits, and auto dealers. We are going to be hiring a business development officer for our manufacturing and construction niches because we want to attack that market to gain dominance. So we will use them in that process.

"Then we have our marketing coordinators who help us make sure the seminars are set up, make sure that the contacts are there, and also make sure that the professionals are involved in generating prospects. If one of my partners says, 'I want to do a seminar and get these people there,' and they totally hand it over to the marketing person, they can't really expect those individuals to fill the seats. We need our partners and senior managers to work with the coordinators to fill the seats. The biggest failure in that process comes when we don't work together with our marketing support."

How to Cope When Worlds Collide

One of Stephen Covey's seven habits in *Seven Habits of Highly Successful People*[3] is "to seek first to understand, then to be understood." Both the marketer and the accountant must take time to understand the other professional.

Marketing and selling is a high-energy, fast-paced culture of innovative ideas and aggressive initiatives, where failure is a part of the business. Marketers have learned to deal with the extraordinary failure rate of marketing and sales. (Even the best salespeople close only one in five sales, and a direct mail campaign can be successful when 99 percent of the mailing produces no results.)

Accounting is a fastidious culture of conformity and compliance where the penalties for mistakes are very high. CPAs generally do not have constitutions that will allow too much experimentation.

Some marketers approach accountants with excellent marketing ideas— but the ideas are better suited for a product-oriented business. "Let's run some advertising, make some cold calls, and mass mail our brochures, and the business will come rolling in," they advise. When the bucks are gone and the business doesn't roll in, the CPA wonders, "Where's the payback?"

Marketers see the tremendous potential for selling accounting services. They see the huge void of marketing talent in the profession. But they do not see the minefield of conservatism. Accountants see the possibility of hiring someone to do a job they don't feel equipped to handle. When this idea person comes in trying to update the reception areas, publish a newsletter, promote community involvement, and go after new business, the CPA freezes and they part company.

A good friend who is a dynamite marketer went to work for a 100-person firm, but within nine months he was burned out and bitter. He had been busy starting good marketing programs. What he didn't expect was the silent negative uprising among the practice partners that cooled the managing partner's zeal. He left the firm, dejected and depressed. He knew that the programs would have worked, but he never was allowed to launch any of them.

We Need Marketers

Marketing professionals are indispensable to today's successful and growing accounting firm. Bob Gaida explains his success: "I was the first partner to hire a marketing professional in our firm. By 1992 I was attracting well over $1.5 million worth of new business a year. I found my time spent, at first, on total marketing to create a practice and, now, serving and facilitating that practice—getting out to the marketplace and making sure that the promises are being kept. So you can imagine that $1.5 million booking pace was starting downward. There are only 24 hours in a day. So my thought was, how could I increase my hit ratio? That was the key to me. Every meeting I need to go to, I really need to have a higher prequalification. It's got to be almost like a no-brainer, that it's worth my time being there, and it's got real benefit coming out of it.

"Well, I didn't know how to fine-tune my own ability to do that. I thought I was already, probably, at the level of being able to do that, so I wasn't going to be able to gain time by making myself more efficient or better educated in the process; not by much, anyway. So I said, what if I could get a person who is used to selling an intangible product? After a few experiments with different individuals, I locked onto one where the chemistry between us worked real well. So this person went out all day long, having a breakfast meeting, having a midday lunch, mid-afternoon dinner, going to various seminars, going to gatherings . . . 'sniffing around.' And he would bring me high-quality prospects. When I went into that meeting, I was well scripted. We already knew who was who, what the background was, who the spheres of influence and top decision makers were, what their challenges were. And I could come in now and pick up from that point and go toward closure. That's how a marketing professional works the best. All of a sudden I was back up to doing seven, eight hundred thousand a year in new business."

Depending on the size and complexity of your firm and the sophistication of your marketing and selling team, you may need one or more marketing support persons in your firm. Firms often give titles to compensate for limited authority and money. Therefore, a person with the title of marketing director may really be operating as an assistant. At the end of this chapter, you'll find some general job descriptions of various marketing positions. These will help you delineate the job responsibilities when you are ready to set up a marketing position.

Introducing Marketing Staff into Your Firm

When new marketing or sales staff join an accounting firm, it is important that they completely understand the firm's services and its people. When my wife joined Xerox, she attended their sales school. The primary focus of the training was gaining product knowledge. Over the next few months, before she was allowed to interact with customers, she studied product manuals, demonstrations, and presentations.

It is crucial that new marketing staff members gain product knowledge early. They also must learn about your firm's culture. Even those CPAs who support marketing initiatives are put off by actions that seem impulsive. Impulsive actions can occur when a new person doesn't understand the business. To be successful, a marketing person has to take into account the conservative nature of the CPAs and their preference for consensus-based decisions. You can't assume new marketing staff know this. They may not have worked with accountants before, and many textbook examples of successful marketing efforts are more "flashy" than most CPAs want to use. So early on, make clear the types of marketing efforts you're willing to pursue and how decisions are reached in your firm.

Newcomers at Work

According to a research study in the Journal of Applied Psychology, *newcomers who received realistic—including negative— information about the organization they were entering had less role conflict and were more productive. The more involved employees acted in their work, the better response from the organization, which, in turn, predicted their future commitment.*

At the same time, encourage marketers to take initiative and reward them for it. If you set it up so that they just do what you tell them they can do, you won't get many fresh ideas and approaches. Be prepared to approve new ideas. If you take weeks to OK a new idea, marketing people often will lose their enthusiasm for the work.

Once the marketer begins to understand your service mix, it is time to focus on the marketing skills of the firm's people. The marketer should spend time in-house with the best marketing minds at the firm. Then the marketer should accompany them when they meet with clients and prospects to observe and determine the factors that make them successful.

The very first market every marketing director must deal with is the CPAs on the firm's staff. Before you can sell successfully to the community, you must sell the value of the firm to the people inside.

Marketing Resources

Directly after the summary in this chapter are two resources that will help your firm's marketing program. I've placed them on separate pages so that you can easily make copies of them for the appropriate people. The first, a Nine-Step Plan for New Marketers, is a blueprint that new marketers in an accounting firm can follow to get your marketing program up and running and on-track.

The second resource is a list of marketing position job descriptions. People who know their specific responsibilities are more likely to perform them.

Summary

Traditionally, the different styles of marketers and accountants have created conflicts and ineffectiveness. Define what you expect from your marketing staff members and tell them what to expect from you. Work to understand people different from you. New business and enhanced client relationships will benefit you both.

Nine-Step Plan for New Marketers

You must know that your first market is your own firm. Use this plan to get started:

1. *Plan to use your first three to six months to get to know each of your firm's key partners.* It is your job to understand each of the partners and key staff people in your firm. Your managing partner is your boss—therefore, "study him until you know what makes him tick," advises Chris Hegarty, author of *How to Manage Your Boss.*

2. *Spend months learning your product lines.* CPA firms tend to have a helter-skelter array of services that have cropped up. You must have a thorough knowledge of each service line. Ask each staff person the strengths and weaknesses of the firm's service line. Ask what opportunities the firm should be developing.

3. *Learn how these proposed new services would benefit clients.* Intuitively you know that those services with the highest benefit will be rewarded best over time. You can make a major contribution if you can stir high-margin cross-selling opportunities into the pot. During the first six months, you should spend up to 50 percent of your time in client offices interacting with your staff, your clients, and the various services that are being provided. You must gain product knowledge.

4. *Conduct a client loyalty survey.* Some CPAs will fight this process, but you must have it. There are ways to obtain the information without formal mail or telephone surveys, such as personal interviews. You must know the market's perception of your product.

5. *Evaluate your competitors to learn their service lines.* What are the unique aspects of your firm vis-à-vis the competitors?

6. *Ask each person during the first six months, to help you with a marketing plan.* Carefully review each of your ideas with each partner before you present them in an open meeting. Otherwise you will run a great risk of having someone second-guess you or ask questions for which you are not prepared. Once you've obtained consensus in an open partners meeting, prepare a simple plan.

7. *Determine the personality style, value system, and business goals of each of the key partners in the firm.* Is your managing partner a dictator, an analyzer, or a socializer? In a CPA firm, many partners will be analyzers. Therefore, you must build trust slowly by being organized, consistent, and steady.

8. ***Develop a concrete list of priority items to implement and present them to your boss.*** This "want list" should be well thought out and carefully planned. Position all of your needs without implying that they are nonnegotiable demands. If you present your needs so that your managing partner can also see clearly the benefits to himself and your firm, your success will be surer.

9. ***Establish an evaluation system for all marketing activity.*** If you set the standards, then you know the targets. For example, if you target 100 referrals next year, track those referrals to contacts, proposals, and new clients. If you run an awareness campaign, perform a survey of clients, prospects, and others to determine its effectiveness.

We make money in an accounting practice by bringing in clients and serving them well. Through marketing, you can also change others' perceptions of your firm members from back-room number crunchers to trusted business advisors. Your success will spearhead enormous energy within your firm.

Job Descriptions of Marketing Positions

Vice President of Marketing and Sales

This partner-level individual leads all practice development activities of the firm. Among other duties, a marketing and sales VP might:

- Prepare a three-year strategic and one-year operational growth plan for the firm
- Develop growth strategies with senior management
- Supervise marketing and sales staff, both in-house staff and outside consultants
- Coordinate sales and marketing activities with each unit of the firm
- Meet with large core clients and significant target prospects
- Supervise advertising, public relations, and speaking events for the firm
- Facilitate internal marketing and sales meetings
- Ensure appropriate levels of sales and marketing training for all employees
- Mentor marketing and sales professionals and other sales leaders in the firm
- Take responsibility for attaining the firm's growth goals and investing the marketing budget

This VP should be knowledgeable about the firm's markets, its competitors, and its internal skill set. He or she should be able to communicate the firm's mission, vision, and values to clients, prospects, and employees. Usually this VP will have a strong marketing education and experience base in accounting or professional services. In some cases, this person can be a CPA, but only if he or she has significant marketing and sales experience as well.

Marketing and Sales Director

Usually the marketing and sales director is a manager who supervises other marketing and sales personnel. This person has many of the duties of the VP of marketing and sales but with less total responsibility. In most cases, this person is not a CPA. He or she reports to a partner or owner of the firm, often the managing partner.

Marketing Director

The marketing director of an accounting firm often has a solid marketing education and experience base. Usually a manager, the marketing director actually directs the firm's marketing plan and activities. In general, a true marketing director:

- Prepares the firm's annual marketing plan and budget, under supervision of a partner
- Assists with the preparation of niche and personal marketing plans of senior people
- Identifies and researches key markets and target clients for marketing and selling activity
- Takes responsibility for the firm's databases of clients, prospects, news media, and referrals
- Conducts marketing meetings
- Reviews or prepares written proposals
- Initiates and supervises all advertising and public relations activities
- Develops and assures proper distribution of marketing support materials
- Supervises the firm's Internet marketing strategy
- Maintains accountability for marketing results

In large firms, this person may supervise a staff of other marketing and sales professionals. In small firms, the marketing director may be a one-person department.

Sales Director

The sales director of an accounting firm is the person who can initiate and close sales with prospects. In many cases, a CPA professional may be involved in the selling and closing process. Many sales directors are CPAs. They are at an advantage because of their significant product knowledge. A sales director might:

- Identify and research target prospects within a market segment
- Develop a communications and sales strategy for key target prospects
- Prepare written and oral presentations and proposals
- Coach partners, marketing personnel, and others during the selling process
- Coordinate marketing support activities with the marketing department
- Maintain accountability for sales results
- Conduct sales meetings
- Maintain contact with target prospects through selling strategy
- Supervise other sales professionals

The sales director is a self-starting individual who will attract a large amount of new business to your firm.

Marketing Coordinator

There is a great deal of marketing-related administrative work in a well-functioning accounting firm.

The marketing coordinator is generally an administrative person who coordinates marketing functions. Marketing education and background is not as important as good organizational and follow-up skills. A marketing coordinator:

- Maintains databases
- Takes charge of distributing firm newsletters and communications
- Operates direct mail campaigns
- Sends welcome, condolence, and thank-you cards; letters; and gifts
- Coordinates open houses and firm parties
- Coordinates speaking events for professionals
- Publishes the internal firm newsletter
- Updates the firm's Web site
- Organizes and mails press releases
- Coordinates advertising, trade shows, referral programs, and other marketing

Sales Coordinator

A sales coordinator is a lead generator for the firm. Through telemarketing, direct mail, and cold calling, the sales coordinator contacts businesses and attempts to develop enough interest for a partner to get involved. The sales coordinator may have many of the duties of a sales director, but usually a sales coordinator cannot close the sale. Normally the sales coordinator is paid largely by commissions.

Other Titles

Some firms have proposal writers, research analysts, database managers, direct mail coordinators, advertising and public relations specialists, publications writers, meeting planners, and marketing training coordinators. Depending on the sophistication of the firm's marketing program, these individuals can be anywhere from helpful to invaluable.

All Selling Is Personal Selling

23 Listening for Dollars, Talking for Dimes

If you think that communication is all talk, then you haven't been listening.

—Ashleigh Brilliant[1]

The title of this chapter is one of the oldest sales sayings I've quoted. Salespeople talk too much and don't listen enough. Even when you are invited to do a presentation, you may be better off listening than talking. For instance, one large company had three professional service firms in to do presentations. Company professionals later complained that all the service firms did was "dog and pony shows." Not one firm had researched the company, not one firm knew about its industry concerns, not one firm asked the right questions. All they did was impressive Power Point presentations about their capabilities and their people.

Almost every book on selling or marketing has a chapter on using questions to determine prospects' needs. Almost every communication trainer encourages the asking of open-ended questions (questions that can't be answered by a yes or a no). Books and trainers teach SPIN® Selling, Dialogue Selling, Partnership Selling, and on and on. In most cases, these books and trainers miss the main point: Communication is as much about the message you receive in response to your question as it is the message you send. The point of asking a question is to encourage your client or prospect to tell you what's on his or her mind. When what is on your client's mind is transmitted to you so that you truly understand, then, and only then, are you prepared to present.

In his book *The Seven Habits of Highly Effective People,* Stephen Covey writes, "If I were to summarize in one sentence the single most important principle in the field of interpersonal relationships, listening is the key." Listening is so important to building relationships. Relationships create a positive environment in which you can sell.

Talk is cheap. Supply exceeds demand.

—John Fogg[2]

We communicate in four major ways: (1) speaking, (2) listening, (3) writing, and (4) "viewing." Viewing includes reading print material as well as "reading" people and situations. High schools, colleges, and CPE programs present many courses on viewing, writing, and speaking. But listening skills are rarely taught in formal education.

Listening to Understand Others

Bob Gaida, whom we met in Day 15, says, "You carefully listen to your clients and you constantly probe to understand their challenges because things change. What my client thought yesterday, he might not be thinking today. And you listen to understand deeply what your client is dealing with. If I pretend to know without listening, he'll see right through me."

Listening for Sales

According to Lucette Comer at Purdue University, research showed that sales reps with higher listening skills were better in all six phases of the sales process: approach, need for identification, presentation, overcoming objections, closing, and after-sales support.

—What's Working in Sales Management[3]

There is no reason to have good questioning skills unless you have good listening skills. You will not benefit from the question but from the answer. Even the best salespeople have had difficulty learning to listen. Terry Orr, whom we met in Day 5, says, "I had been working with clients all those years and suddenly it dawned on me, I need to learn how to listen better. To help clients with their deepest problems requires my understanding first. When I understand completely, only then can I be an adviser on the problem or issue."

Jeff Everly, whom we met in Day 4, says, "I feel it is important to listen to people who are going to make the decision. Listening helps me understand what is going on within their organization. Why they are not happy—or maybe they are happy. Finding out what really makes a prospect happy is an important piece of information. Listening often helps me locate an issue to solve and a person within the organization as an inside coach."

Perception is reality. The important marketing communications are those whose meaning is accurately perceived by clients and prospects, not the ones crafted by the ad writers whose messages get lost in all the cleverness. By the same token, good selling does not come from good questions but from the answers to those questions.

Bill Fingland, whom we met in Day 2, says, "We have a saying that you should learn to listen so you can listen to learn. You have to learn about the client before you can write a good proposal. If you listen to clients, they will tell you where their problems are. They will tell you what to do to make them happy. I used to always try to end the fact-finding portion of my proposals with this question: 'Let me suppose for a moment that we are successful in getting this engagement and that I can be working with you. In a year or two, when I come back and ask you if we are doing a good job, what are the two or three most important things that you will evaluate in my performance?'"

In preparing for a client or prospect meeting, it is crucial to prepare your questions in advance and in writing. Having your questions in writing allows you to focus on listening. If you are busy constructing your next thought or your next question, you may miss the deep message your client is trying to articulate.

 Listen to your customer, and everything else will fall into place.

—John Burgess[4]

Active Listening

To listen, you need to remove as many distractions as possible. Turn off your cell phone or computer screen. Have a note pad, flip chart, or whiteboard available. Listening to your client while taking notes on a flip chart shows that you are actively listening. Try boiling down each point into three to five words that capture the key thought. When you write it on a flip chart, the client will know that you understand the point. This will cut down on repetition. Periodically restate what your client is saying as you are capturing the words. Ask for explanation and clarification. A good question to use at all times is "How do you mean?" Asking this question will encourage the client to talk at a deeper level.

Active listening includes responding so that your client knows you are listening. Phrases like "I see," "Uh-huh," and "That's interesting" all give others feedback that you are in tune with their thoughts. Using these phrases inappropriately shows your client that you are *pretending* to listen. Pretending to listen is one of the quickest ways to break trust with people—and it's all too easy to fall into the habit of pretend listening. In boring meetings, with our children, and at cocktail receptions, pretending to listen has become an art form. One of my young children came to me one day in a panic and said, "Mother wants to be cremated." I said, "Tell her to get her coat and we'll go."

Climb the Ladder to Become a Successful Listener

The six steps to becoming a better listener form a ladder. With each step, you become more highly proficient in listening.

1 Look at the person speaking to you.

2 Ask questions.

3 Don't interrupt.

4 Don't change the subject.

5 Empathize.

6 Respond verbally and nonverbally.

One of the reasons why attentive listening is so difficult is because of the discrepancy between talking speed and listening speed. Most people talk at about 150 words per minute; most people can listen at three to four times that rate. As a lecturer is talking, I can think about my weekend, a difficult person I am working with, a family problem, or a myriad of other topics. If I do not focus on listening to the lecture, often my mind wanders.

While engaged in conversation, most people have a limited capacity to remember things. If your client has five things he wants to talk to you about, it is best to allow him to talk through them once before you begin deep probing of any of the issues. Otherwise, his memory capacity may become overloaded and you may miss his key issue. The key issue often does not come out in the first bulleted item.

Have people ever finished your sentences before you do? Jumped on top of your conversation? I've been told that I do that a lot, but I am constantly working to improve. This comes from the powerful urge to get our thoughts out of our heads, lest we forget them. I am so afraid that I will forget that I sometimes blurt out my thought at the worst time. Rather than jump on some else's train of thought or be distracted trying to remember it, it is better to jot your thought down for later. Put it out of your mind and return to active listening.

> *You'll invariably find the answers—if your ears are open. The average salesperson is a better talker than listener. Listening is not enough. You have to let go of preconceptions and hear old laments as if for the first time.*
>
> —Tom Peters[5]

Sometimes active listeners will ask for a pause from the conversation to process the information. If you have a tendency to pause and process but don't announce what you are doing, your client may think you are slow. One way to pause and process while keeping a dialog going is to recap what was just said. Summarizing the conversation also provides a check that your interpretation was what the client meant to convey. It is important to keep a dialogue moving at the same pace as your client.

> *One of the best ways to persuade others is by listening to them.*
>
> —Dean Rusk[6]

Asking Good Questions

To create a selling environment, good salespeople construct a series of powerful questions that will elicit solid information around which they can sell. *SPIN Selling* by Neil Rackham and *Stop Telling, Start Selling* by Linda Richardson[7] are two excellent books on asking good questions. Rackham's book is based on research into sophisticated selling situations.

While you sit and talk to your prospect at 150 wpm, your prospect is using only a quarter of her thought-processing capability, and she's likely to get bored or her mind will wander. (Don't take this personally. Have you taken any lecture-based CPE lately? Then you know the feeling!)

To engage more of your prospect's thought-processing capability and be more successful at selling in the process, involve your prospect throughout all phases of your sales call, even when you are making a presentation. For instance, you can keep prospects involved in your sales presentation by showing them a list of your references and asking them if they know anyone on it.

One of the best ways to involve prospects is to ask good questions. Here are some questions you could ask a prospect during a sales call:

- **How do you define quality in an accounting firm relationship? Listen carefully to the prospect's answer.** While the vast majority of prospects will say things like "I want you to understand my business" or "I want an accountant who will help me get what I want," some will define quality in other ways.

- **What do you like most about the accounting firm you are currently using?** If prospects answer this question by praising their current accountant extravagantly, they may only be using you to shop for price. However, if they tell you about things they don't like, you can begin to pursue this topic until you discover their unmet need.

- **How do you think I might be able to help you?** Listen very carefully to the answer to this question. Prospects are about to tell what benefits they expect from a relationship with you. Your sales presentation should then be built around proving you can meet the prospect's expectations.

- **What are your goals and priorities over the next three years?** If you can help achieve any of the prospect's top goals, focus your sales presentation on proving how you will be able to do it.

- **Who, besides you, would influence a decision to hire an accounting firm?** Would your bank have any input? Your board? Your family? Sometimes the controller is asked to conduct preliminary interviews of candidate accounting firms, but it is the owner or the CEO who makes the final decision. To succeed in being hired, you must be known to the key decision maker and to as many decision influencers as possible.

It is the province of knowledge to speak and it is the privilege of wisdom to listen.

—Oliver Wendell Holmes, U.S. Supreme Court Justice

Selling to Your Prospects

Invite your prospect to come in for a tour of your office. Seventy-five percent of all games are won by the home team. If you can get prospects onto your home ground, your odds may also improve.

A truly effective and persuasive presentation will create a healthy dissatisfaction in the prospect. This sense of dissatisfaction will motivate your prospect to want to change. That desire to change is an absolutely necessary ingredient to successful selling of CPA services. When you *hear* what problems they care about, you can proceed with questions that raise the anxiety level of your prospects.

The right questions create further dissatisfaction in prospects and a desire to make things different. A note of caution: Never ask a question that will raise negative emotions unless you can solve the problem. If you raise the intensity level of the prospect's dissatisfaction, you create a strong desire to change. If you cannot supply the solution, the prospect will change—but without you!

Last, asking questions that establish the value of your services (i.e., "Is working with a firm that specializes in accounting for the manufacturing industry important to you?") enables you to make the most powerful benefit statement possible. This type of question also allows prospects to put the value of your services in context with the cost. This type of question will differentiate you from other accountants because you are establishing value. This type of question gets the prospect to tell you what your services are worth. You never boast.

Preparation Is the Foundation for Success

How much respect do your prospects have for you when you are not prepared for the presentation? When your clients do not believe you are interested in their businesses and they feel taken for granted, how willing are they to pay your fees? If you could increase your success rate with your proposals from 2 in 10 to 4 in 10, how much could you increase your fees over the next five years?

When you ask better questions, you will encourage your prospects to do the talking and the selling. When they say something, it's more persuasive than when you say it. When you learn to improve your questioning technique, your persuasive powers are guaranteed to get you better results.

Questions are necessary in any sales interview, but if you ask too many of them, they can irritate prospects.

"Problem questions" help you locate a need. If there is no problem, there is no need and there will be no sale.

"Implication questions" prompt prospects to tell you all the bad things that may happen if the problem is not solved. All of these bad images promote a desire in your prospects to make a change. When the prospect has desire, then asking need-payoff questions will get your prospect to actually describe the benefits of your services.

You will make the strongest possible impact when you get your prospect to articulate the benefits and you then reinforce these benefits with strong statements. If *you* say it, they will forget it or doubt it. If *they* say it, they will remember it and believe it. This is the most powerful closing sequence you can use.

The Right Questions

A key issue that most sellers encounter is buyer fatigue. Buyers get so tired of regurgitating the answers to the same old questions that are asked by everybody, such as "Mr. Jones, what keeps you up at night?" or "Would you give me the history of your business?" The reason for buyer fatigue is that buyers are telling you things they know. They are not being challenged. It is a bit like the audit checklists you ask your staff to go over with your clients' controllers. Many clients are irritated and say, "Didn't you ask these questions 10 years ago? I already answered them."

During Rackham's research for *SPIN Selling*, he concluded that certain types of questions created buyer fatigue, whereas other types created buyer energy. A *situation question* is one that elicits information that is purely recitation of data known by the prospect. Situation questions usually gather data that is already known. Other people call these questions "information" or "recitation" questions. You should gather this routine information from others who work for your prospect, not bore the key decision maker with them.

> *Good questioning skills will do more to help you in sales than any "sales techniques" ever could.*
>
> —Neil Rackham, *SPIN Selling*[8]

"Which are best—open-ended or closed-ended questions?" I ask my training seminar participants. The chorus comes back, "Open-ended questions." Then I ask, "What answer do you want to the question: "Mr. Client, would you like for me to handle this for you?" Generally, the class looks puzzled but responds, "Yes." Then I ask, "What type of question gets a yes-or-no answer?" Of course, it is a closed-ended question.

Depending on where and how they are used, open-ended questions and closed-ended questions can be equally powerful. Normally, the answers to open-ended questions are not as predictable as are the answers to closed-ended questions. So, it generally makes sense to ask closed-ended questions at a time during your presentation when you want a predictable answer.

Asking questions that make prospects think transfers energy to them. Questions that get prospects to contrast, compare, project, or speculate will make them think. Linda Richardson calls these types of questions "dialogue" questions. The real point of a dialogue question is to create new thoughts between you and your prospect—new thoughts can lead to your prospect viewing you as a powerful ally in the development of his or her business. Rackham calls these questions "implication" or "need-payoff" questions.

To come across as professional, it is important to ask situation, information, or recitation questions in a way that shows you have done your homework. For example, rather than asking the prospect, "What was your revenue last year?" ask a question based on your homework or research. "We looked you up in *MarketPlace* and learned that your revenues are about $50 million—have you seen a sharp growth or decline in your revenue in the last three years?" is a stronger question. Constructing a dialogue question takes a bit more craftsmanship. But it might go something like this: "We found in *MarketPlace* that your revenue totaled about $50 million, and we read that firms in your industry have seen massive defections of customers to a new technology. Would you tell me about your experiences with these issues?"

One of the biggest mistakes novice sellers make is to only ask questions inside their own comfort zone. For example, an auditor will ask questions only related to the audit. The technology consultant asks only about the computers. Most professionals tend to ask questions that get us what we want to hear. One key way to differentiate yourself is to learn to ask different questions—more holistic ones. Asking questions only about your areas of expertise is a very subtle form of not listening.

42 Specific Questions You Can Ask Your Prospects

Recently a CPA client of mine was preparing to make a presentation and written proposal to an important prospect. The prospect was a $100 million company for which the annual core services fees would exceed $100,000. The CPA and his partners had a series of nine meetings with corporate officers and board members over a period of about two months before being engaged by the client. Here is a list of questions that we prepared in advance of their first meeting. You may find some of them useful for stimulating your thinking about questions you ask can your prospects.

General

1. Please bring us up to date on the success of your business since [insert date or major event].

2. What are some of your most pressing business problems this year? Next year?

3. How do you see us helping you address these challenges?

4. We want to be prepared for your future. Please tell us how you view your business challenges over the next three to five years.

   ■ What growth plans do you have?

   ■ Do you plan to exit any markets?

   ■ Do you expect capital needs? What about new financing?

   ■ Tell us about your new technology investment and how it interfaces with the accounting department.

5. We know you have been making an extensive investment in quality customer service, and so have we. Please tell us the service standards you would like for us to provide you.

Accounting and Auditing

6. What are the vital elements you want from your accounting and auditing service provider?

7. Are there some things, while not vital, that would be nice for us to provide you?

8. How important is regular personal interaction among our executives and yours?

9. How important is assigning our most experienced people to your engagement?

10. How important is it to have continuity of personnel assigned to your work?

11. How important is rapid response on accounting and tax questions?

12. What do you consider rapid response?

13. How important are the national and international resources of our firm to you?

14. Do you see any barriers to working with our firm?

15. How critical is price to you? Approximately what is your pricing expectation?

16. Why are you changing auditors?

17. What did you not like about your former firm that you do not want us to repeat?

18. What are the elements of our firm that can be of most benefit to you?

19. How did you enjoy working with your former firm?

20. Do you envision any other changes in your needs?

21. Would you review with us the best fieldwork dates during which we can interface with your accounting staff?

22. How do you envision your staff availability and capability to provide audit assistance?

23. In addition to the company's annual report, do you anticipate needing other reports from us?

24. If so, what reports and who will be the users?

25. Are you concerned about any of your asset, liability, or income statement accounts where we should pay particular close attention?

Income Tax

26. Do you have any tax savings opportunities we should explore?

27. Are there any tax audits in progress or contemplated?

28. Have you explored any advanced tax strategies?

29. Would you be willing to be very aggressive with your tax payments? Or would you rather take no risks?

30. You are operating in many states and several countries—we noticed that you may be able to restructure some of your operations to avoid or delay large amounts of tax. How would you react to creatively attacking this opportunity?

Technology

31. Will your new computer installation enable you to decrease your SG&A (Selling, General, and Administrative) expenses? Are there areas we can help you explore to help you drive down these costs?

32. How are your computers helping you?

33. Are you having any difficulties with your technology?

34. What would happen if you had a major fire in your main office?

35. We noticed that your systems are being supervised in-house. Do you have any serious issues with this supervision?

36. How would an independent expert review help you?

Management

37. As a part of our engagement, we invest a certain amount of time understanding your business. For example, we are continuously training on and reading about issues related to your business, and studying your business. In what ways do you suggest we best learn about your business

so we can relate your operations to the financial information and so we can be more proactive in helping you maximize your business success?

38. If we invested (nonchargeable time) in attending certain of your internal management meetings as observers, would you be comfortable with this?

39. How would you feel about our partners regularly touring operations in order to better understand your business and find ways to help you be more profitable?

40. When it comes to managing your assets more effectively, are there ways you need for us to help you? For example, your investment in accounts receivable seem to be expanding at a faster rate than your sales each year. Will that cause you difficulties in cash flow? Carry costs? Missed payments? We noticed that your averages for sales growth, SG&A, and cost of sales were a bit lower than industry averages. Tell us about your goals here and how we might help. (What are the industry averages, specific other averages?)

41. Is working with local professionals who have national and worldwide resources important to you?

42. Do you anticipate any mergers, purchases, divestitures, recapitalizations, or reorganizations in the near future?

Summary

Communication is the key to success with clients—and listening is the key to communication. Ask good questions to get good answers. With a client you can do a wonderful thing and simply say, "How are we doing?" and get a feedback on the value that he or she is placing on the relationship. Is it still high? Is it as high as it was the day you were hired? It should be even higher because you should have exceeded the client's expectations. If it's high, then you know you have a ripe environment in which to sell.

24 Advancing Commitment

*[To achieve success more rapidly] double your
failure rate.*
—Thomas J. Watson, Sr.[1]

Believe it or not, in most of your sales contacts with prospects and clients, the ideal outcome is *not* to close the sale. If you expect to close the sale at each contact, you will not only be disappointed, but too impatient and pushy. Superficially, selling is your goal with every contact, but it is unrealistic. In addition, until you know something about the prospects—and they know more about you—signing them up could lead to more trouble than profits. Of course, for each sales contact you *should* have a goal, so you need to have a variety of possibilities in mind.

Closing is that one fantastic moment when a person who was a prospect says yes to becoming a client. However, if you are in the relationship business, you will actually retard the development of a long-term relationship if you put too much focus on closing the sale. And you may start relationships with the wrong types of clients.

Don't Push Too Fast

People buy for *their* reasons, on *their* terms, and on *their* timing—not yours. Bill Fingland says, "We noticed a significant decrease in closed sales when we tried to shortcut the many meetings it took to land a good account."

Meeting a prospect for the first time and expecting the prospect to say yes to your proposal for a long-term relationship is like proposing marriage on a first date. Even if you get a yes, the probabilities are not good for a successful relationship. When you start closing the sale too soon, prospects may conclude that you want the business without regard to their true needs. By the same token, if you view closing the sale as a one-time event, you are missing the vein of gold in the recurring relationship.

"Closing the sale" sounds negative. "Closed" sounds like a final event. And it has received far too much emphasis. Rather than closing a sale, think of opening a relationship. Opening a relationship is a positive event. Opening a relationship is the start of a series of events that becomes a growing process.

Advance the Relationship

Rather than closing the sale, think of each step in the selling process as advancing commitment. Advancing commitment is a series of steps prospects take in response to you that move them along the continuum toward becoming clients. The early steps would be things like agreeing to go on your newsletter mailing list or agreeing that another meeting would be beneficial. Advancing commitment is the most difficult action we have to perform, yet it should be the easiest.

At least 75 percent of your success in selling will come from your ability to influence people to act in everyone's best interest.

Mark Kaland, whom we met in Day 16, says that sometimes he will give away a small service in the proposal process just to demonstrate capability and interest.

Many people view selling as a strategy where you do something to someone. With this perspective, it's no wonder that CPAs shy away from the process. Many of the sales training classes and books seem to pit salespeople *against* potential buyers. Some approaches are "in your face" aggressive. Much of the focus is on manipulative tactics. With this inappropriate approach, the marketing process is not built on a foundation of trust, but of gimmickry.

I would like you to view that moment in time when your prospect says yes to your proposal as just another step in a very logical process. All along the way you will advance the prospect or client's commitment to a higher level. For example, when you meet a prospect for the first time, your objective might be to advance his commitment by visiting with you again. Or, for an existing client, you may wish to advance the commitment to a higher level of loyalty to your firm. You may advance commitment with a new prospect to obtain a tour of her facilities and meet other executives. Or, for a prospect on the verge of making a decision to hire you, you might advance that person's commitment by getting him to talk with one of your satisfied clients.

When you view the process in this way, you will know all along how prospects or clients feel about your proposal; rarely will you ever be surprised.

The Decision

Asking for a decision is easy when you have laid a solid foundation for a relationship. Many times, though, you believe that you are laying a solid foundation but you are not receiving positive feedback from your prospects.

Two key methods will enable you to advance commitment with your prospects: trial closing techniques and asking for the business.

Telling is not selling. The CPAs who are best at gaining new business are those who let the prospects do much of the work of closing the sale. When prospects are talking, you are learning what they want. After you make each benefit statement, a trial closing question will let you know where you stand in the process.

Some Trial-Close Questions You Can Use

Trial closes include questions like these:

- Ms. Prospect, if you were to select us, when would you want us to start the work?
- Mr. Client, what do think about this aspect of our service so far?
- Mr. Client, would you want us to work in your office or in ours?
- Ms. Client, are the fees we are quoting about right?
- Mr. Client, if we got the report to you by . . .

The answers to the trial-close questions tell you where you are in the process. A well-built sales presentation flows naturally into a yes response from your buyer. One of the best ways to do this is through the use of trial closes.

David Morgan, whom we met in Day 1, says, "I just like to let prospects talk. First you want to listen to them and see that you know what it is they want. If I try to sell them what they don't want, it will backfire. Second, you want to know their hot buttons, which they'll tell you. And then you start finding out what is it that they are not happy with where they are. I will tell them how we could solve an issue, and then ask him or her, 'How does that sound to you?' You find out the problems and you know where you are in the selling process."

A trial-closing question calls for an opinion. The prospect's response provides you with a lot of information. When you ask questions and the prospect talks, you will create more trust and a very positive selling environment.

Building Communication

The people who are the very best at influencing others are those people with empathy and sensitivity. They listen closely to what others are saying, and they listen for all the messages—even those being communicated between the lines. The more you listen to what a person is really saying, the more that person will trust you and will be open to your influence. A basic rule is that you should never say anything you could ask in a question. Again, telling is not selling.

With each response that you receive from your prospect, an acknowledgment that you heard the person will strengthen your case. A simple "uh-huh" or "I see" may be all you need most of the time. Take a note or two, but keep your eyes focused on the person with whom you are communicating. Nod, or paraphrase what people tell you. When you are actively listening to prospects or clients, you are building a deep level of communication. When you are listening, your prospect's natural resistance goes down.

A Gallup poll found that the most affluent people in America rated understanding and respect from others as their most important measure of success. It seems that we truly understand and respect ourselves only when we feel that we are understood and respected by others. And we will go to great lengths to garner such respect. When we feel that someone respects us for who we are and what we have accomplished, we tend to be more open to that person's influence.

Dick Reck, whom we met in Day 17, says, "When I really understand the needs and wants of the prospect, I rarely have to give a written proposal. Last year, with over 90 closed transactions, I wrote only two proposals. I'll see a big thick document from one of my competitors on the desk and I'll just go in and talk to the prospect and listen. I spend my time convincing the prospect he needs all our services, that he will make me the preferred provider and the sole source. In the long run, if we have built better communications and satisfied the client's needs, it doesn't matter that it cost 25 percent more to work with us."

Patience is a most necessary quality for business; many a man would rather you heard his story than grant his request.

—Lord Chesterfield[2]

One of your clients' greatest needs is for you to listen without bias. This doesn't mean just listening and waiting for a chance to argue a point or jump in and resume your presentation; I mean totally without bias or assumptions. When you actively listen to clients or prospects, you are demonstrating your high esteem and respect for their opinions.

Advancing Commitment

As you proceed through the commitment process, there will be times when you think prospects should say yes, but they don't. This usually indicates that you have not covered all the bases well. When this happens, try to step back and cover the area of concern. For example, if you hear, "Your fees are too high," that means that your prospect did not see the value in your services. You should go back to this step in your selling and cover all value bases again.

Author Ron Willingham says that clients always weigh the benefits vis-à-vis the cost before making a final decision. Willingham recommends that before you ask for a decision, you are sure the prospect is picturing the value outweighing the cost. This process will enable you to see things from the prospect's point of view, and this is the *only* view that will enable you to advance commitment on a consistent basis.

Advancing commitment is the simple process of asking for a decision at the right time. Advancing commitment with your prospect means you want to obtain a commitment from the person with whom you are meeting to take the next step with you.

You can advance commitment by asking the controller to introduce you to the president, who may be the final decision maker. You can advance commitment by asking the person with whom you are meeting to allow you to spend time in the accounting department reviewing internal controls and documentation. Of course, advancing commitment may also entail asking the prospect to become a client.

Closing Techniques

Whether you are advancing commitment or seeking a commitment to open the relationship, there are several excellent old-fashioned ways to do it. Use these techniques carefully—only after you have built a relationship and the right to ask in a persuasive manner.

Although the following case study appears in Jeff Everly's bio in the Day 4 chapter, it illustrates such a valuable lesson that I'm repeating it again here. When I first heard of Jeff Everly and David Frazier, partners of Yount, Hyde & Barbour (YHB) and leaders of the banking services team, I was working with another client, whom I'll call ABC CPAs. ABC had just lost a proposal to YHB, and they were surprised by this. So the managing partner of ABC asked me to perform a lost proposal review for the firm.

To perform a lost proposal review, among other things, I talk to the decision makers and influencers at the lost client. So I spoke with two of the bank officers—the CEO and CFO. Both generally gave me the same story. Both initially felt that ABC was going to be the winner of the engagement, but they had invited a Big Five firm, a regional firm, and Yount, Hyde & Barbour to provide a proposal. YHB was invited only because the CFO had heard that the firm had some banking experience. The officers did not consider YHB to be in serious running at the beginning, but they had to have three proposals. Yount, Hyde & Barbour partners David Frazier and Jeff Everly appeared before the bank audit committee and made the presentation to it.

At the end of the proposal, Everly and Frazier spoke personally to each person on the audit committee and asked him or her, in a general way, for their business. As Everly and Frazier left the room, they spoke to the CFO and CEO. At the end of the audit committee meeting, the vote was three for ABC and three for YHB. It was tied. The audit committee decided to adjourn and gather additional information. Later that afternoon Everly called the bank's CFO and asked if during the interview process, any additional questions had arisen. The CFO responded, "Yes, there were two questions." Everly responded with an overnight letter. He called the CFO and the CEO the next morning again expressing his interest. The letter was passed out to the entire audit committee members and they voted 6 to 0 to hire YHB.

The audit committee members said to the officers, "This firm seems to want our business. They've answered all our questions." The partners from ABC never called back. They never asked for the business. Members of the audit committee judged this to be a lack of interest and perhaps a bit insulting.

It is *very* important to demonstrate your interest in your prospective client by asking appropriate closing questions.

Types of Closes

The Direct Close.   The *direct close* is the most frequently used closing technique. Using it, you simply ask for the business in no uncertain terms. Terry Orr says, "Sometimes I will just say 'I've gotten to know you and I'd like to work with you. What are some things I could do to help the most right now?'"

The Approach Close.   The *approach close* is used at the beginning of the presentation. It may sound like a trial close, but it calls for a decision. The approach close goes something like this: "Will you tell me, one way or the other, at the end of our meeting today if my service will meet your needs?"

If the prospect answers yes to this approach close, you have advanced his or her commitment to make a decision today. If the answer is no, then you may want to inquire as to the prospect's process and its timeframe.

The Sharp-Angle Close.   The *sharp-angle close* comes at a time near the end of your presentation when the prospect has a request that you can fulfill. The prospect may say something like "I hope you are not going to run a bunch of inexperienced people in on me." In turn you might say, "Ms. Controller, I've heard how other firms do that and I know how it feels. If I could assure you that all of our CPAs will be experienced, would you engage us?"

> *Ben Franklin was very persuasive. Over two hundred years ago, he used what is sometimes called the T-account technique. He drew a horizontal line across the top of a page and a vertical line down the page, forming a "T." On the top of the left side he wrote "Yes" and on the left side he wrote "No." In the column under "Yes" he would write all of the reasons to go forward with the decision; under "No" he would write all of the reasons not to proceed. The graphic presentation when the yeses outweigh the nos is persuasive to both factual, left-brained buyers and emotional, right-brained buyers.*
>
> *The graphic presentation alone is powerful. But to involve your prospect more deeply, you then step back and look at your T-account graphic and ask, "Is there anything you can think of that should prevent our doing business together?" Write down their responses in the appropriate column.*

The Change-Places Close.   The *change-places close* asks prospects to tell you what you need to do to have them sign the engagement letter. The change places close goes something like this: "Mr. Prospect, if you were in my shoes and wanted to do business with your company as much as I do, what would you do?"

The Assumptive Close.   The *assumptive close* asks for a minor decision—assuming that your prospect has made the major decision. Assumptive questions are ones like "With whom should we work?" or "In addition to the items we have covered, is there anything else we should cover before we get started?"

Henry Ford used the assumptive close to sell millions of his black-only Model Ts until creative marketers offered color options. When you assume that your prospect is going to engage you and ask, "Which one?" you have a powerful force working for you.

Pay Attention to Personality Cues

People have different personality styles and each style type responds to the pressure of the decision-making process differently.

Highly analytical people will decide slowly and methodically. If you pressure them too much, they will say things like "If you need to have an answer now, the answer is no." Give a thinker time to process the information, but advance commitment by determining a time in which a decision will be reached.

Highly social people do not want to take the risk of making a decision alone. Their worst fear is making one of their colleagues angry. Help them reach a decision by bringing in people who will help them bear the risk and support them.

Director-type individuals can make decisions as soon as they feel they have a grasp of the situation. They appreciate a straightforward and direct approach: "I'd like to work with you, Ms. Client—when can we get started?"

Summary

If you have a relationship that is built on trust, it will be strong and all selling pressure will be perceived as low. Asking for a decision will be easy. If the relationship is new and weak, however, all decision making will be more tense. If you spend time to build trust, your closing will follow as a natural part of the sales presentation. In fact, if you do not invest the time to build rapport and trust, you really do not have the right to ask for a person's business.

25

Focus: Building a Power Niche

Man who chases two rabbits catches neither.

—Confucius

Last year, the managing partner of a 35-person CPA firm invited me to conduct one of our sales training programs for his entire group of professionals. He was kind enough to offer to pick me up at the airport and treat me to dinner before taking me to my hotel for the evening. He had invited two of his partners to dine with us so I could gain a better flavor of his firm. I figured that this would be a good time to connect with him and his partners, learn more about his firm, and perhaps pick up a few tidbits of information about the firm that would help me the next day.

He had sent me information in advance that indicated that his firm had niches in healthcare, auto dealers, construction, manufacturing, wholesalers, community banking, and not-for-profits. It seemed to me to be a lot of niches for such a small firm. Alarm bells went off because having many niches often means having no niches.

Over dinner, I asked a couple of questions and confirmed my assessment. I asked the partner who said she led the healthcare niche, "How many physicians are there in your city?" Her puzzled expression was the deer-in-the-headlights look I often get when I ask a niche specialist the size of his prospect base. "I've really never thought about it," she said. I later learned that each of the six partners had healthcare clients.

What Is a Niche?

The firm just mentioned had accumulated several collections of similar clients over the years, but it did not have a *niche* in any particular field. CPAs are often confused about what constitutes a niche. A niche is a specific group that has the same problems, regulations, market forces, and concerns.

A niche might be general contractors doing over $10 million a year, retired executives, dental practices, software developers, or auto dealers.

Serving a select grouping of niche clients provides more value for both the client and the CPA. In such cases, clients receive more value because they can lean on the CPA for more unique and in-depth services. The CPA becomes more of an expert and can work with the type of clients he or she likes. By understanding the clients' accounting and tax rules and business issues, the CPA can become more of an advisor instead of just providing basic accounting services. Because clients are receiving more value than they would from a nonniche CPA, they are willing to pay their valued advisor a premium yield. Truly, this is the ideal situation for both parties.

 The idea of being all things to all people is a thing of the past.
—Michael Dell, chairman and CEO, Dell Computer

Dick Reck, whom we met in Day 1, says, "Eight years ago, under the leadership of our then chairman, Jon Madonna, we reorganized into true industry-oriented lines of business. Our firm had always had an industry focus. But this reorganization was based on the theory that KPMG should be organized and go to market in a manner that reflected our clients' markets. We had historically been successful, for example, in our bank practice, where we had followed this focused approach for years. Twenty-five years ago, when I was part of our bank practice, we audited 43 of the 100 largest banks in the United States. That success was due largely to the focus that those partners had in serving clients in just one market. It was on that theory that KPMG established the Information, Communications & Entertainment (ICE) line of business. Back in 1982, when we started this practice (then called the High Tech Practice), we had just 7 partners and managers and 26 clients. In Chicago, we now have a team of about 200 professionals just serving a client base of hundreds of information and technology clients. With this type of focus and market penetration, we have no real competition."

Benefits of Having a Niche-based Practice

When your firm caters to one or more niches, the deep skill set and economies of scale that develop enable staff members to become very efficient in low-value, routine services. Once you become efficient in delivering routine services, you will have the time and resources to develop skills in unique services. I believe in what I preach—my firm works only with CPA and consulting firms.

For many years, PricewaterhouseCoopers has focused its practice on the largest global companies. Before Ernst & Young swallowed it up, Kenneth Leventhal (KL) was clearly the "go-to" CPA firm in the real estate industry. KL was notorious for making money when the real estate industry was moving up *and* when it was moving down. Crowe Chizek, a midwestern CPA firm, has seen its revenue and profits soar as a result of its intense focus on three dying and consolidating industries: manufacturing, auto dealers, and banking. George B. Jones is one of the most profitable and competitive CPA firms in the United States, serving only auto dealers.

The Key Is Focus

It is easy to be unfocused. Many midsize firms have patched together a group of professionals who have attracted a variety of clients. Generally clients are assigned to the partner who made the original contact or who answered the phone when the call came in, whether the partner's skill set serves the client or not. In some cases, firms have merged various skills and clients into a Rube Goldberg type of business structure. It is not unusual to find firms like the one in the opening story, where each partner has a few of each type of client. Often staff members move from a bank to a car dealer to a construction firm during any given month.

Rarely will you find unfocused firms in the high-profit or high-growth category.

> *For many years it has become clear, the firms that are focused make the money. We find every year the divide between the haves and have-nots in the accounting industry gets wider because of this one issue.*
>
> —Art Bowman, editor of *The Accounting Report*

Bill Fingland says, "I specialized in healthcare. In 1982 BKD opened an office with $300,000 of business in Tulsa, Oklahoma. At that point in time we had no healthcare practice in Oklahoma to speak of. At the same time, the Tulsa practice needed someone who had some audit background, and I did. But they also needed to develop a specialty niche, and we were hoping healthcare could be that. In 1982 I was asked if I wanted to go that direction and I said yes. I thought that it was a great opportunity for me to do some things on my own and maybe it was time for the student to leave the nest. So for the first four or five years, I focused almost all my time developing the healthcare practice in Oklahoma."

Fingland became the firm's director of healthcare in 1994 and managing partner in 1997. He led the Tulsa office's healthcare practice to about $4.5 million in Tulsa by 1997. The healthcare specialty represents the most significant industry specialty in that practice. Fingland grew the practice with intense focus and determination, not by trying to be all things to all clients.

Mike Kruse, whom we met in Day 6, built a firm around construction. Starting from ground zero in 1993, the firm had grown to $7.5 million by the end of 2000. Such a growth rate can only be accomplished with focus. Mike says, "A key to success is developing a reputation. The major part of our practice is construction. The major referral sources are bond agents or surety underwriters, so we produce what we call a Surety Underwriter and Bond Agent Seminar. It basically covers what's going on in the industry from our perspective. Here's what we are finding in our clients. They develop confidence that you understand their needs. And typically referral sources come about for a couple of reasons. First, they like you, trust you, and know you would do a good job. Second, the referral source wants you to do the work because they know that you will make their job much easier. If we improve somebody's quality of life or give him a better chance to succeed because we understand the issues, then they want to refer work to us. You can only gain this reputation if you truly offer a focused, deep set of skills."

> *When you are meeting a prospect for the first time, are you asked: "How many other businesses like mine do you work on?" The prospect is really asking "Do you understand my business?"*

Whenever I talk to clients of CPA firms, the most common reason I hear for liking their CPAs is that "the CPA firm understands me and my business and that's the key reason I use them." Clients' most common criticism is that "the partners only understand tax law and do not really understand the nature of my business."

Some CPAs object to focusing deeply into a niche market; they say, "Our clients don't want us working for their competitors." That sentiment *does* exist to a small extent in the marketplace. Dick Reck said, "About ten years ago, I lost a proposal to a prospective client because I did work for his competitor. Last year that prospect became a client of KPMG because we did work for all his competitors." Focusing as Mike Kruse, Bill Fingland, and Dick Reck do will make you irresistible. So long as the prospect can trust that you will not divulge company secrets, your depth of knowledge is compelling.

Developing Your Niche

How can you develop a niche? To do so, a firm must take four steps.

1. Choose a champion—a person who will dedicate him- or herself to leading the niche.
2. Do whatever is necessary to assemble a critical mass of clients under this champion.
3. Commit to a deep set of skills, which includes training beyond the typical industry CPE classes offered by state societies.
4. Develop a communications program to the marketplace, including clients, prospects, and referral sources.

Choosing a Champion

A champion must be a senior-level person who truly loves the industry that he or she is being asked to lead. If the champion doesn't care about the industry, this plan won't work. A few years ago one of my CPA clients wanted to develop a medical niche. I asked one of the firm's partners to lead the medical niche team because he was the only one left without anything to do. Big mistake. After about six months that niche had gone nowhere. After meeting repeatedly with the partner, I finally learned that he didn't like doctors. Rather, he really enjoyed working with the construction clients he had brought in. We decided he would instead lead a niche in construction. He committed himself to developing the niche and has attracted over $1.5 million of new clients in just a few years. Liking the niche is fundamental to being a champion.

Assembling Clients under the Champion

At least 60 percent of the partner's clients should come from the industry niche. Many firms will have to adjust the compensation plan to reassign clients. Some firms will have to overcome the culture of eat-what-you-kill, so the champion can have this critical mass.

Lou Mills says of Moss Adams, "We are very niche focused in our firm. Instead of doing many things halfway, we focus on doing one thing extremely well. Our management decided that to be successful, we had to focus intensely. Many local firms say they are niche focused. I can tell you that when you dig into the numbers and you dig into the client relationships, they are not really niche focused. They don't really allocate the clients in that firm to a specialist team. For example, in our firm I am responsible for the manufacturing distribution team. That means you are working primarily 75 percent of your time on manufacturing distribution clients."

Many firms have a culture that the partner who first worked with the client is the partner who should forever serve the client. But when you adhere to this philosophy, you are actually doing your client a disservice if one partner is championing the client's niche and has a deep set of skills in that area. You are also not doing what is best for your firm if you refuse to transition your client to the champion. For a niche program to work, all partners must work together.

Jeff Everly, whom we met in Day 4, says, "The key to our success has been that all banking clients are assigned to a team headed by Dave Frazier and me, and all medical clients are assigned to a team headed by Mark Rudolph. Several years ago our partners had to make this critical decision for the good of the firm. When you try to be all things to all people, you just scratch the surface. I'd rather us be strong in a few things than mediocre in many things."

If the firm's compensation system is based on a certain book of business, it is easy to develop a "bridge plan." A bridge plan will compensate partners who assign their clients to a niche specialist for several years. It will also protect the assigned partner. A good compensation system for owners of a CPA firm will minimize the impact of book of business and length of employment and will maximize productivity. In some firms partners with a large book who have been with the firm for many years actually strangle the firm's growth potential. To build a niche, you sometimes must give up what you have for what you could become.

Jim Belew says, "We reorganized our firm into service delivery units, or SDUs. The people in the SDUs perform most of their work with the industry clients in that unit. We had to make some choices for the good of the clients and the good of the firm. The choices were not always popular with members of our management team because they had formed good relationships with their clients. They felt an obligation to those clients and wanted to continue their good relationship. But when each person saw how much better his or her life would be under this structure, we all agreed to proceed."

Developing Deep Skills

Many people recognize that traditional services of CPA firms are becoming more of a commodity. If you are among those accountants who focus only on the commodity side, you will be increasingly under both price pressure and the threat of losing your clients to someone bringing more value to them. In his book *Beyond the Billable Hour,* William Cobb presented a figure similar to the one on the following page.

At the low value-added end of the figure are traditional services, such as audits and tax compliance work. At the high end of the value curve are services such as estate planning, strategic planning, and technology consulting when they are performed in a unique way for a client. To provide these high-value services, the proactive CPA must invest in a deep set of skills, skills that are often beyond what can be learned from the state society's CPE programs. For instance, developing legal or insurance (Continuing Education-type) courses in estate planning will help you fashion unique, personalized services for your client.

Concentration is the key to economic results. Economic results require that managers concentrate their efforts on the smallest number of activities that will produce the largest amount of revenue.

—Peter F. Drucker[1]

Communicating Your Niche Skills

To convince clients that you are developing deep skills, it is important to communicate about the niche. Regular contact with prospects and referral sources will keep you in mind. Bill Jenkins developed a strong commitment to educational programs at Kennedy & Coe a number of years ago: "We believe that education comes before consulting." His firm has made a commitment to three industry groups: financial institutions, manufacturing, and agriculture. He says, "In all three of these niches, our firm offers a variety of educational programs for our clients and prospects. We believe in investing our resources to help our clients succeed. That is our best source of new clients. Our firm has tremendous intellectual property in the minds of our partners. Demonstrating this through our educational programs is vital to our growth."

Greg Anton, whom we met in Day 11, says, "The real key for me has been the integrated series of communications my firm has allowed me to set up within the SEC community. People are invited to my seminars at the state society level. I make an attempt to personally meet as many as I can. After the seminar, I call those participants whom I think might be good prospects.

We place them on our mailing lists for newsletters and so forth. I periodically send them a note or article."

Summary

To have a profitable, enjoyable practice, you must offer superior skills to a clearly identified niche. Your prospects and clients must believe that you are a specialist with expert skills in their areas. Once you establish your expertise, then you must communicate it to prospects and clients. Niche specialization is the key to future success. I recommend that you get started now.

26 Selling Value, Not Discounts

If your services are generic, the potential client might as well just take the lowest bid. It's up to you to show people why you have unique capabilities for meeting their needs.

—Rick Crandall, Author and Consultant

Your success in selling is not measured by the number of times you win the business. You profit from the number of times you win engagements *without* giving up an overall discount. Winning engagements as the *highest*-priced competitor is the ultimate selling thrill. Winning engagements as the lowball bidder should be scary.

Winning with a higher price confirms that prospects engaged you because you'd convinced them of the expertise you bring to the engagement. Winning with a higher price starts your relationship off with a new client as a value-adding partner. Obviously a higher initial price allows you to profit from the engagement in the first year. But it will also allow you more room for reasonable price increases in future years.

Don't Discount

Discounting fees is a bait-and-switch strategy used by sophisticated sellers with a wide range of services. Discounting low-value commodity work to get the high-value-added extended services is one method of matching pricing to the perceived value of each service. Matching prices of services to value perception is an appropriate way to price your services.

Unfortunately, many hapless CPAs discount their fees just to attract clients. Discounting is their *only* strategy. The hapless sellers do not have a strategy to provide value-adding services at premium prices. All too often, the client pegs your hourly rate at the discount. Then when you provide any value-adding service, such as strategic, financial, or estate planning, the lowball hourly rate sticks. My experience has shown that clients who buy you because of your low price will leave you more quickly than clients who buy your value.

Tom, a client of mine in Atlanta, is a partner in a large CPA firm. A partner whose motto was "Get the client at any price, we'll get them up later" coached him throughout his younger years. I asked Tom to select some clients who had been obtained this way for a review. He concluded that every single client who had been obtained using a discount had either left the firm or was still a pricing headache. His firm had not been successful in obtaining a reasonable yield from any of those clients.

Get the confidence of the public and you will have no difficulty getting their patronage. Remember always that the recollection of quality remains long after the price is forgotten.

—H. George Selfridge[1]

Go for Value

Always being the highest-priced competitor may be a bit too optimistic. David Morgan, whom we met in Day 1, says, "We win some proposals when we are the highest priced. I wouldn't say often. But I would say that we are rarely the cheapest. There are times we lose business just over prices. If we lose over price, then it may not have been a good fit for us anyway. I think to overcome pricing pressures you have to show real differentiation. Prospects will pay more for us if they look at all the different things we can bring to the table."

CPAs are the most respected business professionals in the United States. Because of this position of respect, you have built-in persuasive powers. Often you have the opportunity to make a persuasive presentation to a prospective client. These presentations can be written or oral. In building his firm to over $9 million in revenue in seven years, Mike Kruse says that he has probably written fewer than 10 proposals. Many times the presentation is oral, but the document is an engagement letter. In other cases, a formal written document along with a PowerPoint demonstration will be the process to follow.

Five Keys to Winning Proposals

During the years I have worked with accountants to improve proposal success, I have discovered 5 factors in winning proposals and 10 factors to avoid. The 5 keys to winning are:

1. Win the emotions.
2. Uncover key information.
3. Obtain a strong endorsement.
4. Plan your proposal.
5. Use the right words at the right time.

Win the Emotions

"Winning the emotions" refers to the strong development of liking and trust with key decision influencers so that prospects want you to win. This is so important that I devoted much of the Day 4 chapter to this subject. In many proposal situations that I have studied, the client personnel always genuinely liked the service provider selected. Yet all too often, CPAs forget the emotional side of decision making.

David Morgan believes you should demonstrate your responsiveness and professionalism during the proposal process. He says: "I believe you should get to them right away. The worst things you can do are get your proposal in at the last moment and drag out the process. That sets a bad tone. Prospects will believe that you will be slow to respond to their needs when you become their accountant. We landed a $40 million distributor recently—I believe, because we reacted quickly. Their accountant had been slow in reacting to their requests. On Wednesday I gathered the information, and on Friday I called to tell them our proposal was ready. We met on Monday and they hired us. If we can demonstrate our responsiveness, we will win the emotional game."

Uncover Key Information

When prospects trust you, often they will share information with you on which you can build a winning proposal. This is one reason so many current CPAs win proposals. They know inside information and use it to their benefit. When you don't uncover this important information, your proposal appears to be inept. This is because you did not structure your proposal to meet the client's real needs.

Bill Fingland says, "When I am selling to the right concerns of the prospect, my proposal can be very short. I think the shorter, the better. When your proposal is short and is focused on the client's key issues, he or she knows you have done your homework. Long, voluminous proposals often signal that you haven't done your homework and boiled it down for the client."

The best way to learn what your prospect's needs are is to listen carefully. To begin, simply ask two questions:

1. What is the situation today?
2. How would you like it to be?

The difference between the answers to these two questions is the problem you want to solve—how to move prospects from today's situation to their ideal situation. Once you have defined a problem, probing more deeply may enable you to uncover information that your competitors miss.

> On a recent proposal, a client I'll call Joe learned that he was competing with three other CPA firms: an incumbent and two others. During a dinner with the CEO, arranged by a lawyer friend of the two, Joe learned that the CEO had doubts about his CFO. This bit of information had not surfaced during the formal interviews. Joe probed deeply and learned that the CEO felt trapped with his incompetent CFO because he'd fired three in five years. The CEO admitted, "I don't think I know how to pick a CFO who will be both accurate and timely."
>
> The CPA asked a variety of questions around this issue, showing his complete understanding of the issue. Alternatives, training, executive search, and outsourcing were discussed. My client won the engagement. During my interview with his new client, the client said, "Joe got to my real needs. He understood me. I'd had many doubts about the best way to hire a CFO. Our former accountants seemed to think our situation was normal. But I wanted more."

Obtain a Strong Endorsement

As you know, referred leads are the most successful selling opportunities you have. Many successful CPAs have gone to by-referral-only selling systems. A true referred lead should get you in front of a prospect without competition. Naturally, this is a highly successful selling situation.

In many cases, you are proposing among competitors. Your entrée came from being on a list of possible sources. Thus, you must engineer a strong endorsement. There are several ways to do this. One method is to ask a mutual friend to call or write your prospect with a solid endorsement.

Depending on your friend's relationship with the decision makers, you can elevate yourself to number one very quickly.

Avoid Dated Testimonials

Don't date testimonials—it will keep your literature fresh longer. Even when the testimonial is current, the date can distract the recipient from the message.

—C. Richard Weylman, *Opening Closed Doors*[2]

Another method is to ask your prospect to call your references. If you really want the business, say: "Ms. Smith, we maintain confidentiality and care with our valuable clients. I hope you can appreciate that. You have asked for some references, and I will provide them to you if you will promise me that you will call them. You see, I must contact my client first to assure he will take your call and you will receive priority. This is the minimum courtesy my clients expect from me. Will you call them?" Now you have entered a moral contract with your prospect. If she says no, then you know you are just being priced. If she says yes, you know she is serious.

Plan Your Proposal

Have you ever left a meeting and thought of all the things you should have said? Such an experience demonstrates that even when you know what to say and do, if you are not thinking quickly enough, you may miss the target. Planning your presentation will enable you to be prepared with the right words at the right time.

All authorities agree that the preproposal stage is the most important phase of selling CPA services. In this stage you gather the information you must have to make an effective proposal. This information should enable you to understand your prospect's situation so you can plan the appropriate questions to ask and statements to make during the crucial interview process. If you cannot spend the time up front to gather the necessary data, or if prospects will not devote the time to you to help you learn about their business, then your odds of winning the proposal decrease dramatically.

Often the key to improving your batting average in proposals is to decline to propose in at least 25 percent of your opportunities. The box lists signs warning when you should not submit a proposal to a prospect. When you focus your attention on fewer prospects, your success rate will improve.

Good selling takes preparation time. How many times have you headed out of your office with a proposal in hand with the paper still hot from the

Four Signs that You Should Not Submit a Proposal

1 You cannot spare the time to do a professional job.

2 Your prospect will not allow you sufficient time or access to key decision influencers.

3 There is no problem for you to solve.

4 There is no up-front commitment to make a change in the way business is done.

printer? You will improve your presentation dramatically when you rehearse before an audience of your associates. Have you ever given the same speech several times to a succession of audiences? Remember how each time your speech improved? That was because your past performances before live audiences improved your understanding of your material so well that you could focus on the audience rather than the material you were presenting.

During the planning phase, you should begin to prepare your questions. You will be able to ask powerful questions if you plan them out in advance of your meeting. All great attorneys take thorough depositions in advance of the trial and then carefully plan the questions they will ask at trial.

Use the Right Words at the Right Time

People buy for their own reasons, not yours. There are dramatic differences among feature selling, advantage selling, and true benefit selling. You increase your persuasive skills tremendously when you talk about what your prospects want and then show them how to get it.

Whenever you sell anything, there are three possible "languages" you can use. *Feature language* describes the physical characteristics of a product or service. Feature language is the least persuasive language of all. In fact, much research has shown that feature language has a low to negative impact on the selling process. Feature selling—when you talk about the size of your firm, its age, all the services you may offer, your international offices, your headquarters, and your downtown location—may run up the price concerns of your prospects. This type of selling is a killer when you are trying to cross-sell services.

Advantage language is more powerful than feature language because you speak to the possible benefits for a client or prospect. Each feature of your firm or its services has one or more advantages. What are the advantages of each of the features of your accounting firm?

Bob Gaida on the Importance of Using the Right Words

One of my early endeavors, when I was 27 years old, was to bring on a new client. When I brought a large client on board, it was quite exciting. No one in the New York office thought there was a 27-year-old who could bring in a large client. Someone should have said, 'He probably cannot get this done, but we should support the motivation of this individual.' That's what I would do today if I had a 27-year-old. But that was a different time.

A partner took over the proposal process from me, after I had established rapport with the prospect. He made a flip chart presentation about things in which the client had no interest. As this presentation droned on, I noticed the owner had to catch his head once, when he was nodding off. I was in a real quandary.

So I took a risk and said, 'Let me jump in here a little bit. I do have the advantage, and I should have helped you better. I've been working with these people for the last several months.'

And I turned to the owner and said, 'Pat, I know we've thrown a lot at you and you've got to digest it. But if we were your accountants, we would have filed your last two tax returns in the following manner . . . and we would have brought back to you $75,000. You would be $75,000 richer. Now, the good news is, we can still do it.' He said, 'You can go back and get me $75,000 now . . . legal? All that?' 'Yes.' He says, 'Good.' Turned to his son and says, 'Sign them up.' And he walked out of the room.

Being able to speak the right words to the prospect at the right time takes planning and rehearsal. And sometimes it can be risky.

At a minimum, the training program for each staff person in your firm should include memorization of the features of your firm and all the advantages of each feature. Without a thorough knowledge of the features and advantages, an accountant cannot possibly cross-sell a client.

A word of caution: If you present your firm's features and all of their advantages in a long string of boastful statements, advantages begin to sound like features to the prospect. This is called the spray-and-pray technique— you spray the prospect with all the features and the advantages of each service and pray that some of them will be relevant to the prospect's needs.

Some professionals are successful with this approach because they are able to predict with some degree of accuracy prospects' possible interests.

Advantage language is particularly powerful in the early stages of a presentation to pique prospects' interest levels.

The most powerful selling language of all is *benefit language*. All advantages are possible benefits. The only way you can truly speak in benefit language is to talk about the particular advantages of your service, which are in direct response to a need or want statement from the prospect. Sometimes prospects will tell you what they need or want. But more often than not, you must probe to learn their true problems, wants, and needs, so you can craft benefit statements that persuade.

Using the Puppy-Dog Close

Perhaps the best way to win a proposal competition is to eliminate your competition. Have you ever taken a puppy home "just for the night" to see how the kids would like it? You now own it, don't you? After your family spent a few hours with the puppy, you were hooked. The same is true with various products and services.

Four Ways to Make the Puppy-Dog Close Work for You

1 **Sell the trial, not the service.** It is much easier to sell someone a free profit-improvement review than it is to sell an audit.

2 **Gain the prospect's confidence.** Make it clear that this service does not create any obligation. During the trial period, your goal should be to get the prospect to like you and trust you.

3 **"Bear hug" the prospect.** During the trial period, turn on your winning ways to really get to know the prospect and the prospect's business. Your goal is to get the prospect to enjoy working with you.

4 **Use your findings to close the sale.** If you have uncovered any improved ways of doing business with prospects, they will be very open to hiring you. Help prospects find reasons for engaging you by appealing to their buying motives and using the trial results as proof of the benefits of doing business with you.

The puppy-dog close works on the principle that once a person has experienced the benefits of a product or service for a short time, he or she hates to give it up. What about your services? Can you think of a puppy-dog close that would work? Three possibilities might be: (1) a "free" profit-improvement assessment, (2) a tax-reduction review, or (3) a trial use of a module of your accounting software. With a little creativity, any accounting firm can create more sales using the puppy-dog close.

10 Proposal Pitfalls to Avoid

In my experience over the years, I have found 10 significant reasons why proposals are unsuccessful. Use this checklist to see how your firm stacks up.

❏ *Use of boilerplate.* Whether written or oral, if the prospect suspects you have cut and pasted from someone else's proposal, you look cheap.

❏ *No differentiation.* If you can't make a case for why your differences from your competition are important to your prospect, why should a prospect select you? If there are no value differences, clients will select based on price alone.

❏ *No focus on risk reduction.* Whenever companies change their accounting provider, the decision makers perceive risk. Often the risk of change is perceived as greater than the risk of staying put. You can minimize risk by identifying it and mitigating it.

❏ *Missing the deadline.* Being late with a proposal implies you will be late with the work. Missing the deadline is a killer.

❏ *No eye appeal.* Proposals that do not appeal to both right- and left-brained people risk being dismissed. Content and eye appeal both are crucial to success.

❏ *The professional does not drive the process.* Turning over the proposal process to an inexperienced professional or a marketing coordinator who does not understand the client's issues will result in a weak effort. If you cannot devote the time to drive the process, don't bother.

❏ *Mailing the proposal.* Mailing the proposal shows your lack of concern. By doing so you miss valuable face time with the prospect. A client or prospect who insists that you mail the proposal is probably not serious.

❏ *Lack of thorough interviews.* The investigation and interview process is crucial to a well-directed proposal. Without information, you'll have to use the ineffective spray-and-pray technique.

❏ *No preview.* Previewing your proposal with the prospect in draft form is the same process you would use to prepare a set of draft financial statements for a client. Failing to preview shows your lack of professionalism.

❏ *No focus on prospect's business.* Focusing on your firm and not your prospect's business is the kiss of death. Focus on how you are going to solve clients' problems and meet their needs and wants. Prospects will dismiss quickly long pages of boilerplate on how great your firm is.

Summary

You shouldn't buy work by discounting. Sell value and your unique expertise. When you are successful, you will avoid most competitive and written proposal situations. The preproposal work is what will get you the job. Find out key issues and build rapport. Then focus on benefits to the client. A losing proposal is rushed boilerplate with no eye appeal or differentiating characteristics. It doesn't show an understanding of key issues in the prospect's business. A good initial high-value sale lays the groundwork for the type of mutually satisfying client relationship you want to have.

27 Your Differences Will Handle Objections

I love different folks.

—Eleanor Hodgman Porter, *Pollyanna*

The Bilbrey Furniture Company was the most successful store in the small town where I grew up. The owner, Lee Bilbrey, provided personal service in an unusual way. As the Wal-Marts and Kmarts began arriving on the scene with their discounted furniture and other items, many businesses died, but not Bilbrey Furniture. Whenever customers would visit Bilbrey's store, Lee Bilbrey would let them browse without interruption for a few minutes, all the while observing them. Then with his detailed knowledge of the items the customers were looking at, he would comment on the items' fabric or construction. He would ask a few very gentle questions and then make a presentation about the furniture the customers were interested in.

If customers did not purchase and Bilbrey felt they would be well served with quality furniture, he had a unique wrap-up to his presentation. Bilbrey would say, "I know you have choices in buying furniture. You could travel all the way to Knoxville and you could buy some cheap stuff at the Kmart. But there is one thing you won't get when you buy from those other places. You won't get me. You have me standing behind your purchase, helping with the arrangement and free delivery and setup. You won't get that anywhere else." Then he would walk over to a freezer and get a quart of ice cream to hand to the customer. Inevitably, the customer would thank Bilbrey and then drive home to put the ice cream in their freezer. Most would talk about how nice that man was and return to buy his furniture. (Having ice cream melting in the car also ensured that customers didn't stop and shop at other stores on their way home!)

Bilbrey understood how to differentiate himself and his business. First of all, he knew his products inside and out, a rarity at the discounting stores. His detailed knowledge was very impressive to his customers. Second, he stressed the key differentiator of his business: himself. He knew that people begin to decide which product to buy based on differences.

Your Uniqueness

How do you differ from your competition? What are your mission and your vision for serving clients? Is it your niche focus? Is it your size? Is it your commitment to certain levels of customer service? Is it focus on certain services? Whenever you can match up your differences with the needs of certain clients, there is a natural fit. When this natural fit occurs, you will easily overcome the objections that may arise in a selling situation.

In order to be irreplaceable, one must always be different.

—Coco Chanel

Objections arise because prospects sense that your services are not a perfect fit for his business. Whenever a prospect senses this perfect fit, you will have a new client. If there is a perfect match, the prospect will pay more for your services because she values your differences.

Think about it this way: The audit committee has completed its interview of three firms and one of the members says, "They all looked the same, quality work, CPAs, nice proposals, blue suits, smart people, and specialized in our industry." How will they choose? If all things appear the same, the choice will come down to low price. That is another reason you want to focus on your differences. When the prospect values those differences, price becomes less of an issue.

To be successful in business, you must be unique. You must be so different, that if people want what you have, they must come to you to get it.

—Walt Disney

Jim Belew describes it this way, "In public accounting, we deliver a commodity-type service that is extremely customized. During my youth I worked at a gas station. Gasoline is a commodity. The margin on the gasoline is very competitive. But the profit potential on all of the other products is enormous. The gas station I worked at focused on auto repair and other fluids for your car. Today the gas stations sell milk, bread, prepared fast foods, and souvenirs. While the services have changed, it's the same concept.

When you bring value to customers, they reward you with their money. Same thing in what we do—yes, you can deliver a tax return, but you focus on some of the real needs: for example, paying less taxes, personal or business budgeting, cash flow, credit and the right kind of debt. Are they investing in the assets to get the right kind of return? Are they putting money away for retirement? You are adding value above and beyond just providing a commodity set of tax returns or books. This is what makes us different."

A major portion of your prospect investigation should be to determine the needs and wants of the client and then to match up your differentiators to fit the needs.

Your Competition

Bob Gaida uses a "service gap" message. He says, "Across America, there are companies or clients who are being underserved by their local accounting firm or by a Big Five competitor. Our middle-market firm has an opportunity to fill the service gap created when a perception of this occurs. When I am talking to a specific prospect, I focus on these differences. The local firms and the Big Four know of these, but they can't match them. Clients who are well matched for us will value the service gap message. I never slam my local or Big Five competitors. But I do point out truthful differences."

On the following pages are some charts to help you sort through your differences from your competitors (see Exhibit 27.1). Fill them out and see how they help you.

Clarifying your differences from your competitors will handle most objections before they arise. But there is rarely a perfect fit, so you must help prospects deal with some of the imperfections.

In a competitive selling situation, the CPA who successfully uncovers and sells to the objections of the prospect will gain a winning edge. How often have you left a competitive proposal feeling really good about your presentation only to learn later that the prospect either selected another CPA or stayed with the current one? And how often did you really know the reason why you lost the proposal?

Handling Objections

A great seller will anticipate and cultivate objections. If you do not know areas of potential client concerns, you cannot address them. And if you do not address them, the objections will stay hidden from you and will kill your chances of proposal success. Begin searching for possible objections the moment you realize that you will propose. Some objections should be handled

Exhibit 27.1

COMPETITION DIFFERENTIATION WORKSHEET

LIST YOUR COMPETITORS:

International Firms _____

_____

National Firms _____

_____

Regional Firms _____

_____

Large Local Firms _____

_____

Sole CPA Practitioners _____

_____

National Brokerage Houses _____

_____

HOW ARE YOU DIFFERENT FROM YOUR COMPETITORS?

I. When you compete against a big firm,

Your advantages are:	Describe the various benefits to clients:
1.	
2.	
3.	
4.	
5.	
6.	
7.	
8.	
9.	
10.	

When you compete against a big firm,	
Your weaknesses are:	*Describe the impact on clients:*
1.	
2.	
3.	
4.	
5.	

II. When you compete against a small firm,	
Your advantages are:	*Describe the various benefits to clients:*
1.	
2.	
3.	
4.	
5.	
6.	
7.	
8.	
9.	
10.	

When you compete against a small firm,	
Your weaknesses are:	*Describe the impact on clients:*
1.	
2.	
3.	
4.	
5.	

(continues)

Exhibit 27.1   *(Continued)*

III. When you compete against a firm about your size,	
Your advantages are:	*Describe the various benefits to clients:*
1.	
2.	
3.	
4.	
5.	
6.	
7.	
8.	
9.	
10.	
When you compete against a firm about your size,	
Your weaknesses are:	*Describe the impact on clients:*
1.	
2.	
3.	
4.	
5.	

during your presentation and some after the prospect brings them up. The rule generally is this: If your answer to an objection is weak, deal with the objection during the early part of your presentation.

If, during your presentation, your prospect brings up an objection such as "Your fees are too high" or "We're happy with our present CPA," there are specific steps you should take to handle it.

Seven Ways to Deal with Objections during Presentations

1 *Listen carefully.* Let your prospect talk it out. The worst thing you can do is anticipate what the prospect is going to say. You may answer an objection your prospect doesn't have yet.

2 *Never argue.* This will push the prospect into a defensive mode. When prospects become defensive, they will begin to think of new objections and you will find yourself in a wrestling match you cannot win.

3 *Restate the objection.* Restating often is a way to get prospects to answer their own objections. If you are presenting to multiple decision makers, many times one of them will handle the restatement for you. J. P. Morgan said that a person generally has two reasons for doing things: one that sounds good and the real one.

4 *Question the area of concern.* Often when you ask prospects to elaborate, they will determine that what they thought was a problem is not very important in the whole scheme of their decision. You will also gain valuable insight into the concern and give yourself a little time to mentally prepare your answer.

5 *Provide a short answer.* Minimize the mental impact of the objection by providing a well-rehearsed, concise answer. Do not be vague, but be as brief as possible.

6 *Confirm your answer.* If you do not clear the air before proceeding with your presentation, prospects will still be thinking about the area of concern while you are talking about something else. Say something like "That clarifies the issue for you, doesn't it?"

7 *Proceed with a trial close.* After you have satisfied a prospect as to one of the voiced areas of concern, you may be able to get your prospect's commitment.

In a competitive proposal process, you have wasted your time if you do not win the business. There is no silver medal for coming in second. Often the key to coming in first is to discover any possible reason, real or imagined, that your prospect may have for rating you number two in any area of your service. Anticipating and handling objections is crucial.

Handling Specific Concerns during the Presentation

Below, I discuss some of the concerns you might encounter during your meetings.

Fees, Price, and Value

When presenting to a prospect, when should you mention the fee? Not until you have established the value of the benefits provided.

Because non-CPAs have difficulty selecting among professionals, they often ask, "How much would it cost me?" Such a question baits you into discussing price before creating a context of value. Price is relevant only when compared to value. Price without value is exorbitant under any circumstances.

If you can avoid price until you have determined the needs of your prospect, you will be in a position to propose the service that will provide the greatest satisfaction.

Don't ignore a specific request for fees, but answer it vaguely until you can clearly establish value. Say something like "Our fees are comparable to other CPAs, but we may find ways that you can save substantially," or "Our average billing rates are $105 per hour. But before I give you a quote, let me see if there are ways I can make you a profit from our relationship."

Market pricing is a coming issue for accountants. You will be able to market price only when you establish value before quoting a fee. Selling value will distinguish you from competitors and may allow you to realize many times your standard fees from delighted clients.

We're Happy with Our Current CPA

Are there ways you can respond when you hear this comment from your prospects? Or should you just congratulate them for their excellent choice and bid them adieu?

Most businesses have a relationship with an outside CPA. Rarely will they share small problems with another CPA until the intensity of the complaint is large. But, if you follow these five rules, you may learn there is great opportunity for you.

Rule 1: *If you cannot find dissatisfied people in the business, your chances of success are nil.* The person with whom you are talking may not be unhappy, but another person may be. You may be talking with the CEO who is satisfied with the current CPA firm, but the CFO may hate the firm. Ask your contact, "Who comes in contact with the outside CPA firm?" or "Who has an impact on engaging outside CPA services?"

Rule 2: *Never slam a competitor.* Congratulate your contacts and say that you are glad they are receiving great service, because many businesses are not. Let them know that you realize business must be earned over time and you are willing to make that investment. Tell them that you would like to be their second choice in the event that something should happen to their first choice or when they have a need that number one cannot fill.

Rule 3: *Anticipate the comment that prospects are happy with their current CPA.* "While you are probably happy with your present CPA, our firm has helped many of our clients become more profitable." Tell contacts that many businesses their size often split their business between two CPA firms so they won't be dependent on just one for advice or pricing. It is very common for businesses to utilize numerous law firms, for example.

Rule 4: *Offer a service that none of your competitors provides.* Doing this will differentiate you and allow you a better chance to serve. When offering such a service, insure that you can do it profitably and extremely well.

Rule 5: *Try to keep your courtship confidential.* This may be impossible, but the moment your competition learns of your advances to its clients, the other firm will rush into action and clean up its act.

Summary

A key factor in impressing prospects and getting new clients is to be able to articulate your differences from your competitors and to make your prospects understand how those differences are benefits to them. Know yourself first, then your competition. Be prepared to deal with common objections about price by instead selling value. Be prepared to show why it's worth their effort to change accountants.

28 Pricing to Maximize Value

*When dealing with people, remember you are not
dealing with creatures of logic, but with creatures
of emotion, creatures bristling with prejudice, and
motivated by pride and vanity.*

—Dale Carnegie

There are at least three ways to make more money in your firm: You can lower costs, add new business, and charge more for your current clients. The last point—raising prices—is the quickest way to increase both your gross and your profits. Pricing your services is an art, not a science. However, it's safe to say that most of you are underpricing too many clients.

Recently, at Chicago's O'Hare airport, I passed a water fountain on my way to purchase a 16-ounce bottle of water for $1.81. I was struck by the irony of the situation. I paid $1.81 for something I could have gotten for free, just ten feet away at the water fountain. As I had 45 minutes before my next flight, I stayed near the water fountain and watched 12 other people pass it to buy water. Only two people drank from the water fountain, while 12 paid the two bucks. Why?

A few months ago I bought a similar bottle of water at the St. Louis airport. After sipping from it for a while, I noticed that fine print: "This water is a product of the St. Louis Water Works." It was tap water. I could have had the water free at the fountain, but I chose to pay for it. Why?

As in the case of the water, your clients don't always make the lowest-cost choice. Despite price competition, good clients buy on value. While they don't want to pay more for less, they don't mind paying more for more value. It's your job to provide a clear sense of increased value for clients and to deliver it.

Until recently, pricing has been relegated to a function of the accountant's cost accounting systems. Most MAP (Management Accounting Practice) studies compare billing rates to staff member costs. Because pricing is so difficult, many accountants prefer to avoid dealing with the issue. Management consultant Dave Cottle asks participants in his meetings, "How many of you could charge $15 more per hour and not lose any clients?" Most accountants raise their hands. Then he says, "Why don't you?" Usually the room is silent till someone says, "Well, that would be 3.3 times our salary cost and we charge out at 3." In other words, because of inertia the CPA is leaving $15,000 to $20,000 per year on the table that clients are willing to pay.

Demand Pricing

Many accounting firms are keep-busy oriented. The badge of honor is the number of worked or chargeable hours per year, not profits. As Cottle regularly points out, CPAs acknowledge they are leaving money on the table. The most important rule of market pricing is: Charge each client the most that client is willing to pay.

A few years ago I devised a simple system for an accounting firm to use. We identify the largest clients who make up 50 percent of the revenue of the firm. That usually amounts to 5 percent of the clients. In a firm with 1,000 clients, 50 clients will add up to about 50 percent of the revenue. For each client on the list, I ask the partner responsible, "Would you lose the client with a 5 percent increase?" If the answer is no, then I ask about 7 percent, 10 percent, 12 percent, and 15 percent. Answering the questions causes the partner to evaluate the client's perception of value rather than the cost structure of the firm and the hours necessary to complete the job.

In some cases, it is best to ask the clients some questions to determine their perceptions of value. I ask clients, "On a scale of one to five, with five being the most, what value do you receive from your accounting firm?" When the client answers "five," I know we have a client who can absorb a substantial price increase.

There are two dimensions to the pricing decision: willingness and ability to pay. The client's willingness has a great deal to do with his own attitudes of frugality and the level of service you are providing. The ability to pay has more to do with the profitability of the enterprise or the budget allocated to your services. In evaluating these situations, you must ask yourself a number of questions: Who are you dealing with? People deep in the organization may have more price sensitivity than do the senior officers. CFOs may have more price sensitivity than do CEOs. If your primary relationship is with the CEO, your ability to raise prices is enhanced.

Are there competitors in the arena with you? If your competitors are pricier, can you raise prices? If your competitors are less pricey, can you build your value?

How profitable is your client's or prospect's business? If the business is very profitable, the ability to pay is higher.

Who are the other suppliers to the business—the banker, the attorney, and so forth? If the business is using a higher-priced group of other advisors, your ability to price higher may be enhanced.

Ron Baker, in his book *The Professional's Guide to Value Pricing*, refers to the practice of charging different prices to different customers (for the same service) as price discrimination. For me, the goal of price discrimination is to maximize profits while at the same time to keep my client. The first rule of good accounting firm pricing techniques is to bill according to the value perceived by your client. Therefore, you should charge different prices to different clients for the same service.

When performing a client loyalty survey, I want a client to rate the accounting firm with 5s (5 = outstanding, 3 = as expected, 1 = unacceptable) on quality, responsiveness, and deliverables. I really do not want my accounting firm to receive a 5 on value received. I'd prefer a 3 on value. With high marks on satisfaction and average to good marks on value, we know that we have a profit-maximized client. This client thinks our services are first rate and thinks the value she's getting for her money is about right. I want the client to say "You are expensive, but worth every penny of what I pay."

Baker is a true evangelist. His mission is to wipe out the billable hour as a method of pricing for CPAs. Reading his book or listening to his presentation will convince you how serious he is. A former KPMG accountant who is an expert on economics and pricing theory, Baker is an authority on pricing issues for accountants. Of all the books that I mention in these chapters, Baker's book is the one that I would say is a must read for the serious leader and manager in the accounting business.

You're Worth What You Ask For

The managing partner of one of my CPA clients was terrified by the idea of raising his prices. He said, "The last time we raised prices, our clients were very angry." I asked, "How many clients were angry?" He said, "Most of them." I asked, "How many did you actually lose?" After thinking for a few moments, he said, "Well, actually, none." Because a few clients were angry, he didn't want to raise prices. In many cases, you must understand that negotiating a "half cent a ton" price concession is a sport with many of your clients. What you perceive as anger is really a test of your entrepreneurial mettle. The client screams and you bend.

> *It takes great service, not just good service, to insure differentiation from competitors, to build solid customer relationships, to compete on value without competing on price, and to inspire employees to create repeat business.*
>
> —Leonard Berry, *On Great Service*[1]

Terry Orr says, "Many of our clients are quite successful because they have made a business out of buying low and selling high. Sometimes I help clients negotiate with a supplier to reduce costs. And I know they turn those skills on me. When I have a good sense of what my client is trying to accomplish and where he is trying to go, I get a sense of the value he places on me. When I am able to get this sense, we can get a higher price for audit or tax work. But it has been the result of sitting down and understanding where the company is going. We understand they need an audit, but before we start the process of pricing we want to spend some time talking about where the company is today—what their objectives are to take the company over the next three years, and five years."

The one-price-fits-all philosophy does not work. If you charge the highest price your most willing and able client will pay, you'll only have one client. If you charge the lowest price so that you will get all of the clients in your market, you will never make a profit. The hourly billing method is a midpoint selection that assures you of a moderate profit but provides a windfall to your clients to whom you provide the most value. The clients who get the most value from you can afford to pay you the most.

Rules of Pricing

Rule 1: Bill according to the value perceived by your client.

Rule 2: Determine what your client is willing and able to pay, then provide a package of services around that price so you obtain the maximum.

Another method of pricing is to determine what your client is willing and able to pay, then provide a package of services around that price so you obtain the maximum. In some cases, the client may not want a comprehensive consulting engagement. If $40,000 were the maximum price the client is willing to pay, would the client implement the project if you perform the investigation phase of the assignment?

How do you determine the maximum? One approach is to tell the prospect, "We have different types of clients, some who value all of the things we bring to the table and some who want the cheapest price. What do you value the most, our range of services or our prices? Another approach is to tell the prospect, "This package of services could run you $40,000, $60,000 or $90,000, depending on the range of service and degree of detail. Would you give me a sense of which of these fits your budget?"

Another method is to present the job as a fixed price for the basics with optional add-ons. Recently I asked two roofing contractors to bid on replacing the roof on my home. The one I selected bid $6,400 for a 20-year roof. But he provided me a variety of options, including a 25- or 30-year shingle, a tear-off or nail-over option, and some different venting options. I ended up spending over $10,000, but I felt in control.

Tips from Successful Negotiators

- *Once you name your price, "shut up." Watch and listen. Don't say anything. Your silence demonstrates your confidence.*

- *Ask for the budget in a direct and determined voice. People will feel compelled to answer you.*

A New Way of Thinking

Using these pricing methods requires you to change the way you are doing things. Change is always difficult. Jim Belew says, "All of our partners are working to price our services based upon value. We are in the learning process. It will take time."

Mike Kruse, whom we met in Day 6, says, "We work hard to price our services on value added. So if we've got a project, and we know that it is very important to a client and that we are one of the few that can deliver it, or it takes some approval and we've got contacts on a regulatory board that can walk it through, we value bill. As an example, we had a situation about a year ago when a contractor from out of state needed a contractor's license. I talked to him on a Friday afternoon. The licensing board was meeting Tuesday morning, and he was in violation of the construction law. So if we couldn't make it work, he was in big trouble. We went into high gear and set up a new company. He capitalized it on Monday. We performed an audit on that company and met with the licensing board. I had four or five hours in it and I billed him $10,000. He wasn't paying me for the time but for the result. He made over $100,000 and he wanted us to do the project. Many accountants would not have been able to act quite so quickly because of their lack of construction experience."

Sell Wants, Not Needs

Here is a test for you to use on 10 of your friends. Open a discussion with each person on the subject of needs and wants. Talk about what some of their needs might be. Then chat about possible wants. Ask each friend to write down the name of one tangible item he needs. After it is written down, ask your friend to write down the name of one tangible item he wants. Then ask your friend to place a price tag on each item. You write the price tags in the chart shown in Exhibit 28.1.

Exhibit 28.1   Price Tag Chart

Friend's Name	$ Amount of Need	$ Amount of Want
1.		
2.		
3.		
4.		
5.		
6.		
7.		
8.		
9.		
10.		
Totals	$_____	$_____

Once you have asked 10 friends these questions and tallied up the costs of the needs and wants, answer these questions.

- Do you think your clients might react the same way?
- Do the price tags of all your friends' needs fall in the same range?
- What about the price tags on your friends' wants?

- Is there a dramatic difference between the totals of the needs column and the wants column? (There should be; wants are generally more expensive than needs.)

- If you had this kind of information about your clients, would it help you allocate your resources if you could supply some of their higher-priced wants?

Value Your Time

Most of us have only so many hours we can work per year. In other words, we have a finite amount of time we will apply to our business. Don't apply the same amount of your resources to clients with low levels of needs and wants as you do for clients with high levels. Utilize an appropriate pricing schedule to get the highest yield from your time *and* deliver the greatest value to clients who need it.

In his book *Revenue Management,* Robert G. Cross[2] defines revenue management as "the application of disciplined tactics that predict consumer behavior at the micro-market level and optimize product availability and price to maximize revenue growth. In even simpler terms, revenue management ensures that companies will sell the right product to the right customer at the right time for the right price."

Many accountants separate services into Type 1 or Type 2. Type 1 services are generally those that are compliance related. Helping clients prepare tax returns or compile financial statements would be examples of Type 1 services. Type 2 services generally are those that clients want, such as strategic or tax planning. As we saw in the Day 26 chapter, Type 2 services can be further separated into three categories representing different levels of value of the service. Type 2 services are typically the more value-adding services. Firms that focus on Type 1 services tend to have clients who are very sensitive to price. Therefore, the ability of these firms to increase pricing using some of the methods I described earlier in this chapter will be very limited.

Type 1 services can be delivered cost effectively with the aid of technology. Firms that successfully compete in the Type 1 market make large investments in technology in order to drive down transaction costs. For example, through the use of technology, H&R Block attracted nearly $1 billion in tax return business away from CPA firms who were slower to adopt new technology.

Those firms that add at least 15 percent of their services mix in the Type 2 category will begin to see their clients' price resistance go down. Firms with larger percentages of value-adding services seem to have the least amount of price resistance for all services. You will experience the ability to price even Type 1 services at a premium by adding the valuable brand, experiential, and unique services to your mix.

> *Nurture your relationship with each customer . . . selling more to fewer is more efficient . . . and more profitable.*
>
> —Don Peppers and Martha Rogers, *The One to One Future: Building Relationships One Customer at a Time*[3]

Value, Value, Value

Accountants have the best ability to price services based on value rather than on cost compared to almost any other professional. It is crucial that you focus on price rather than costs when balancing supply and demand. You have a limited supply of time and talent; if you focus on cost, you will never be able to maximize your profits.

Because you sell your services to segmented small markets of business-to-business users and not to mass markets, you can determine the willingness and ability to pay of each one of your clients. Once you have determined this, you must save your services for your most valuable customers. Too often, accounting firms allow the tax season to blur the necessity for this. Ask yourself these questions: Am I exhausting myself and my workforce during tax season serving nonstrategic clients? Does my focus on nonstrategic clients during tax season keep me from proactively serving my most valuable clients?

Once you have an appropriate pricing mechanism in place, it is important to continually assess your revenue opportunities. Your clients' wants and needs are changing constantly. And so are their willingness and ability to pay for your services. Your supply of talent and intellectual property may also fluctuate, as may the market's. To maximize your profits, you must continually assess your opportunities.

Factors Involved in Pricing

To develop a good market pricing system, evaluate each service you are providing each client using this list:

Input	Output
▪ Time	▪ Value
▪ Effort	▪ Results
▪ Cost	▪ Benefits
▪ Input	▪ Output
▪ Hourly rate	▪ Market rate

The left column, Input, represents practice management systems. If your services are focused more on the left side of this chart, you will always have pricing pressures.

In some of our Rainmaker classes on pricing strategy, we ask the attendees to evaluate the pricing strategies of other service and product providers to determine a pricing strategy for themselves. Some you might consider are:

- **Airline pricing.** There may be 50 different prices for an airliner with 120 passengers on board.

- **Cosmetics.** The same product with the same ingredients is sold in different channels at different price points.

- **Children's food prices at restaurants.** Often these meals are at lower prices or free to encourage parents with kids to eat there.

- **Broadway shows.** Expensive seats are sold first to prevent the purchase of cheap seats and patrons from moving to unsold expensive seats.

- **Senior discounts.** Seniors are not poor; but they do have more time on their hands and will patronize establishments that offer discounts to them.

- **Marriott Hotels Concierge Services.** These services provide Marriott a 90 percent margin from those willing to pay.

- **Nightclubs and bars.** Free early admission, drinks, and happy hours are used to attract crowds early so the clubs are "happening" places by evening, when owners can extract a cover charge.

- **Newspapers.** A cheap price to subscribers boosts circulation in order to increase advertising rates.

- **Daimler-Chrysler.** Mercedes and Dodge are made by the same company; is price difference same as cost difference?

- **Doctors.** They charge more to the wealthy. Do they incur a different cost? Is there a greater malpractice risk?

- **American Express Cards—Green, Gold, Platinum.** Is this cost-plus pricing?

- **Telephone services.** Phone companies charge less to residential customers. A variety of billing methods exists using price discrimination.

- **Grocery food.** Coupons issued by manufacturer are doubled by the grocery. Consumers can purchase an item for one of three price points.

I am going to propose an invoicing and collection process in this chapter that will help you cross-sell more services to your client base and collect a higher yield on those services. You can do this without spending any additional hours. Instead, you can accomplish this by appropriately matching your service delivery and collection processes to your clients' emotions.

Clients buy two things from you: solutions and emotions. Clients will tend to pay commodity prices for your solutions, but they will pay a premium for positive feelings.

Think of the goods and services you purchase. For example, your automobile provides you transportation. If transportation were all you were buying, you wouldn't spend $20,000, $30,000, $40,000, or more for your automobile. Reliable transportation can be had for much less than what you are paying. Much of what you bought when you purchased your automobile was emotional. You purchased an image as well as transportation. People make decisions emotionally and then justify them with logic.

Your home provides protection from the elements; that's the solution. Could you pay less money for shelter in other parts of your community? Do you need as much shelter as you have? The emotional aspects of buying a home center around things like pride of ownership, image, and comfort.

Marketers have come to recognize that pricing strategy should take into consideration the psychological as well as the economic aspects of price.

—Robert J. Kopp and Humbert D. Hennessey,
How to Write a Marketing Plan

Clients are dealing with you in the same way. Most of them have the intellectual ability to prepare their own financial statements and tax returns and make their own business decisions. A hundred years ago most businesspeople did all of that themselves. But society was relatively slow-moving compared to today. In our fast-paced business world, smart businesspeople focus on what they do best and use professionals and consultants to help them in areas outside of their core competencies.

Pricing Emotions

Clients deal with three emotions when discussing pricing and when receiving invoices from you:

1. Price resistance
2. Price anxiety
3. Payment resistance

Price Resistance

Otherwise known as sticker shock, price resistance is the emotion people have when the immediate cost of something is higher than expected. Unless clients are able to emotionally get over the hurdle of price resistance, they will not buy your services. The only way clients can jump over this hurdle is to be emotionally convinced that your value exceeds your cost. Think of it like a seesaw with value on one side and cost on the other; the value must weigh more than the cost.

Value means a good price for the quality you offer. You don't have to be the least expensive to be the best value.

Client may feel sticker shock at many times during an engagement, For example, when they hear your price, clients may think or say, "You are way too expensive for me." That may not be the case at all, but if clients are thinking or saying this, they are feeling price resistance.

If clients get over the price shock *prior* to engaging you or committing to additional services, they feel in control. If clients deal with price shock *after* you have completed your work and sent the invoice, they feel less in control. The more in-control your clients feels, the easier it will be for them to deal with your price.

Dealing with price before allocating resources to work for clients will allow you to discuss value issues with clients at the time when they are in control. If the value discussion (convenience, peace of mind, image) is not convincing to clients, you may be able to rescope the engagement to a budget with which you will both be happy. If either clients are not convinced of the value or you haven't been able to rescope the engagement, then price concessions are your final alternative to make the engagement work.

Many experts suggest that you never lower your price to acquire a customer because these customers take time and resources away from more valuable customers who pay full price. However, I disagree. There are many reasons you want to build your value to its highest level but also come off your highest pricing in certain situations.

This is the real world. Pricing is always a negotiation with a newer client and if it takes a price concession to obtain a valuable long-term client, then I believe you should do it. In the Day 7 chapter, we discussed selling to 10s —those prospects who are both interested and qualified. The only price concessions I would recommend would be to prospective clients who are high on the qualification scale. If a prospect is a 10 in terms of interest alone, there is no reason to discount.

Some firms offer pricing discounts on certain services to entice clients into a larger relationship. Recently a few brokerage firms have been giving free stock trading to certain qualified accounts. Certain accounting firms give away personal tax returns to obtain the larger corporate relationship. Mike Kruse has used the "business physical" as a way to build an early relationship with a prospect. The business physical entails either giving away or discounting the first service. Kruse has used this process very well to attract new clients who later pay premium fees.

A key strategy to always use when discounting to highly qualified prospects is to clearly remind clients that your normal pricing will be different. Tell them that you are willing to make an early investment in the relationship, which you ultimately expect to be built on value. Most good clients appreciate this and will remember the discussion when your fees increase.

In other cases, you may set an initial price that builds in an extraordinary margin. For example, let's assume that Joe (a sole tax preparer) is preparing 10-hour, $1,000 tax returns during the month of March. Let's assume he does not want to work more than 40 hours per week and he already is committed to three returns per week. Joe might price the next four returns at $2,000 and be willing to negotiate down to $1,500 if he really wants the clients. In some cases, rather than discounting his fee, Joe might offer to provide the client two to four hours of tax and financial planning during the summer months. This pricing process will help improve his overall yield on his business. Once Joe locks in the newer clients at the higher fee level, he has an opportunity to improve pricing on his older client base during the next year.

One of the worst practices I've seen among my newer CPA-firm clients is the willingness to discount pricing *during tax season.* Many accountants work themselves to death during tax season and still discount fees! They could make more money and have a better life if they would follow Ron Baker's advice and be more aggressive with pricing.

The Great Discounting Debate.   Ron Baker, author of *The Professional's Guide to Value Pricing,* disagrees with me on discounting. He says: "I remain completely unconvinced by your arguments on when it's proper to discount. We both know there is empirical evidence that CPA customers are not price sensitive—they don't pick CPAs based on price and they don't leave based on price. Once you discount, you set the precedent, and the customer will expect that treatment in the future. By definition, it shouldn't take a price discount to obtain a 'valuable' client.

"Once you discount, no matter what you say to the client, you have cut the value of your services in the client's eyes. Clients do not value that which they get for free.

"The next point is a classic example of cost-plus pricing, trying to price based upon internal work flow and capacity issues. This contradicts what you say in the Day 26 chapter about pricing on value, not costs. It doesn't matter to the client what time of year Joe does the tax return, unless you focus the client on your internal workload rather than the external value. I can't think why Joe would want to cut his price $500, nor do I think it would make a difference to the client."

Price Anxiety

Price anxiety occurs in two situations:

1. When clients regret that they have committed such a large and expensive project to you
2. When there is an open-ended budget and clients feel the project is out of hand

The first issue arises out of buyer remorse. The buyer made an emotional decision when convinced of your value, but later regrets the decision. The second issue is a form of delayed price resistance.

One way to minimize a client's price anxiety is to stay connected with your client throughout all phases of the engagement. Lou Mills says, "During a significant client engagement, I visit the staff and meet with the client. I encourage my partners to be visible in the field as much as possible. This keeps the client happy with our work. They don't feel like we have turned it over to a group of juniors."

Staying connected and continuing to build the relationship reinforces your quality and personal service value to your client. The more fieldwork performed by partners and others at the client's office, the less price anxiety the client will feel. Jim Belew says, "One of our strongest beliefs is that you complete the work in the field. The more the client sees you working, the less he will complain about the invoice."

Payment Resistance

Payment resistance is the emotion people feel about paying out money. Everyone, to one extent or the other, feels this emotion. Businesspeople often delay payments to their CPAs for a long time. They place your invoices last, not because they don't value your work, but because their first priority is to pay for services and goods that keep their businesses running on a day-to-day basis.

Because of this tendency, it is important to establish pricing and payment terms right up front with clients. Waiting until the engagement is over can be disastrous. If you wait until the end of the engagement to invoice all of your work, clients must get over price and payment resistance after you have turned over the product. Now you are vulnerable. If a client complains, you will be more prone to discount because you have no leverage. If a client wants further delay in payment, you have no teeth. Most clients know that you probably won't sue.

Five Keys to Getting Paid

Follow this simple five-step formula for negotiating and collecting your invoices to dramatically improve your yield on your work:

1. Establish price and payment terms before you commit to the engagement.
2. Negotiate for a retainer and progress payment arrangement.
3. Clearly set forth a change-order process.
4. Communicate all aspects of your engagement process with all members of your team.
5. Follow the process.

Establish Price and Terms Ahead of Time

I am appalled at how many CPAs talk about their wonderful service, but do not discuss pricing and invoicing with clients. You must make certain that your clients deal with your price before you commit your time and resources. Otherwise, you run the risk of antagonizing clients.

Some professionals use a high price as a screening device. Because some people believe that a higher price equates to higher quality, quoting a high price screens out those people for whom price is an issue. There is an old adage, "If you have to ask the price, then you can't afford it."

Bob Gaida says, "I want our clients to know, right up front, that we are not the cheapest service provider. If they find it out after we have performed the work and sent them a invoice, everyone loses."

Quote a fixed price for every engagement right up front. Doing this avoids the mutual mystification that seems to occur when neither the CPA nor the client knows what the engagement will cost. Quote an exact fee, not a range. Don't say, "The engagement will cost between ten and fifteen thousand dollars."

Clients will always hear ten. Instead, tell clients, "Your investment will be fifteen thousand. If I can find some ways to save, I'll certainly do it." That helps your clients over the price resistance and anxiety at the appropriate time.

If you're unable to state a price ahead of time for the defined scope of work, how confident can a client be in your competence? If you're shy about bringing up price with your client, what does this say about your relationship? Use discussions of price to clearly establish value and client expectations. Then plan to exceed those expectations.

Negotiate a Retainer and Progress Payments

Professionals like lawyers get a retainer before they start work. If the job is small, the retainer is an estimate of the total cost. If the job is larger, a retainer is followed by a series of progress payments—payments that are tied to a schedule of work completion.

These arrangements will help your cash flow and planning, increase your professionalism in the eyes of your clients, and reduce uncollected invoices.

If clients won't accept a retainer and progress invoice arrangement, you may decide not to take the engagement. If clients will not pay a retainer, I wonder whether they will pay my invoice after the work is complete. Send the problems of collecting six-month-old accounts receivables to your competition.

Clearly Set Forth a Change-Order Process

When you are working with clients on one problem or process, it is natural for them to ask you about other issues. This is a good cross-selling opportunity. However, there are also occasions when clients may exploit your good will to get free work out of you. This is why you need a change-order process.

Change orders are probably best known in the construction industry. When owners or architects change the plans or specifications while construction is under way, it usually creates new problems. All such changes should be documented and have prices calculated.

When the scope of the work required for an engagement is different from what you were told, you need a change order. You don't have to get too formal. A verbal understanding followed by a memo may be sufficient. This also gives you a chance to think out the implications of a surprise change. Even if you are working on an hourly arrangement (which I discourage), change orders are useful documentation to avoid client surprises when they receive your invoice later.

Don't nickel-and-dime clients with change orders. Build in to your quotes some contingency for surprises. But do protect yourself by communicating about important changes promptly.

Communicate All Details of the Engagement to Your Entire Team

Discussing the cost of the engagement up front with clients will help you clarify the exact scope of the work. Don't allow a senior partner to delegate a vague engagement to an associate who then delegates it to staff.

All staff members who work on a job should know what's involved—what the clients' expectations are. This allows all team members to understand what they need to do and to recognize when change orders are necessary. That's all part of your training process so juniors can move up efficiently.

Follow the Process

Establishing detailed procedures makes work—and getting paid—easier. Not following a set procedure wastes time, demoralizes staff, and causes inefficiencies that clients notice. Don't be afraid to adjust your invoice processes, but don't be afraid to apply them either.

Summary

Many accountants routinely discount their pricing after the fact. To receive more than commodity prices and full realization, you must deliver both solutions and good feelings. It is best to deal with price resistance and slow payment before you start an engagement. Be clear about a fixed price ahead of time and arrange for progress invoicing. Be visible at the client's site and use a change-order process. By setting up the right procedures, you can increase profits and client satisfaction, and achieve better yields on your units of work.

Extend Your Profits

Keeping Clients Sold: Service after the Sale

I have invested many years in networking in the community and building relationships. If I did not pay more attention to my client service than I did to selling new clients, our reputation could be destroyed quickly.

— Jack Amundson[1]

In 1998 I met with a CPA with whom I had worked at Price-WaterhouseCoopers (PW) in the 1970s. He had operated as a sole practitioner since leaving PW. I had heard that he was doing well. But that year things were not so good for him. He was perplexed as to why he had lost two of his largest clients within the last 12 months. He told me, "I saved the owner of one of the businesses over 10 times the amount he'd paid me in fees." He'd helped the other client obtain bank financing and implement a succession plan for a business.

With his permission, I contacted the former clients and performed a lost client review with them. Those clients told me that my friend was highly qualified, but they felt he had taken their business for granted. In other words, he didn't bother to resell his existing clients every year. Their comments were like a bolt of lightning for me. I, too, had my focus on obtaining the new client. Those clients' comments changed my life and my approach to marketing and sales.

Why do we take clients for granted? Perhaps human nature plays a role. My wife wonders aloud sometimes how I can be so nice to strangers and so curt with her. Perhaps boredom sets in. There is excitement in chasing a new account. There is exhilaration in winning a new client. All of us need that sort of validation from time to time.

When asked, almost every CPA admits that client service is crucial. Yet most accountants focus most of their marketing efforts on attracting new clients. Not only is this a reckless neglect of your clients, but also it is costing you tremendous profits. Your biggest incremental income will come from taking better care of your good existing clients and from selling them new services.

Not only is service crucial to keeping clients, but research confirms that it is crucial to your profits. Research by Bain Consultants reported in *The Loyalty Effect*[2] showed that reducing client attrition by 5 percent could increase profits by 25 to 90 percent! This leverage comes about through reduced marketing costs and increased referrals.

You may say, "My clients love me and wouldn't leave me." Or you may think, "I give my clients a Mercedes product at a Chevy price. Why would they even consider moving their accounts?"

Or perhaps you would rather not know exactly how your clients really feel about you. Just how satisfied they are with you or how loyal they are to you is a subject you'd rather not discuss.

Repeat-Customer Value

Taco Bell has determined that a repeat customer is worth about $11,000 in lifetime total sales. At Sewell Cadillac, that figure is $332,000. Xerox has learned that a very satisfied customer is six times more likely to repurchase Xerox equipment than a merely satisfied customer. A recent study found that reducing customer defections by just 5% resulted in an 85% profit increase in a bank's branch system; a 50% profit increase in an insurance brokerage; and a 30% increase in an auto service chain.

—Achieving Breakthrough Service[3]

The Costs of New Clients

Stop for a minute and calculate your investment in marketing over the last year. Include both time and dollars. What percentage of your marketing was devoted to your clients? To your prospects? If you devoted less than 50 percent of your marketing to your current client base, this chapter is for you.

If you are interested in a new and better way of investing your marketing efforts, this chapter is your key to success. I want to stimulate you to market to your clients as you would to your best prospects. Think about this: Your best clients are someone else's best prospects.

A partner in an Atlanta accounting firm told me about chasing a Class A prospect for over two years. (An A prospect is one that would fit as one of your largest and 10 best clients.) He'd spent hours schmoozing the prospect's executives and finally was about to enjoy a luncheon with the CEO and his attorney. Across the restaurant, this partner spotted *his* best client having lunch with another Atlanta CPA!

This scene is played out all too often all across the country. In trying to build their practices, accountants are communicating with prospects—including clients of other accounting firms. The end result finds many accountants swapping clients with other accountants. Swapping clients with your competitor creates a poor return on your marketing investment. There is a better way of investing your marketing time and dollars.

> *We are in the midst of a revolution . . . those organizations and individuals who can create new relationships with customers will find themselves with unimagined competitive advantage. Those who don't will lose.*
>
> —Larry Wilson, *Stop Selling, Start Partnering*[4]

The Times They Are a-Changin'

Since 1977, radical changes in many business fields have occurred that affect us all. Computers have taken over much of the number-crunching work accountants used to perform. Today competition isn't just from other CPA firms; clients and customers are demanding more and better service from all of their business vendors.

Tax revenues and A&A at the largest accounting firms have been relatively flat for a number of years. To grow their revenues, most firms have aggressively pursued consulting services. Couple these factors with potential major tax simplification and we are in an industry that finds itself in what Georgetown professor and author Peter Vaill calls "permanent white water" —an ongoing state of change that is fast-moving and dangerous.

In *Stop Selling, Start Partnering,* Larry Wilson writes, "We're in the middle of massive turbulence. If you look for precedents, there aren't many. The future can no longer be predicted by remembering the comfortable signposts of the past." For accountants who have relied on audit and tax work, the future is more uncertain than ever before.

As an accountant, your future and your growth potential rest in that deep vein of gold that you call your client. Deepening your relationship with your clients and learning to serve them in a more effective manner is the key for your future success. You may need to shed your worn-out concept of objectivity and independence in order to succeed. You may need to "bear hug" your clients. In the future, you must first build your clients' businesses in order to build your practice.

Invest in Relationships

Abram Serotta, managing partner of Serotta, Maddox & Evans in Augusta, Georgia, developed a client investment system. He allocates a certain number of hours to each professional and for each client for time spent and not charged. He says, "Our clients are the lifeblood of our business. We don't want them worrying that we are charging them for everything we do. So we tell our professionals to make client investments—'Tell the client she is not being charged for your time, that we are investing in the relationship.'"

According to studies by Arthur Andersen and Deloitte & Touche, it costs six times as much to find a new customer as it does to retain an existing one.

Many accountants will invest many hours and dollars chasing a prospective client and yet will invest no unbilled time in their Class A accounts. Even though reselling next year's engagement requires much less time and worry than chasing a new account, and subjects you to no rejection, most of us don't bother because we take our existing clients for granted.

When I give a training program on client marketing, I ask the accountants to evaluate various instances of great and poor service they have received. When asked why they changed service providers, over 70 percent of them say that they changed because of the way some individual treated them. A few leave because of price, and perhaps a few more leave because of the technical quality of the service they received.

The reasons are the same from industry to industry and from profession to profession. People leave because of the personal treatment they receive— or don't receive. Whenever people engage you and your firm, they hire you for two things, not just one. Technical competence and good feelings are both required for an excellent client-accountant relationship to exist.

In a 1994 national study on why clients choose auditors and why they switch, Professors Lon Adams and Brian Davis of Weber State University found that personal relationships led all other factors in the decision process. Three of the top reasons clients switched related to poor service: not proactive in delivering services, not responsive to understanding of client's business, and lack of communication.

Mark Kaland, whom we met in Day 16, stresses that outstanding client service is the primary focus of the entire Clifton Gunderson firm. He says, "Some partners aren't comfortable going out on new prospect calls. They do a great job of serving existing clients. Their goals might be to keep a client

Relationships Build Loyalty

Decision makers were asked: Would you consider buying from anyone else?

Bought because of:	Would consider another vendor:
Features	94% Certainly
Benefits	91% Probably
Helpful salesperson	99% Absolutely not!

—10 Secrets of Marketing Success [5]

for life. They get to know those clients really well. Even the traditional bean counter can learn to build strong client relationships. I think this is the total secret to having great growth in a practice office."

It is clear from the results of numerous client satisfaction surveys performed for accountants that clients are highly satisfied with technical issues. But satisfaction with technical issues is only one of the things that clients want from their CPAs. Clients want to receive positive feelings. Technical competence earns you satisfaction and a modest fee. Positive emotions will earn you loyalty and a premium fee.

Jim Belew, whom we met in Day 3 says, "We invest heavily in visiting with our clients and creating a dialogue. I personally visit 20 to 30 of our firm's clients each year. Clients with whom I don't personally work are the ones I visit. I'll ask our marketing director or another partner to visit my clients. I want to make sure we are listening to and serving our clients' changing needs."

Bill Jenkins, whom we met in Day 7, periodically goes on a listening tour of his clients. He says, "I encourage each of our partners to craft a few open-ended questions that will prompt our clients to talk. Then we must be quiet and listen to their concerns, their needs, their fears, their wants, their loves, their hates, and their unique natures. This is how we serve our clients the best."

Ask yourself: "From whom do I buy a product or service who I do not like?" If you are like most people, you only buy from those people you like, unless you absolutely must do otherwise. I drive past several printers to buy from my printer because I like him.

Return on Relationships

Lou Mills, whom we met in Day 9 says, "Retention of clients is a major part of our sales process. If you have an unhappy client, they are going to tell 15 or 20 people that they are unhappy. Seattle is a small town even though you may think it's big. If you falter, a lot of people are going to know about it. I take those professionals who are both technically and client service oriented. I say, okay, they are helping us sell, hopefully selling other services to those clients besides just our tax and audit services. I think they can learn to sell our value-added services, for example. I think that's an easy sell because you are not developing a new relationship there. You are dealing with an existing relationship. We hire individuals who have interpersonal skills to develop those relationships further."

Calculate the impact on your business if you lose one of your largest 10 clients. Multiply the loss over a 10-year life expectancy. Factor into your equation the referrals you lose from this client. Then add the impact of your lost clients telling your potential clients why they chose another firm.

How much time and effort would you invest into marketing if you knew you could obtain a new client who would generate $10,000, $25,000, or $50,000 —whatever would qualify to be one of your top-10 largest—a year in fees? How much would keeping this client for 10 years mean to you? How much marketing effort would you be willing to invest to keep a client of this size?

Increase Contact with Your Best Customers

Maintaining relationships with your best customers builds loyalty to protect against competition. For example, in financial institutions, about 20% of customers generate most of the profit. Keep in contact by card, note, letter, special promotion, invitation, or event. About 68% of the attrition in financial institutions is a result of ignoring customers; only 14% leave because of a bad experience.

—Thomas J. Winninger, *Price Wars*[6]

Action Programs

Assuming you are now reasonably aroused to start or improve your client-marketing program, where do you start? Normally, the best place to begin is listening to your clients—really listening.

To listen, you must place yourself in proximity to your clients. In a recent study conducted by the marketing research company Huthwaite, Neil Rackham described a comparison between CPAs and product sellers. Customers of product sellers said 52 percent have a caring attitude whereas only 35 percent of CPA clients rated the CPAs as caring. Yet businesspeople consistently report that CPAs are their most trusted business advisors. How can this seeming contradiction be explained? Rackham replies, "Because accountants are highly rated in candor and competence, clients will judge accountants to be their most trusted business advisors. That does not necessarily mean that clients will increase or keep their business with you." There is a difference between client satisfaction and client loyalty.

Spend time with your best clients, listen to them, and keep them informed —these are the most important marketing activities you can perform. There are hundreds of ways to do this, but a few high-touch, high-impact methods include writing a client newsletter, performing a client survey, scheduling specific nonchargeable visits with your best clients to build loyalty, and holding a client reception,

A Client Newsletter with Impact

Client newsletters are great marketing tools for CPAs. They were covered in detail in the Day 18 chapter. Newsletters are one of the most efficient ways to communicate with a large client base. However, for your largest and best clients, you should carefully highlight, personalize, and elaborate items in your newsletter that you think would be relevant to them. For significant issues, call them and say, "Sara, this issue is covered in depth in our newsletter this month but I wanted to make sure you had all the information on this you needed."

A client of CPA Jennifer Bowers of BKD, LLP, in Houston, Texas, told me, "Jennifer took the time to highlight areas of the newsletter she thought I would be interested in. This kind of personal service is why I am a loyal WPM client."

Client Surveys Are Crucial

The best way to learn what clients want is to ask them. The best way to ask them is in person, one on one. Take every opportunity to ask clients two key questions: "How am I doing?" and "How can I do better?" An accountant said to me, "I don't want to ask the question because perhaps the client hadn't considered the complaint till I mentioned it." My response was "Would you rather ask the question and hear the answer or risk your competitor asking the question?" Good sellers probe for problems, then close around the solutions.

Client surveys can be performed through the mail, via phone, as well as in person. If you haven't performed one, do one now.

There is a major difference between client satisfaction and client loyalty. CPAs are fooled when clients rate you with a 4 or a 5 (out of a possible 5) on their satisfaction and a 3 or no answer on loyalty. Clients can be very satisfied and still change firms. Satisfaction means you're doing okay. Loyalty means your clients really like you and the relationship. When performing a client survey, do not shy away from asking questions about loyalty. Questions like "Would you refer me to someone else?" or "Will you return next year?" are critical. You are at as much risk of losing satisfied clients whose loyalty is questionable as you are of losing clients who are highly dissatisfied.

The Emotional Link

University of Texas marketing professor Robert Peterson had studied customer satisfaction for years, but he couldn't find significant correlations between customer satisfaction and repeat business.

Peterson was puzzled by this lack of relationship. Eventually he found that in order for a customer's experience to lead to repeat business, there had to be an emotional link between the customer and the product or service provider.

Nonchargeable Client Business Reviews

For your large business clients, a formal business review is one of the most powerful marketing tools you can use. The client business review (CBR) is designed to build client loyalty.

How CBRs Work

Every year, select one of your A clients for review. These should generally be your firm's largest accounts. Each CBR involves about 14 hours of partner and manager time and about 6 hours of staff time. With an average billing rate of $120, a CBR represents an investment of about $2,400 of time at regular rates. But since most CBRs are performed in May through December, when you have some nonbillable time on your hands, your true cost is much lower.

Once your key account has been identified, call your client CEO and say something like this:

We would like to offer you a review of your business. The meeting would be about three hours long, and we can hold it at your office, ours, or at a neutral location to limit distractions. Please bring your CFO and if possible, your heads of sales, operations, human resources, information management, and administration.

We will include all of our personnel who work on your account. We will not charge you for this event. For us, it's an investment in our relationship. We want to learn about your goals, problems, and plans. We believe the more we know, the better we can serve you.

Here's a sample agenda for the first two hours of the CBR:

- The CEO reviews the current state of the business and the industry.
- The CEO reviews past three years' performance, the company's objectives, and whether those objectives were met. What were the causes for success or failure?
- The CEO reviews business goals for the next three years. The CEO's key officers are asked about their key goals and how they plan to achieve those goals. What obstacles lie in the way? These could be competition, markets, new products lines, or other organizational or governmental issues.
- How can our CPA firm better help the company in achieving its objectives?
- What aspects of the CPA's services could be improved?

Once these items have been discussed, tell clients that your intention is to provide the best possible value at the most efficient pricing. If you have suggestions on how the company can save some dollars, tell them.

Then ask, "Do you feel you are receiving your money's worth for our services?" Spend the last 30 minutes of the meeting reviewing the ways you can help your clients achieve their objectives. They will not expect you to solve all their problems. But the extent to which you are aware of their problems and your attempt to help will seal the clients' loyalty to you.

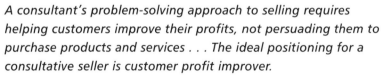

A consultant's problem-solving approach to selling requires helping customers improve their profits, not persuading them to purchase products and services . . . The ideal positioning for a consultative seller is customer profit improver.

—Mack Hanan, *Consultative Selling*[7]

Ending the CBR with a convivial luncheon will enable you to get to know your client's people on a more personal basis.

The primary benefit of CBRs is that they foster client loyalty. In fact, CPAs who use these reviews rarely lose a client who has undergone a CBR. Frequently a CBR will uncover the need for additional services, which translates into new billings. Most of all, the CBR is a way to market to existing clients as if they were your best prospects. Wouldn't you spend 20 hours schmoozing a Class A prospect? Then why not do it for your client every two to five years? CBRs can also be an enjoyable change of pace for your staff and can help train them in general consulting.

Net fees collected from clients who have undergone a CBR increase at a faster rate than fees from other clients. CBRs are also a great way to train staff to market to clients. These staff members can perform CBRs on your firm's second tier of clients, with less partner time involved. And finally, a CBR will elevate a client from "satisfied" to "delighted." Delighted clients are the ones who provide the best referrals and are the most loyal.

Client Receptions

Get your clients together as often as you can. An annual reception, seminar, open house, or party are all good excuses. Positive group dynamics occur when clients are together with you and your staff. You need not invite every single client to every event.

Concentrating on the best clients will create the impact you need. Let clients know you care. Firms that offer annual client seminars, whether there is a major tax change or not, are the ones that engender strong client loyalty.

The independence and objectivity training that is so good for our profession is often carried too far. Sometimes clients perceive our independence as aloofness and lack of concern. Sometimes they perceive our objectivity as hostility. Client receptions, seminars, and get-togethers are great ways to show that we accountants are human beings and a chance to give our clients more than technical competence and candor.

Please don't misread or misunderstand me. A CPA's independence, integrity, and objectivity are great assets when used properly. But when used as an excuse for aloofness and indifference, independence and objectivity will repel clients.

Client Visits Seal Relationships

To really learn about and understand your clients, you must visit them in their environments. In their book *Successful Large Account Management*, Robert Miller and Stephen Heiman[8] describe the various levels of client relationships. Delivering commodities that meet specifications is at the lowest level of a customer relationship. Many accounting and tax services have become commodities. I saw a headline last year that read, "Big Companies Buy Audits by the Pound."

When you follow a regular client visitation program, you will make yourself more valuable to your clients' organizations. You will better integrate your services with your clients' needs and build the important human bonds necessary for strong relationships.

> *You never persuade clients of anything. Clients persuade themselves. Your function is to understand the issues that matter to your clients. You have to feel their problems just the way they feel them. You have to sit on their side of the table and look at the issues from their point of view.*
>
> —An executive cited in *The SPIN Selling Field Book*[9]

Summary

The message of this chapter is simple. It's much more costly to obtain a new client than it is to keep an old one. But merely doing a good job is not enough to retain clients. You have to strengthen the relationships. Clients want the work done *plus* they want to receive good feelings and know you care about them. Implementing programs like client business reviews, personal contacts, and client receptions will show you care, build the relationships, and get you more business.

30 Clients Come Second: Five-Star Service

The most significant thing we have done in our firm in 25 years is dedicate ourselves to Five-Star Client Service.

—Jim Belew[1]

The *Customer Comes Second*, written by Hal Rosenbluth,[2] is an excellent resource. Rosenbluth built his own service business to a dominant position in the tough travel industry by involving his staff in unique ways. His company was ranked among the top companies to work for in the United States.

In the book Rosenbluth discusses a subtle secret to delivering great customer service that is still seldom emphasized. To deliver great service, you have to enlist your employees and staff in the effort. You do this by treating your *employees* well. Only then will they deliver consistent, great service that thrills your *clients*. This is particularly true in a service business like accounting, where the service received by your clients depends largely on a number of employees.

For instance, Extractions Systems of Massachusetts markets contamination measurement and control products for ultra-clean environments. After a survey found that employees ranked their job satisfaction only as average, Extractions implemented programs to improve the workplace environment. In a follow-up survey, satisfaction jumped to the top 15 percent of companies surveyed. And the willingness of employees to recruit friends to work at Extractions went up 20 percent.

Extractions stated: "Clearly, satisfied and happy employees translate into satisfied customers and shareholders. Based on this fundamental management principle, we embraced the mantra: 'The customer comes second.' Logically, it is impossible to satisfy customers with unsatisfied employees." Employee satisfaction action plans are now part of the yearly Extractions business plan.

If you analyze the interactions of your clients with your firm, you'll see that the majority of the company-client interactions probably don't involve only accountants. They involve other professionals, receptionists, and the people who take messages or answer phones. You need to "sell" your staff on being extraordinary in how they treat clients. If you treat your staff first class, they are more likely to treat your clients that way.

What Makes a Client Really Loyal to You?

From the clients' point of view, a great interaction is one where they are treated as special. In a business sense, your employees are aware of the client's concerns and can proactively offer solutions. It is beyond just being on time and returning phone calls promptly. At the same time, in a personal sense, clients are treated as special *individuals.* Your people know their names and show that they like them.

If you're like me, you're not treated this way very often. Likely your clients aren't either. And few firms have standards like this and train for them. On average, good service in this country is merely *professional* politeness. All the words are right, but there is nothing personal behind them. People say, "How are you today?" but it's an empty phrase. Think about your bank interactions. Tellers are usually polite but impersonal. You might as well be using the automated teller machine.

Most accountants think that good service is doing the work on time and on budget. They don't understand that clients largely judge by other things because they can't judge the quality of the work.

An important distinction that is almost never discussed in client service is that *not doing anything wrong is not the same as doing things right.* Some little-known research on employee satisfaction seems to apply well to clients also. If employees are underpaid or subjected to bad working conditions, they are unhappy. But eliminating these same factors is not enough to make them happy. That is, good pay and good working conditions do not make employees *happy.* More generally, some factors are necessary to *avoid dissatisfaction.* But other factors are necessary to *achieve positive satisfaction.* The positive factors are things such as being involved in decisions, interesting work, and colleagues they respect.

The same is probably true of your clients. They *take for granted* that you are qualified to do the work and technically competent. If these are missing, you are graded down. But you are not given positive credit for them. To achieve positive satisfaction—the type of loyalty that leads to unsolicited referrals—

you need to provide positive factors so clients receive more than ordinary satisfaction out of interactions with you.

Training for Great Service

To provide superior service to your clients, you need to train your staff. But more important, they have to want to deliver great service.

Some people are just plain "nice" in client interactions. They tend to treat people personally and clients like them. Hiring this kind of person for client contact roles can go a long way to better service. However, the only way you can be sure of a quality service level is to decide what you want and train for it. Some examples of things you might train for are:

- Greeting clients by name
- Asking clients about their interests, children, and so forth and "remembering" information in a database so they can be asked about them later (In his first book, *Swim with the Sharks Without Getting Eaten Alive*, Harvey McKay presented his list of things to find out about prospects.)
- Using a warm, personal tone of voice when talking to clients
- Making eye contact
- Listening skills
- Training in recovery from errors

How to Create Great Service

Most companies expect their people to give *good* service, and most people do give good service as they understand it. But *good* service is not enough. To give *great* service, you need to help your people in three ways:

1. Set standards, train for them, and reinforce performance.
2. Get out of people's way!
3. Treat your employees the way you want them to treat clients.

The first point is fairly standard, even though it is often not done well. To set standards for client service, you need to spend some time researching what makes for happy clients. Here you'll need to think out of the box with a focus on nontechnical factors. The second point involves empowerment. Usually the administrative "rules" require approval to do something unusual for a client. This should be set up the opposite way, as with the mail-order company Lands' End. There employee have to get permission *not* to fulfill a customer request! In other words, the expectation is that all employees are empowered to do what customers want. In practice, most firms act the opposite way.

Once employees know what to do and how to do it, further bureaucracy and administration tends to have a negative effect. Employees shouldn't have to ask permission to do something extra for clients. They should be encouraged to experiment with ideas, even if "the bosses" don't think they will have much effect. As author Ken Blanchard says, when you don't get exactly the performance you want from staff members, you have to reinforce them for being approximately right. With encouragement, they'll get better.

Another way to demonstrate this attitude to your clients *and* your employees is to offer a money-back satisfaction guarantee. Although this encourages new clients to try you and old ones to refer you, of interest here is its effect on staff members. When you offer such a guarantee, they know you are *serious* about satisfying clients. The guarantee encourages them to make an extra effort to please clients. It empowers and motivates them.

Such a satisfaction guarantee might put pressure on employees in a negative way. But instead it seems to motivate them and tell them that their complete efforts are appreciated. Since staff members take pride in working for a superior firm, all your efforts to deliver great client service also improve employee retention. And you can't have long-term client support without long-term employees.

The third point is to treat your employees the way you want clients treated.

Although we generally think of internal customer service as how the "bosses" treat employees, the situation is actually much more complicated. Much of a positive organizational climate depends on how coworkers treat each other. Employees are each other's customers in many ways. Managers look good only if their employees pull behind them. Employees need managers for training, political support, and assignment selection. A partner is a client of the receptionist. The partner depends on the receptionist taking messages correctly, putting visitors in the right mood, and so on. And the receptionist obviously depends on the partner for job ratings, raises, and the like.

More subtly, there can be conflicts between external and internal service in unexpected directions. It's up to the boss to fire workers who hurt the organizational climate with their treatment of other employees, even if they provide good external service. For instance, in one consulting firm, one long-time employee spent about half time training clients and about half time with administrative work. Clients liked her, so she was providing fine external service. And she hid behind her external service value to be a negative influence internally. Other employees—and even the boss—disliked her because she didn't follow through on internal tasks and was generally unreliable. They put up with her too long because she was good at external service. When they finally fired her, the whole organization felt better.

There are two important aspects to "internal customer service." The first is *top-down expectations*—the standards that the top partners set up and reinforce. The second is how employees treat each other. A positive organizational tone can be pushed from the top, but ultimately it depends on employees to treat each other as well as they treat customers.

What are your partners doing to create a positive service atmosphere in your firm? A firm must develop the set of standards that will lead to happy, loyal employees. Then it needs to develop a specific action plan to create the organizational climate necessary to produce the desired results. For instance, in one attitude survey by Watson Wyatt Worldwide, only 55 percent of employees said they have the power to make decisions to satisfy customers.

Organizational climate can be measured on many dimensions, from attitudes toward coworkers to liking for the boss or the work. Research in this area has covered literally dozens of areas of employee satisfaction that can contribute to overall job satisfaction or performance.

A Shared Vision

Creating a service-oriented organizational climate is no easy task. And the fact that you need to start with how you treat staff makes it even more complicated. First you need a clear vision for the firm that employees will buy in to. People have made fun of "the vision thing," but all great firms share some vision, even if they don't think of it that way. You may have gone through various exercises to create some sort of vision statement at a firm retreat. When done right, a vision can energize a firm. When done wrong, nothing but increased cynicism results.

The logical vision to start with in this area is to provide great client service. It is much easier to enlist people in this vision than in a vaguer core value about being a profitable firm. It's much easier to feel proud of being in a firm that has the best client service than one that makes the biggest partner profits.

Now add the value to be a firm that treats its people great and you can enlist everyone in defining how they can give great client service. Examples of how treating your people well and giving great external service go together are easy to find. For instance, most firms have a shortage of accountants with five to seven years of experience who can hit the ground running to do the work. Yet many women accountants leave the field to raise a family or endure stressful schedules trying to maintain their jobs while having a family. If you offered true flextime *and* a chance to be a partner with a part-time schedule, you might have your pick of talented people.

Your people can go on to make a big list of things that give them the confidence and flexibility to deliver great service *and* feel good about their jobs. These things might include things as simple as a lunch budget to take clients out to lunch, business cards for secretaries (and rewards for bringing in clients), empowerment to make decisions about clients, and money-back service guarantees.

You Get What You Reward

To create the internal service atmosphere you want, you must define it, train for it, and reward it. Useful training develops employee skills and self-esteem. This training makes employees better at service and increases their value to your organization. Simple thank-yous for jobs well done, by fellow employees or bosses, may be all that you need to turn your organizational climate into a strongly service-oriented one. But you must act to create the right reinforcements. Your employees will never go the extra mile unless they want to. If you don't reward them, they won't reward internal and external clients with great service.

Benefits of Satisfied Employees

Most employees are *generally satisfied* with their jobs. But they are not *delighted* with them. They do their jobs, but they don't put their hearts and souls into them. This will lead to average client service.

A less-than-happy employee:

▪ Costs your firm opportunities

▪ Gives average customer service

▪ Dampens other employees' enthusiasm about your firm

▪ Doesn't talk up your company to your customers and prospects

Having happy employees translates to great customer service for several reasons:

▪ Happy employees are enthusiastic about their jobs and do them better.

▪ Clients can tell when employees are positive, and they take that as a "referral."

▪ Happy employees take pride in their firms and their client service reflects that. They become role models for other employees.

- They recruit employees similar to themselves, and they also bring in client leads.

In too many accounting firms the organizational climate is "harried." Everyone is stressed, waiting for things to get better "after tax season." (That's also when they hope to get around to marketing so that they'll have better clients next year.) When you have happy, involved employees, you create a positive feedback system. Happy employees stay longer and do their jobs better. This supports a positive work climate that further supports employees and leads to happy clients. Positive clients, in turn, make your employees' jobs easier and more pleasant.

Involve All Staff Members

Getting input from all staff members can be crucial in improving both internal and external client service. In most firms, staff members can quickly highlight a number of factors that would make their jobs easier and please clients. Staff morale will increase just because you are making an effort to improve their situation. By obtaining staff input, you also increase cooperation with any new procedures put in place to improve your organizational climate.

The way to deliver great external service is to treat your employees like your most important clients. Depending on the size of your firm, either sit down with each employee or conduct a brief "organizational climate" survey. Measure things like morale, job satisfaction, and empowerment to serve clients. Calculate your turnover rate and what it costs you, combined with difficulties in obtaining new staff members who fit your needs. You'll see that investing in staff internal "service" can pay off on a number of dimensions.

A satisfied employee will create and keep satisfied customers.
A dissatisfied employee will cost you customers.
—Michael Le Boeuf, *How to Win Customers and Keep Them for Life*[3]

When I interview partners in firms where sales are flat, I hear pleasantries and platitudes about customer service, but most of what I hear is only lip service. Five-Star Client Service for CPAs is patterned after the service you would receive in a five-star restaurant. It is a training course we at The Rainmaker Academy deliver to CPAs throughout the world to help them focus more on providing outstanding service. The concept of Five-Star Client Service for Accountants was originally developed by the late Tim Beauchimin,

---

Benefits of Employee Satisfaction

Companies that have distinguished themselves in the way they hire, train, and treat employees have experienced the following positive benefits.

- *Increases in service, quality, and customer satisfaction of over 50%*

- *Growth rates 60% to 300% greater than their competition*

- *Return on sales 200% to 300% greater than their competitors*

- *Return on assets 150% to 300% greater than their competitors*

- *Direct impact on employee retention, which in turn leads to customer satisfaction, which leads to profits*

—William Fromm, *The Ten Commandments of Business and How to Break Them*[4]

---

a brilliant consultant to the accounting industry. Our firm is honored to be able to carry on some of his work.

Bill Gates, in his book *Business at the Speed of Thought,*[5] predicts, "Only a few businesses will succeed by having the lowest price, so most will need a strategy that includes customer service." In a rapidly change environment, dedicating yourself and your firm to great client service is a high-payoff activity.

To deliver Five-Star Service, accountants must focus on the concepts of connecting and recovery and on a five-step process based on these concepts.

Connecting

Connecting is the concept you use when proactively investing in building the relationship with your client. It is based on the principle that long-term relationships are built on regular communication that fosters trust, caring, and confidence.

Neil Rackham of Huthwaite Market Research reports that two-thirds of CPA clients said their accountant didn't care about them. How do you think your clients feel about you? Emphasizing the connecting phase of Five-Star Service can help your firm avoid having clients feel you don't care about them.

The purpose of connecting is to build and strengthen all parts of the relationship. The concept of connecting touches all of the steps included in Five-Star Service.

Jack Amundson, whom we met in Day 10, says, "The most important thing in my business life is my relationships with my clients. I work extra hard to spend time with them, off the clock, to let them know I care."

Last month, I sat in the reception area of a large accounting firm for about 20 minutes while waiting for an appointment with the managing partner. I was struck by how "cold" the reception area felt. Then I noticed that as the firm's employees walked through the lobby area, no one spoke. The staff members didn't greet or acknowledge each other, let alone me. No one knew who I was. I could have been a client or a prospective client. Had I been either, I would have gotten a poor impression.

Contrast the above visit with a visit to the offices of Simpson & Osborne in Charleston, West Virginia. Upon entering the lobby, an expected guest feels welcome. There are bowls of candy on the tables. Marcie Jividen, the receptionist, greets me by name and asks, "How is your day, Mr. Waugh?" After listening to my reply, she says, "Mr. Simpson is expecting you, I will let

---

One Person Sets the Tone

Our staff is loaded to the gills with résumés to die for. Then there's Leslie McKee, the receptionist. I've never seen her résumé. But she has taken our company and turned it around. You see, Leslie is amazingly upbeat, courteous, funny, patient, upstanding and professional, smart, outrageous, and helpful. I don't know what our official "core values" are. We've never written them down. (Whoops.) But I know what they are unofficially: They're Leslie.

Customer Service Wonder
Clients love Leslie. She, of course, is our Commander-in-Chief of Client Service. Her manner—energetically cheerful—gives us a foot in the door with whoever is calling. Leslie makes sure you end up talking to the right person (no small thing), or are otherwise handled efficiently and effectively and feel good about it.

Once a week or more, it seems, she takes some totally amazing personal initiative to research something for a client. Often as not, it's unrelated to anything we do; it's just plain helpfulness. (Reading "praise Leslie letters" from clients eats up a lot of my time these days.)

—Tom Peters

© TPG Communications. Reprinted with permission of Tribune Media Services, Inc.

him know you have arrived. What would you like to drink during your meeting?" Marcie is a great "Director of First Impressions," but the connecting did not stop with her. Every person who came through the lobby either smiled, caught my eye and nodded my way, or said hello. The staff members at this firm start connecting with you the moment you walk in the door—that's the way every business should be.

> One of the dangers is that people think of customer service as somebody else's job. We say to ourselves, "my job is sales" or "my job is data processing." But each of our jobs is broader than that—it's creating relationships and partnerships.
>
> —Kristin Anderson, coauthor,
> *Delivering Knock Your Socks Off Service*[6]

How would you feel if, after you had placed your order in a fine restaurant, the waiter did not check back with you? Many CPAs commit this error for various reasons: tight work schedules, a fear that the initial order wasn't taken right, communication reluctance on the part of the service provider, a lack of care, or just a lack of awareness of the importance of connecting with the client.

Recovery

It's time for all organizations to think of complaint handling as a strategic tool . . . rather than as a nuisance or a cost.

—Janelle Barlow and Claus Møller, *A Complaint Is a Gift*[7]

Even the best CPAs make mistakes. But it's how you recover from mistakes that can make or break you.

Most great service businesses have a specific process to recover from an error or customer complaint. When a process is communicated throughout your organization, employees become empowered to meet client recovery needs rapidly.

I recently chatted with a CEO who is a client of a large CPA firm. He told me about a senior accountant who had made a serious error. The CEO said that when the error was discovered, the senior canceled a personal weekend trip and spent the weekend with his accounting staff correcting the problem and preparing financial information to meet the deadline. The senior apologized, and the CEO thought he had recovered extremely well.

But what most impressed the CEO was that the firm's managing partner appeared on Monday morning with an additional staffer and an apology and assurances that the CEO would not be billed for the firm's error. The CEO recognized that the managing partner's visit signified that the senior had the trust to tell his superiors and get them involved. He said, "The error could have caused us to leave the CPA firm. But the way they recovered from the mistake and the teamwork and trust within the firm will make us a long-term client. I understand how humans can make mistakes, but it is how a CPA firm reacts when they err that tells me the true value of our relationship."

Mike Kruse says, "The most important thing our professional staff and partner must know is 'Do the right thing in the circumstances.' Even if doing the right thing hurts us, it is important that our people and our clients know that we stand behind our work."

In many firms, mistakes get buried, or blame gets tossed back and forth. But in the most successful firms, accountants at all levels take responsibility for mistakes. What about in your firm? Do your staff members trust you enough to save a client like this?

Recovery is the systematic series of steps you take when you make a mistake or are presented with a problem. If handled correctly, recovery is a valuable opportunity to strengthen client loyalty to your firm. Memorable recoveries can create stories about you that are passed on to other clients.

Legendary Service

"Legendary service" describes service so good your customers want to brag about it. . . . The most important part of creating legendary service is story generation. If your customers are telling positive stories about you and your service, you could not ask for better publicity. One of the best sources for service stories is all-out recovery. Recovery means if you make a mistake with a customer, you do whatever is needed to fix the problem and create or win back a devoted customer.

—Ken Blanchard[8]

Usually, there are four basic types of human errors in accounting firms:

1. Communication errors
2. Procedural errors
3. Knowledge or technical errors
4. Price errors

When you have built a relationship with clients through a systematic process of connecting, they will be quite forgiving when a mistake occurs, regardless of its magnitude. If you have failed to invest in connecting, however, the smallest error can lose you a client. If you have a weak connection with a client, then when you make an error, you have problems—the smallest errors can lose a client for you. On the other hand, when you have been proactively building the relationship, the connection is stronger. You can make a very large mistake and the client will be very forgiving. You have a choice: be proactive or reactive. The more you invest in proactively building the relationship, the less you must invest in recovery.

A Five-Step Service Process

Step 1: Taking the Order

Waiters who take your order in fine restaurants have a big responsibility. Incorrect orders result in enormous cost increases from the rework of your food. Aren't you amazed by servers who are so well trained that they are able to get your order correct without writing it down? For most of us, this is not possible.

If your order is incorrectly taken, it cannot be delivered correctly. Reworking the order is not only costly for the restaurant immediately, but also in the long term. Your perceptions are negatively impacted when you must wait for your dinner to be corrected. The timing of your entire evening can be destroyed when the order is not taken correctly.

Training our staff members to properly take the order from the client and from each other has saved us tremendous budget overruns in time and money.

—Jim Belew, Founding Partner, Belew Averett, LLP

In an accounting firm, when the order is not taken correctly, review notes and reworks abound. If you track your cost overruns and delivery delays, most of them would relate to not taking the order exactly. Many times a partner takes the order from the client and then plays "pass-it-on" to an associate. At each level of pass-it-on, the message becomes garbled. In some cases, the client intimidates the partner and the partner, in turn, intimidates an associate. The person lower on the totem pole does not want to press the issue of vague misunderstanding. He or she wants to move forward with the work and will do so without a clear picture of the order.

To take the order correctly, partners must commit to a few more minutes with clients. It is necessary to listen carefully, take notes, and repeat the order back to the clients. Associates must do the same, even though the partner may seem eager to move on and associates may feel rushed.

Firms that focus on taking the order correctly will dramatically reduce reworks and review notes and improve the client delivery schedule. Clients also report dramatic improvements in perceptions of service quality.

During the first step of taking the order, it is crucial that you review your client's investment or cost. If you do not review cost at this point, you may set yourself up for serious misunderstandings later on. If your cost estimate is too high, you can adjust your services and the client can still feel in control.

Step 2: Delivering the Order

When you take the order from clients, an expectation level was established. The delivery is a moment of truth: Did you meet, exceed, or fail to meet your clients' expectations? Your clients' expectations are the only ones that counts. To show you care and to determine how well you've met clients' expectations, it is important that delivery be done in person.

In-person delivery also gives you an opportunity to reconnect with your clients and protect your profits. If, for some reason, you failed to meet a client's expectation for service, you want to know about it quickly. Waiting to learn that you failed will increase the cost of reworks or redos.

Terry Orr says, "I enjoy delivering our major projects personally. The client is most happy when I sit down and go over the product with him. We will almost always pick up new projects. I think the client is so pleased that he envisions we could do more." During a good delivery, begin the meeting by summarizing the services you have provided your client. This allows you both to review the expectation level set originally. Personal delivery is a good time to present other findings through management or internal control suggestions.

Goodwill plus good service brings sales success that no competition can possibly undersell.

—Harry F. Banks[9]

While meeting with clients to deliver the order, it is important to cover the benefits of what you have done from each client's perspective. Ask the client questions: "Michelle, tell me how it helps you that I prepare the financial statements and forecasts for you each quarter. Does it allow you to make better decisions? Does it enable you to focus on selling your company products rather than worrying about the finances?" By asking these types of questions, you are getting clients to say back to you what the benefits are of doing business with you.

Last, it is important to review clients' investment (cost) in your services. Reviewing the on-budget, overbudget, or underbudget status of the service will enable you to discuss the situation openly with your clients.

Step 3: Ascertaining Satisfaction

Many studies have shown that most clients will not volunteer a complaint—you have to ask. The only time you may learn if you met the clients' expectations is when you give them permission to tell you. You can do this by asking two key questions:

1. What did I do you liked?
2. How could I have improved?

Former Mayor Ed Koch of New York City became famous for asking people "How am I doing?" He would give people permission to tell him the vital information he needed. Bill Jenkins does a "listening tour" with clients. Jim Belew and his partners will visit 20 clients a year and ask a series of key questions that get their clients talking.

Step 4: Offering Dessert

How would you feel if you went for a wonderful dinner and the waiter did not offer dessert? Even if you don't eat dessert, most people enjoy the presentation. We smile and say, "Just the sound of that adds a couple of pounds." Or we might split a dessert or have one of our own. At great restaurants, you will pass the dessert cart on the way to your table. These restaurants suggest dessert early in your dining experience.

Bill Fingland says, "Clients really appreciate the way we help with business issues. A number of years ago we developed a profile of a good client: one who engages us for the same amount of consulting as compliance work. In other words, a $25,000 compliance account should be a $50,000 client if we have done our job well."

If you develop the habit of offering "dessert" to your clients, they will appreciate it. On the other hand, clients who learn of your other services after they have purchased them somewhere else may become angry that you didn't tell them. Most people don't like to have dinner in one location and stop for dessert in another.

Mark Kaland says, "In Clifton Gunderson, we invest heavily in developing skills our professionals can use to help clients. We find clients trust us and want to know about our services. If we don't tell them, they seem disappointed." In the next chapter, I talk more about "offering dessert" and the importance of developing a process for it in your firm.

Step 5: Collecting the Check

To collect the appropriate amount of fees from your clients so you make a profit, you must take into account client emotions. Clients value your services the most at the time of delivery. Every moment you wait to bill your client until after the delivery process increases your risk of not collecting an appropriate amount.

Bob Gaida says, "I believe in giving premium service to my clients. I want to serve them in ways they will not receive anywhere else. And I expect a premium price in return. If the client is not willing to pay a premium, then I must ask myself, 'Is this a good client for me?'"

I discuss collecting the check in more depth in the Day 31 chapter. But it is important to set a foundation for it here. You must discuss the fee when you take the order and again when you deliver the order. It is best to establish a billing arrangement that will provide you a retainer up front, progress payments along the way, and a final bill on delivery. Such an arrangement will work with client emotions more evenly while providing you the most profit and your client the most satisfaction.

Summary

The key to long-term profitability in any business is loyal customers. Because clients have been coming back year after year does not necessarily mean they will continue to do so. The CPA who is proactive in delivering outstanding service will keep the good clients and attract more of them.

The most important thing you can do to increase your work—and your profits—is to really focus on customer service. You must set up a process to send the message to your staff and clients that service is your number-one priority. You must also have a process for delivering service, recovering from problems, and making sure clients get more than they expect.

31 Invest First, Then Reap Powerful Profits

You have to spend money to make money.

—Anonymous

"Give me heat and I'll give you wood," said the freezing man. There was no reply from the stove.

How much should we spend on marketing and sales? What elements should be included in a marketing budget? Should the salary of a marketing director be included? What about the hours that professional staff members spend on networking, entertaining, and proposing? Is sales a part of the marketing budget? How do I track the results of marketing expenses?

These are questions frequently asked of me by CPAs who are nervously contemplating marketing programs. Sometimes I speculate that the questioners would rather not spend anything or are looking for an excuse to reduce the cost of marketing. Bruce Marcus, in his book *Competing for Clients in the '90s,*[1] says, "Professionals have one foot on the boat and one foot on the dock when it comes to commitment to marketing."

CPAs are better trained in expense control than in revenue generation, and thus they are biased in that direction when it comes to their own firms. No wonder confusion exists about how best to assemble a marketing budget. CPAs lack confidence that marketing can add to their profitability. They also worry about how much to invest and where it should be invested. Add to these factors the long selling cycle for accounting services and the results orientation of many accountants, and we can begin to understand the difficulty.

But CPAs *are* experts at budgeting. Why then is constructing a marketing budget so difficult? I don't think the problem is with the budget. The budget is simply a marketing plan quantified; the problem really is developing and managing the plan. Failing to commit to a budget after the plan has been agreed on is the CPA's way of keeping one foot on the dock.

Marketing Is an Investment Activity

A paradigm shift is necessary for many CPAs when they plan marketing. To successfully plan and budget, CPAs should view marketing as an investment rather than an expense. Expenses should be reduced, but well-managed investments increase firm value and partner income.

"Marketing dollars are strategic, and strategic costs are the long-term life-blood of the business. Marketing investment must be maintained in good times and bad," says management consultant Bob Fifer in his book *Double Your Profits*.[2] Many CPA firm managers miss this point when they employ their "blood from a turnip" marketing-budget reduction strategy.

CPAs are not the only businesspeople who are skittish about a budgetary commitment to marketing. Lee Iaccoca, quoting John Wannamaker, once said that he knew that most of Chrysler's advertising budget was wasted and that if he only could identify the successful portion, he would spend only that. But in spite of his skittishness about advertising, Iaccoca dramatically increased the marketing budget of the ailing Chrysler Corporation. More important, Iaccoca managed the marketing budget wisely so that he achieved consistency, integration, and leverage from his marketing investment.

Both Iaccoca and Fifer define strategic costs as all those things that clearly "bring in business" and improve the bottom line. "Nonstrategic costs are all other costs which don't bring in business," says Fifer.

An accounting firm has two investment commodities: cash and time. Assembling a marketing budget should encompass both. David Maister, author of *Managing the Professional Services Firm*, says, "A major responsibility of firm management is to set the ground rules for investment of firm funds." Marketing is fundamentally an investment decision. Maister says, "A competitive advantage doesn't come free."

Most CPA firm accounting systems treat all strategic costs as expenses rather than as investments. According to Maister, "Partners subject to the ongoing financial control systems of the firm postpone or avoid investment activities for fear of being judged as missing their income target."

How Much Should I Invest?

Various MAP (Management Accounting Practice) studies and the AICPA survey indicate that most accounting firms spend 1 to 3 percent of their firm's revenue on marketing. Most of these surveys account for only the out-of-pocket marketing costs and generally do not include an allocation for part-time staff costs. Anecdotal information indicates that some of the more aggressive firms spend upward of 6 percent on marketing. One consultant told me that if a firm would not commit at least 3 percent to marketing, he would not work with them.

Some CPAs have had significant success with aggressively stimulating new business through well-managed marketing. Because of the high gross-profit margin, increases in revenue can improve profits dramatically. The objective is to increase fee volume with as little erosion in gross margin as possible. Most accounting firms have a variety of products, some of which provide recurring fees. Marketing spending directed at generating a recurring income stream could be viewed as an investment amortized over several years rather than only one year.

Hypothetical Return on Marketing

A $33,000 investment produces $100,000 new revenue:

Total revenue per year	$100,000
Gross margin percent	33%
Gross margin	$33,000
Life expectancy of client	7 years
Profits over seven years	$231,000
Discounted value @ 10%	$161,000
Marketing costs (investment)	$33,000
Total profit	$128,000
Annual average (after payback)	$18,000
	(55% annual return)

This income statement assumes that one-third of every incremental revenue dollar is direct cost, one-third is overhead, and one-third is profit before partner compensation.

A model called the available gross margin theory provides a gauge for measuring the upward limit for marketing investment. If a 33 percent profit is generated from each incremental dollar of new business, then an investment of up to $33,000 in marketing to generate $100,000 of new business would be profitable in the first year. Generating $100,000 of recurring business with a 33 percent margin, a firm would receive payback in year 1 and $33,000 additional profits each year thereafter. The discounted value of $100,000 of additional revenue over a seven-year client life expectancy, with a 33 percent margin (using 10 percent interest), would be $170,000. Investing $33,000 in acquisition costs would reap a 55 percent annual return after payback.

Using these calculations, we can understand the significant potential for a well-managed marketing program. In the short run, a CPA firm could gain up to a 67 percent margin on each incremental dollar of revenue generated at standard rates. Investing the full 67 percent into marketing could be a wise decision, particularly if the income were of a recurring nature. After obtaining a new client, cross-selling additional services and price optimizing can raise the margin significantly.

Do not set your marketing budget at 33 or 67 percent of expected revenue. That is a range for new client development only. A solid marketing budget will allocate a similar amount of investment to existing client building and some portion to positioning.

Setting Your Marketing Budget

Once you decide your marketing objectives and action plans, you can set a budget amount. For example, a practice grossing $1.5 million that seeks $75,000 in new client recurring revenue could budget up to $50,000 (dollars and time). If the revenue were totally nonrecurring, $7,500 to $15,000 (10–20 percent) would be the upper limits, barring any unusual factors intervening.

A well-balanced marketing budget would allocate about 45 percent for new business, 45 percent for existing clients, and about 10 percent for positioning. Using our example of a firm investing $50,000 in new client acquisition ($1.5 million gross billings), the total marketing budget would be approximately $110,000 (7.3 percent of past revenue and 6.6 percent of future revenue). The budget may be made up of 50 to 60 percent time and 40 to 50 percent dollars. Firms maximizing chargeable staff hours (utilization rates over 75 percent) would allocate more dollars. If staff utilization is below 60 percent, then management of the available time for marketing would be warranted.

What Methods to Use

A marketing budget based on affordability, competitive parity, or industry ratios can be set up easily. But these are the least effective and most wasteful methods. Discussed in order from the poorest to the best, here are the five methods CPAs use in setting a marketing budget.

1. *Investing what you can afford in marketing encourages impulse spending after good months and discourages marketing after poor months.* This method violates the rules of consistency and integration. A retail CEO once remarked that CPAs market like the retailer who didn't advertise in December because he was too busy stocking the inventory. After tax season, when CPAs are flush with cash, they begin to market: at a time when prospective clients' needs for their services have diminished. Affordability is the worst criterion on which to set your marketing budget.

2. *Matching the competition forces you to react, not lead.* "Most truly successful and profitable businesses outspend their competition in marketing either in absolute dollars or as a percentage of sales," says Fifer. Accountants have the potential for an excellent return from their marketing investments, but they must commit enough to make a difference.

3. *Allocating a percentage of past sales impedes growth.* "If you look backward to determine your marketing budget, you are looking in the wrong direction," says Jay Conrad Levinson, author of many *Guerrilla Marketing* books.

4. *"Investing based on projected revenue forces you to look into the future to act instead of react, to make and keep a commitment, and to be consistent,"* recommends Levinson.

5. *Using the objective/cost approach enables you to allocate the marketing budget among competing programs and to maximize profit.* This method requires you to set objectives and marketing needs and then determine the cost to attain the objectives.

Detailing Your Marketing Budget

To prepare a good budget for marketing, two key elements of information are important:

1. How, and on what, have we spent our budget in the past?
2. What are our current objectives?

To determine what has been spent in the past usually requires accountants to reformat the firm's income statement into functional rather than natural categories. A functional statement will delineate every aspect of the revenue stream (price increase, product mix, discounts, etc.).

The expense side will delineate and contain an allocation of full-time and part-time employee costs devoted to marketing as well as out-of-pocket marketing items. However, perks for employees, such as country club dues, donations, and similar items, should be excluded unless they truly are used for marketing purposes.

There are five key elements in the market planning and budgeting process:

1. Market communications
2. Client decision process
3. Media
4. Personal selling
5. Push versus pull

Functional Statement

Product Lines	Audit	Accounting	Write up	Tax Prep	Tax Planning
Average charge hours for each staff level					
Hourly rates for each staff level					
Blended hourly rate					
Hours billed					
Gross fees					
Markups (initial)					
Markdowns (continuing)					
Net fees before bad debts					

Prepare a separate budget for each of these marketing areas:

- Market positioning, selection, segmentation, product planning, and pricing
- New client attraction systems, target marketing, creating awareness, and differentiation
- Client sales (new and existing)
- Existing client building, loyalty, price optimization, cross-selling, and developing referrals

Within each budget, use the functional expense categories in the box on the next page.

For a firm wishing to have a balanced marketing program, these rules of thumb would apply:

	Dollars	Hours	
Marketing communications (All reallocated to the functional areas; develop a budget worksheet for this.)	40%	15%	
Positioning	10%	10%	
Internal marketing	50%	75%	
Breaks down as:			
New client attraction		17%	25%
Client sales		17%	25%
Existing client building		17%	25%
Total	100%	100%	

This formula is not a pat answer for allocating the budget. A brand-new firm may allocate 80 to 90 percent of the budget to new client attraction and sales, whereas a mature firm that has a recent history of client turnover may devote 75 percent to existing client building. Two problems tend to occur if a mature firm with no recent client losses focuses too much marketing on new clients:

1. Clients begin to feel they are being taken for granted and their loyalty declines.
2. The potential revenues from price optimization, cross-selling, and referral building are missed.

Marketing Objectives

Market share should also be considered when allocating the budget. Often it is very difficult to increase your market share if you already have a large share. If your market share is high, your marketing focus should be to optimize profits through building client loyalty, cross-selling, and raising prices.

Now, prepare the marketing objectives in concert with the firm's overall objectives. Before setting a budget, establish a set of marketing actions, such as networking or newsletters, to achieve the objectives. The marketing budget represents the quantification of each of the programs.

A good marketing plan should have consistency, integration, and leverage. Consistency is simply a good fit between the various elements of a marketing plan. For example, a firm that seeks to market estate planning services would not achieve consistency with a yellow pages ad. Yellow pages shoppers are primarily impulse or price shoppers and typically are not in the market for an estate plan.

> *Picture the ideal client you want to reach. Then coordinate your different marketing efforts to reach them in different ways but to appeal to them in a consistent way.*
>
> —Rick Crandall, *1001 Ways to Market Your Services: Even If You Hate to Sell*

Integration suggests that there is a harmonious interaction among the elements of your marketing plan. To continue to use the estate planning example, your marketing would be well integrated if there are elements of market positioning, new client marketing, and existing client marketing in your plan to sell your estate planning service.

Leverage comes into play when each element of your marketing plan is used to its best advantage to support the total marketing mix. For example, the awareness portion of the marketing budget is focused on a group of prospects who later in the selling cycle may be candidates for estate planning. Throughout the marketing cycle, estate planning is mentioned to help pave the way for the later sale.

Once the objectives are in place and the budget step of the marketing process is set, ask these questions before finalizing the plan and budget:

- Are the marketing budget elements consistent?
- Do the elements form a harmonious whole?
- Is each marketing program being used with its best leverage?
- Does each marketing program meet the needs of the target market?
- Do the marketing communications programs and target markets build on the firm's strengths?
- What information will be communicated? How receptive are the target consumers? How complex is the message? What is the number, heterogeneity, and accessibility of prospective clients?
- Does the marketing mix create a distinct personality in the market and offer any protection from your competitors?

Summary

Of all professionals, CPAs should be experts at budgeting for marketing. Remember that marketing is an investment that should bring measurable returns. The best marketing can pay for itself in the first year, plus provide ongoing revenue. Budget to achieve specific marketing objectives. Focus on existing clients more than prospects and choose from the many marketing methods available. Then track your results and build your practice.

Notes

Day 1

1. Ellsworth M. Statler (1863–1928) was a U.S. hotel businessman. He built the first Statler Hotel in 1898 in Buffalo, Texas. (It was the first hotel having a private bath and running water in every room.)
2. Harvey Mackay, *Swim with the Sharks Without Getting Eaten Alive* (New York: Ballantine Books, 1988).
3. Thomas J. Stanley, *Networking with the Affluent and Their Advisors* (Irwin Professional Publising, 1993).
4. Philip Kotler, *Kotler on Marketing* (Simon and Schuster, 2001).

Day 2

1. Thomas Watson is former CEO of IBM.
2. Lou Pritchett, *Stop Paddling and Start Rocking the Boat* (East/West Books, 1999).
3. Tom Peters is a consultant, author, and speaker.
4. Bob Fifer, *Double Your Profits* (Lincoln Hall Press, 1993).
5. Zig Ziglar, Chairman of the Zig Ziglar Corporation, speaks each year to hundreds of thousands of people throughout the world. He is the author of several bestselling books.
6. Michael LeBoeuf, *How to Win Customers and Keep Them for Life* (Putnam Publishing Group, 1988).

Day 3

1. Tony Alessandra et al., *Non-Manipulative Selling* (Prentice-Hall, 1987).
2. Harvey Mackay, *Swim with the Sharks Without Being Eaten Alive* (New York: Ballantine Books, 1988).
3. Barbara Geraghty, *Visionary Selling* (Simon and Schuster, 1998).
4. Tom Peters is an author, consultant, and speaker.

Day 4

1. Jay Conrad Levinson, *Guerilla Marketing Attack* (Boston: Houghton-Mifflin, 1989).
2. Al Ries and Jack Trout, *Positioning: The Battle for Your Mind*, 3rd edition (McGraw-Hill, 2000).

Day 5

1. Tony Alessandra et al., *Non-Manipulative Selling* (Prentice-Hall, 1987).

Day 6

1. Claude C. Hopkins (1866–1932) invented test marketing, coupon sampling, and copy testing, all standard practices in modern advertising.
2. Dale Carnegie (1888–1955) was a pioneer in public speaking and personality development.

Day 9

1. Ivan R. Misner and Robert Davis, *Business by Referral* (Bard Press, 1998).
2. Rick Crandall, *1001 Ways to Market Your Services: Even If You Hate to Sell* (McGraw-Hill, 1998).

Day 10

1. Harvey Mackay is a sales, management, and leadership author and speaker.
2. Thomas J. Stanley, *Networking with the Affluent and Their Advisors* (Irwin Professional Publishing, 1993).
3. Harvey Mackay, *Dig Your Well Before You're Thirsty* (Currency, 1999).
4. Philip B. Crosby, *Quality Is Free* (McGraw-Hill, 1979).
5. Don Gabor is an author and professional speaker.
6. Terri Mandell, *Power Schmoozing* (McGraw-Hill, 1996).
7. Rick Crandall, *1001 Ways to Market Your Services: Even If You Hate to Sell* (McGraw-Hill, 1998).
8. Susan RoAne, *How to Work a Room* (Chrysalis Books, 2001).
9. Tom Stanley, *Networking with the Affluent and Their Advisors* (Irwin Professional Publishing, 1993).
10. Ibid.

Day 11

1. Peter F. Drucker is a professor of social science at Claremont Graduate School and the author of more than 30 books.
2. William Penn was a Quaker who helped found the American colony of Pennsylvania.

Day 12

1. Paul Thurow is the author of over a dozen books about Windows, the World-Wide Web, and software development.

2. Jordan Lewis, *Partnerships for Profit* (Free Press, 1990).
3. Richard Glickman, *Journal of Accountancy* (January 2000).

Day 14
1. Charles M. Schwab was an entrepreneur of the early steel industry in the United States who served as president of both the Carnegie Steel Company and the U.S. Steel Corporation.

Day 15
1. Rick Crandall is an author and consultant.
2. Peter F. Drucker is a professor of social science at Claremont Graduate School and author of more than 30 books.
3. Neil Rackham, *SPIN Selling* (McGraw-Hill, 1988).
4. Harry Beckwith, *Selling the Invisible* (Warner Business Books, 1997).
5. Harvey Mackay is a sales, management, and leadership author and speaker.

Day 16
1. Gerald D. Ford was the 38th President of the United States.
2. Ben Feldman, serial entrepreneur, was previously an investor and COO of MDeverywhere. Ben recently founded rapidata.net, a pharmaceutical marketing research firm.
3. W. Edwards Deming is a consultant in statistical studies.

Day 17
1. Tom Peters, an organization and business expert, is the author of *In Search of Excellence* (Longman, 1986).

Day 18
1. Tom Peters, an organization and business expert, is author of *In Search of Excellence* (Longman, 1986).
2. Elaine Floyd, *Marketing with Newsletters: How to Boost Sales, Add Members, Raise Donations and Further Your Cause with a Promotional Newsletter* (Lifetime Books, 1991).
3. Rick Crandall, *Marketing Magic: Proven Pathways to Success* (Select Press, 1996).

Day 19
1. Miriam Otte, *Marketing with Speeches and Seminars* (Zest Press, 1998).
2. Ken Blanchard is an author, speaker, and business consultant.
3. Granville N. Toogood, *The Articulate Executive* (McGraw-Hill, 1995).
4. Art Sobczak, *Telephone Selling Report* (Business by Phone, 1996).
5. Paul LeRoux, *Selling to a Group* (Harper Resource, 1984).
6. John Newstrom and Edward Scannell, *Games Trainers Play* (McGraw-Hill, 1980).
7. Richard L. Hudson, *70 Steps to Speaking Success* (Business by Phone, 1996).

Day 20

1. Dick Reck is partner in charge, KPMG Illinois High Tech Awards Program.
2. Jack Amundson is with Larson Allen Weishair & Co.
3. Rick Crandall, *Celebrate Marketing: Secrets of Success* (Select Press, 1999).

Day 21

1. Bill Gates is chairman and chief software architect of Microsoft Corporation. The quote is from his essay "Content Is King," 1996.
2. William D. Ruckelshaus is a lawyer, businessman, and two-time head of the Environmental Protection Agency.
3. Norman Augustine was a U.S. aircraft businessperson.
4. Jay Conrad Levinson and Charles Rubin, *Guerrilla Marketing on the Internet: The Complete Guide to Making Money Online* (Judy Piatkus Publishers, 1995).
5. John Audette is an Internet marketing pioneer. In 1995, he founded the Multimedia Marketing Group.

Day 22

1. Stephen R. Covey, founder and chairman of the Covey Leadership Center, is author of *The Seven Habits of Highly Effective People.*
2. Ken Blanchard, *The One Minute Manager* (William Morrow & Company, 1982).
3. Stephen Covey, *Seven Habits of Highly Successful People* (Simon and Schuster, 1990).

Day 23

1. Ashleigh Brilliant is an English cartoonist and author.
2. John Fogg is the author of *The Greatest Networker in the World* (Three Rivers Press, 1997).
3. *What's Working in Sales Management* is an online newsletter for sales managers, published by Progressive Business Publications, *www.pbp.com.*
4. John Burgess is the head of International Profit Associates, known as IPA, based near Chicago.
5. Tom Peters, organization and business expert, is the author of *In Search of Excellence* (Longman, 1986).
6. Dean Rusk (1909–1994) was U.S. Secretary of State from 1961 to 1969.
7. Linda Richardson, *Stop Telling, Start Selling* (McGraw-Hill, 1997).
8. Neil Rackham, *SPIN Selling* (McGraw-Hill, 1988).

Day 24

1. Thomas J. Watson, Sr. (1874–1956) was president of the International Chamber of Commerce.
2. Lord Chesterfield, *Letters to His Son* (1752).

Day 25
1. Peter Drucker is a professor of social science at Claremont Graduate School and the author of more than 30 books.

Day 26
1. George Selfridge is founder of Selfridge and Co., Ltd., a leading department store in London. He is credited with coining the saying, "The customer is always right."
2. C. Richardson Weylman, *Opening Closed Doors* (McGraw-Hill, 1997).

Day 28
1. Leonard Berry, *On Great Service* (Free Press, 1995).
2. Robert G. Cross, *Revenue Management* (Broadway Books, 1997).
3. Don Peppers and Martha Rogers, *The One to One Future: Building Relationships One Customer at a Time* (Currency, 1993).

Day 29
1. See "Portrait of a Sales Leader" in Day 10 for Jack Amundson's story.
2. Frederick Reichheld, *The Loyalty Effect* (Harvard Business School Press, 2001).
3. This quote comes from "Achieving Breakthrough Service," taught by Jeffrey F. Rayport under the Executive Education program at Harvard Business School. Rayport is founder and chairman of Marketspace™.
4. Larry Wilson with Hersch Wilson, *Stop Selling, Start Partnering* (Oliver Wight Publications, 1995).
5. Rick Crandall, *10 Secrets of Marketing Success: How to Jump Start Your Marketing* (Select Press, 1997).
6. Thomas J. Winninger, *Price Wars* (Saint Thomas Press, 1994).
7. Mark Hanan, *Consultative Selling* (AMACOM, 2003).
8. Robert B. Miller, Stephen E. Heiman, and Tad Tuleja, *Successful Large Account Management* (Warner Books, 1992).
9. Neil Rackham, *The SPIN Selling Field Book* (McGraw-Hill, 1988).

Day 30
1. Jim Belew, who is quoted throughout this book, is a founding partner of Belew Averett, LLP.
2. Hal Rosenbluth, *The Customer Comes Second* (HarperCollins, 2002).
3. Michael Le Boeuf, *How to Win Customers and Keep Them for Life* (Berkley Trade, 2000).
4. William Fromm, *The Ten Commandments of Business and How to Break Them* (Berkley Trade, 1992).
5. Bill Gates, *Business at The Speed of Thought* (Warner Books, 2000).
6. Kristin Anderson is coauthor with Ron Zemke of *Delivering Knock Your Socks Off Service* (AMACOM, 2002).

7. Janelle Barlow and Claus Moller, *A Complaint Is a Gift* (Berrett-Koehler Publishers, 1996).
8. Ken Blanchard has authored many books on management and customer service.
9. Harry F. Banks is an author.

Day 31
1. Bruce Marcus, *Competing for Clients in the '90s* (Probus Pub., 1986).
2. Bob Fifer, *Double Your Profits* (HarperCollins, 1994).

Bibliography

American Institute of Certified Public Accountants. *Marketing Advantage II.* New York: AICPA.

Baker, Ronald J. *The Professional's Guide to Value Pricing.* San Diego, CA: Harcourt Professional Publishing.

Beckwith, Harry. *Selling the Invisible, A Field Guide to Modern Marketing.* New York: Warner Books.

Bly, Robert W. *Selling Your Services.* New York: Henry Holt & Company.

Crandall, Rick. *Marketing Your Services for People Who HATE to Sell.* New York: McGraw-Hill.

Godin, Seth. *Permission Marketing.* New York: Simon & Schuster.

Hanan, Mack. *Consultative Selling,* 5th ed. New York: American Management Association (amacom).

Herman, Fred. *Selling Is Simple (Not Easy, But Simple).* New York: Vantage Press.

Hopkins, Tom. *The Guide to Greatness in Sales: How to Become a Complete Salesperson.* Scottsdale, AZ: Tom Hopkins International, Inc.

Kantin, Robert F., and Mark W. Hardwick, Ph.D. *Strategic Proposals.* Dallas, TX: Minehan Quality Press.

Levinson, Jay Conrad. *Guerrilla Marketing Attack.* Boston: Houghton Mifflin Company.

Lill, David J., Ph.D. *Selling, The Profession, A Relationship Approach.* Nashville, TN: DM Bass Publications.

Mackay, Harvey. *Dig Your Well Before You're Thirsty.* New York: Currency.

Maister, David H. *Managing the Professional Services Firm.* New York: The Free Press.

Misner, Ivan R., Ph.D., and Robert Davis. *Business by Referral.* Austin, TX: Bard Press.

Rackham, Neil. *SPIN Selling.* New York: McGraw-Hill.

Ries, Al, and Jack Trout. *The 22 Immutable Laws of Marketing.* New York: Harper Business.

Seybold, Patrica B., and Ronni T. Marshak. *Customers.Com.* New York: Times Business Random House.

Shaw, Robert Bruce. *Trust in the Balance.* San Francisco: Jossey-Bass.

Wilson, Larry with Hersch Wilson. *Stop Selling, Start Partnering.* Oliver Wight Publications.

Index